813.24

D0906264

James Fenimore Cooper and the Development of
American Sea Fiction

PS 1442
S4
P45
1961

JAMES FENIMORE COOPER

AND THE DEVELOPMENT OF

AMERICAN SEA FICTION

Thomas Philbrick

HARVARD UNIVERSITY PRESS

Cambridge, Massachusetts

1 9 6 1

JUL 1962

74452

© Copyright 1961 by the
President and Fellows of Harvard College
All rights reserved

Distributed in Great Britain by
Oxford University Press, London

Publication of this book has been aided by
a grant from the Ford Foundation

Library of Congress Catalog Card Number 61–15276

Printed in the United States of America

TO M.F.P.

Preface

This book grew out of my conviction that *Moby-Dick* is too often thought of as the first appearance of the sea in American literature. It seemed to me that Melville's inheritance from the rich and varied store of sea fiction which Cooper and his contemporaries had created was as essential to the making of *Moby-Dick* as his debt to the Bible, to Shakespeare, to the seventeenth-century writers of metaphysical prose and the nineteenth-century writers of cetological treatises. Once engaged in the study, I became increasingly appreciative of the intrinsic value of Cooper's art and the historical importance of the work of his contemporaries. Viewed as a body, the hundreds of nautical novels and short stories that were produced in this country during the first half of the nineteenth century offer a revelation of the surprising depth and range of American interest in the sea and its affairs. They suggest that before 1850 the American frontier was primarily a maritime one, that the sea rather than the continental wilderness was the principal focus of the yearnings and imaginings of the American dream. And in the work of the ablest writers, above all Cooper, we have evidence of the still deeper and wider meanings that the sea can hold for the artist and thinker, meanings that enable the ocean to function as the symbolic ground for the profoundest explorations of the nature and condition of man. If those explorations were most extensive in the novels of Melville, the fact remains that the work of his predecessors has interest not merely as the background of his fiction; it is significant in itself as a gauge of the shape and quality of a vital segment of the American popular imagination and as a demonstration of the rich potentialities of maritime materials as a subject of art.

A central concern of this book, then, is the significance of the sea both for the writer and for his audience. It is an attempt to find answers to a number of important questions: What accounts for the great quantity of sea fiction in the period? Why did maritime materials interest writers and their readers, and what meanings were they used to express? What changes can be observed in the fictional treatment of the sea, and how do those changes relate to the course of the national experience and to the general evolution of literary theory and practice? Perhaps it should be pointed out that, in pursuing these issues, I have not attempted to conduct a comprehensive survey of all instances of the extensive use of nautical materials by American writers; rather, the discussion concentrates its attention on a fairly small sampling of the whole body of fiction. Moreover, the relative emphasis that is given to the various stories and novels is not always directly proportionate to their literary value. Although my selection of the works to be discussed is biased in favor of artistic merit, I have tried to deal with all the major shifts and changes in the development of American sea fiction, and hence I have been forced occasionally to deal with inferior works. The poor quality of many of the stories that are discussed in Chapter V, for example, is in itself evidence of the decay of interest in the sea in the late 1840's, a phenomenon that needs analysis and explanation.

The structure of the book centers on the work of James Fenimore Cooper, the originator of the sea novel and the

writer who contributed most to its subsequent development before the appearance of *Moby-Dick* in 1851, the
year of his death. Cooper's lifelong involvement in maritime affairs and his steady devotion to the sea novel as a
literary form are still largely unknown to general readers
and are usually ignored or given cursory treatment by
specialists in American fiction. For the first seventy-five
years after his death, Cooper was regarded almost exclusively as a novelist of the forest frontier, a writer whose
lasting appeal was limited to the adolescent lover of adventure stories. The revival of interest in Cooper that began
in the 1920's not only led to the discovery of the wider
significance of the Leatherstocking Tales as myth and
symbol, but, in calling attention to Cooper's social criticism, it revealed a whole new dimension of his mind and
art. As yet, however, students of Cooper have not fully
reckoned with the fact that his knowledge of and interest
in the continental frontier was secondary to his concern
with the significance of the sea in the past and future of
America, that more than a third of his novels focus on
maritime life, that his sea fiction was regarded as his major
achievement by many of his contemporaries, here and in
England. Accordingly, another central aim of the book is
to explore this neglected aspect of Cooper's work, to place
it in its historical perspective, and to weigh its importance.

From the dozen or so novels by Cooper that may be
classified as sea fiction, I have chosen three for extensive
discussion. In making that selection, I have again been
guided by a desire to illustrate the major phases of his development, as well as by the criterion of intrinsic narrative
value. Thus *The Red Rover* was chosen as the best integrated expression of the extreme romanticism which characterizes Cooper's early treatment of maritime life. *Afloat
and Ashore* seems the most successful embodiment of his
attempt in the middle years of his career to treat nautical

materials realistically and to relate them to common human experience rather than to isolate them in the realm
of the glamorous and the exotic. *The Sea Lions,* Cooper's
last sea novel, is the most neglected and the most interesting of the lot. Read simply as another tale of maritime
adventure, it is manifestly not one of Cooper's better efforts: its characters are drab; its plot is slow-moving; its
details often seem irrelevant; its style lacks the verbal
grandeur that Cooper, at his best, is capable of attaining;
and, most annoying of all, its narrative is interrupted again
and again by passages of conventionally pious (and very
tedious) moralizing. But to read *The Sea Lions* in that way
is, I believe, to mistake its intention and to overlook its
achievement. As I hope my discussion of the novel indicates, Cooper's last exploration of the fictional uses of
nautical materials led him to transform the sea novel into
symbolic narrative, to view the voyage as an allegory of
regeneration. If Cooper was no Goethe and no Melville,
if his metaphysical imagination was circumscribed by the
doctrines of Anglican theology, his conscious and coherent
use of symbol and allegory in *The Sea Lions* as means for
probing the ultimate nature of man's condition nevertheless constitutes the most important extension of the scope
of the sea novel since its inception, an extension that at
once reclaimed for modern fiction the traditional union of
maritime experience and moral significance and pointed
the way to the fulfillment of the artistic potentialities of
that union in *Moby-Dick.*

In pursuing the course of American sea fiction before
Melville, I have incurred many debts of gratitude. In particular, I wish to thank Professor Kenneth B. Murdock,
who directed the dissertation from which the present work
has grown. I am grateful also for the friendly and efficient
assistance of the staffs of the Harvard College Library, the
American Antiquarian Society, the Brown University Li-

brary, the Essex Institute, the University of Vermont Library, the Munson-Williams-Proctor Institute of Utica, New York, and the Marine Historical Association of Mystic, Connecticut. No acknowledgment can express my gratitude to Professor Howard Mumford Jones for his help and encouragement or to my wife, Marianne Dennis Philbrick, for her sustained and sustaining interest in this book.

                                  Thomas Philbrick

Burlington, Vermont

CONTENTS

CONTENTS

ILLUSTRATIONS

James Fenimore Cooper and the Development of
American Sea Fiction

Chapter I

Dread Neptune's Wild Unsocial Sea

THE SEA IN AMERICAN LITERATURE
BEFORE 1820

DURING the first half of the nineteenth century the sea occupied much the same place in the imaginations of many Americans that the continental frontier was to fill after 1850. The sea exerted the same appeal to the individual: it offered adventure, quick profit, the chance to start anew, and freedom from the restraints and obligations of society. The same national values were attached to the sea: it represented the arena of past glories, the training ground of the national character, and the field on which wealth and power were to be won for the country.

This concept did not spring full-blown in the national consciousness. Rather, it grew out of the cumulative effect of the history of maritime enterprise in colonial America; the naval victories of the Revolution, the undeclared naval war with France, and the war with the Barbary States; the steady expansion of American trade throughout the world in the early years of the new republic; and above all the astounding naval successes of the War of 1812, which seemed to indicate unmistakably the road by which the national aspirations of America were to be achieved. In the words of one popular literary magazine in 1813, "the glorious achievements of our navy" had "kindled a new and holy spirit of nationality, and enabled the humblest citizen among us boldly to say to the world that he too has a country." It now became the duty of American literature to keep the flame of maritime nationalism burning brightly, for, the magazine proclaimed, "poetry can have no higher office among us than to embalm, in its purest essence, these brilliant deeds of heroism; to reflect, in all their lustre, the images of great and glorious triumphs; to familiarize the national mind to acts of high and generous heroism; and thus, by preserving the lofty tone of its patriotism, make the remembrance of the old become the cause of future victories."[1]

Not all of the future victories at sea were to be won in war. With the end of hostilities in 1815 the country entered what has aptly been called the golden age of American shipping, a period of thirty-five years during which American seamen came to challenge and even to displace the British hegemony of many of the most important areas of maritime activity. To the West Indian, Baltic, and Mediterranean trades, established in colonial days, and the Northwest and Canton trades, first explored in the 1780's, were added new ventures. Massachusetts vessels carried spices from the Fiji Islands, Madagascar, and Zanzibar, rubber from Brazil, sandalwood from Hawaii, and hides from California in exchange for nails, firearms, blankets, rum, and even that most abundant of Yankee commodities, ice, which, cut from Fresh Pond in Cambridge and Walden in Concord, enabled the priest of Brahma to drink at Thoreau's well. In 1816 a group of merchants in New York organized the famous Black Ball Line of packets with such success that by the late 1830's, when Cooper was creating the packet *Montauk* to serve as the fictional stage of his novel *Homeward Bound* and Melville was getting his first taste of the sea as a green hand on board a Liverpool packet, the United States com-

pletely dominated the passenger trade between New York
and England.

The more prosaic elements of American maritime life
displayed an equally remarkable vitality. By the 1840's the
American whaling fleet comprised more than three quarters of the world's total. The deep-sea fisheries of Maine
and Massachusetts, the traditional school of American
seamen, enlarged to the point that in 1850 the tonnage
of the American fishing fleet was over five times greater
than it had been in 1815, while in the same period the
flotillas of schooners, brigs, and barks that ferried cotton,
sugar, lumber, coal, and granite between the ports of the
Atlantic coast quadrupled in tonnage. In response to the
demand from all quarters for more efficient vessels, American shipyards were developing the succession of designs
that culminated in the 1840's in the perfection of the fast
and beautiful clipper ship.

2

It was inevitable that this wide and varied maritime
activity should find expression in the literature of a people seeking to create a national identity, for, in the first
half of the nineteenth century, the ocean seemed to be as
much America's peculiar domain as it had been England's
in the preceding century. But if the introduction of the
sea to American literature appears inevitable from the
perspective of history, it seemed a difficult and doubtful
venture to those who first undertook the experiment.

When American writers turned to the literature of
eighteenth-century England in search of precedents and
prototypes to guide their attempt to shape native maritime materials to the uses of fiction, they found little that
answered their immediate needs. In the eyes of Cooper
and his contemporaries, British nautical literature was

dominated by the figure of Tobias Smollett, who had made extensive use of naval characters and settings in his novels *Roderick Random* (1748), *Peregrine Pickle* (1751), and *The Adventures of Sir Launcelot Greaves* (1760–1761). But Smollett's work was severely limited in scope. In the first place, he employed nautical materials only incidentally: the scenes aboard H.M.S. *Thunder*, rich in vivid detail though they are, represent only one in the seemingly endless series of locales to which Roderick Random's wanderings take him; characters like Commodore Trunnion and Tom Pipes are of interest, not so much as seamen, but rather as two particularly colorful specimens in Smollett's collection of eccentric variants of the human species. Moreover, Smollett restricted his nautical sketching to the life of the Royal Navy. His emphasis is on the traditions of the service, on the workings of a massive organization that dominates and sometimes crushes its individual members, on the pressures and restraints to which men crowded between the decks of a man-of-war are subjected by the daily routine of naval discipline. That emphasis was appropriate to a people whose interest was focused on their huge navy as the prime instrument of national power and to an age which, committed to the values and attitudes of neoclassicism, regarded man primarily as a product and component part of the machinery of society. But American writers in the early years of the nineteenth century were addressing a nation whose naval traditions, in so far as it possessed them at all, centered on the daring exploits of heroic individuals rather than on the long history of an institution that had built and defended an empire. They addressed, too, an audience whose political philosophy was based on the value and importance of the individual, and whose literary taste was shaped by the romantic concern with external nature; man's relation to society was no longer the all-engrossing object of concern.

Smollett's most serious limitation, however, was his tone. True to the neoclassical dictum that heroism is incompatible with the realistic treatment of familiar materials, he consistently viewed the life of the forecastle and the waterfront from a satirical stance. The noblest qualities he allows his nautical characters are the dog-like fidelity of a Lieutenant Bowling or the childlike simplicity of a Tom Pipes. The stereotype that Smollett prepared for the sailor of fiction proved as durable as it was entertaining. The frank, openhearted and openhanded tar whose fun-loving temper buoys him up in his sea of hard knocks and whose salt-encrusted speech and briny eccentricities of manner separate him from the landsman (and very nearly from the entire human race) came to walk the decks of many an American fictional ship. But clearly the stereotype had outlived its usefulness for major characters; whenever the occasion called for a demonstration of the ennobling effects of long association with the sublimities of wild nature or for a democratic assertion of the common seaman's capacity for heroism, it had to be discarded.

Smollett's handling of the sea and the ship was still less useful as a pattern for American writers. Sharing the neoclassical distaste for the wild, primitive aspects of nature, he gave scant attention to the ocean, allowing it to hold the narrative foreground only in moments of storm. But for Smollett there was no suggestion of sublimity in a wind-swept sea; it was chaos returned again, a scene of desolate, inhuman violence that could evoke only terror and astonishment. Nor was the ship the embodiment of grace and the symbol of freedom that it was to be to the early Cooper. Rather, it was the microcosm of a corrupt society, a pesthouse suffused by the stench of putrid stores, a prison whose inmates were tormented by fleas and floggings and governed by malice and incompetence.

For the most part, the nautical novel in England during the first half of the nineteenth century retained the pattern established by Smollett. By the time the main stream of romanticism swept into prose fiction, Trafalgar had been fought, and England turned her attention to the consolidation of her empire and the industrialization of her economy. The front rank of British novelists relinquished the sea to a succession of retired naval officers, Marryat, Chamier, Howard, and their imitators, who, between 1829 and 1848, recalled their youthful days of service in picaresque novel after picaresque novel. If, as Cooper believed, these productions were prompted by the success of his own early nautical romances, they almost invariably turned to Smollett rather than to him for their substance and tone.

The work of Frederick Marryat, the best known of the group, is representative. In taking the scapegrace and the poor devil to sea in novels like *Midshipman Easy* (1836), Marryat's technique was to expand and multiply the naval episode of Smollett until it engrossed the major portion of the book. The result is a narrative that focuses its attention not on the seaman, the ship, or the ocean as such, but on the British naval service, an institution which is viewed both as a legitimate outgrowth and a necessary segment of society. In the loving concentration on the traditions, manners, and techniques of the Royal Navy, the individual retreats to the background, and the sea and the ship function only as the habitations, local and general, of the institution. Although Marryat's tone lacks the note of outrage that had converted Smollett's man-of-war into a chamber of horrors, it still does not permit his treatment of maritime life to move in the direction of the ideal. No less antiheroic and antisentimental than Smollett's, Marryat's tone is distinguished only by a cynical flippancy which so diminishes his characters that the reader is tempted to share his usually complacent acceptance of the more brutal forms of naval discipline as the proper means of governing the human animal.

If British novelists were content to follow in Smollett's wake, their American counterparts in the first half of the nineteenth century felt compelled to take a different tack. The American writer might not be fully conscious of the basis of his sense of the inadequacy of Smollett's work for his own purposes, but he could justify his experiments by regarding Smollett's treatment of nautical materials as so perfect of its kind that any further use of it could not go beyond mere imitation. As Cooper surveyed, at the end of his career, his own first attempts at the novel of the sea, he recalled that "Smollett had obtained so much success as a writer of nautical tales, that it probably required a new course should be steered in order to enable the succeeding adventurer in this branch of literature to meet with any favor." "This difficulty," he continued, with a sideways glance at his British competitors, "was fully felt when this book [*The Red Rover* (1827)] was originally written, and probably has as much force to-day as it had then, though nearly a quarter of a century has intervened."[2]

Where, then, could Cooper and his American contemporaries turn for precedents offering alternatives to the satirical realism of Smollett's approach to maritime life? One possible line of development, shunned for the most part by Cooper but adopted by some American writers of short fiction, was indicated by English songs and comic drama of the later eighteenth century: the sailor could be sentimentalized, transformed into a curly-locked, graceful lad whose heart beat true for his Susan, his Nancy, or whatever sweet girl he had left behind him at the dockside in Portsmouth. The seaman had been a familiar figure on the English stage since Congreve created Ben Legend in *Love for Love* (1695), but throughout most of the first half of the century the stage sailor remained, like Ben Legend himself, a sea monster, a rough, hearty caricature of the kind Smollett introduced to prose fiction. In the latter half of the century, however, the sentimentality that was sweeping through English and continental literature at last began to color the treatment of maritime life. Although Smollett's tar remained the dominant type, in a few dramatic productions like Isaac Bickerstaffe's operetta *Thomas and Sally; or, The Sailor's Return* (1760) and in the immensely popular sea songs of Charles Dibdin the sailor underwent a significant modification. The frankness and simplicity of Smollett's characters were retained, but instead of emphasizing the seaman's grotesque eccentricity of manner and outlook, the new sentimentalism suggested that the sailor might be capable of feelings broader and more universal than his well-known fondness for piping winds, roaring seas, and flowing cans. It was now discovered that even the seaman might have a mother, a truelove, or a wife and children; that a very young sailor might feel the pangs of homesickness, and that a very old sailor might know the hardships of poverty, loneliness, and disability. If the sentimental situations in which the seaman was cast tended to make him merely pretty or merely pathetic, they at least reunited him with the rest of the human race and, in so doing, offered his feelings and concerns as subjects worthy of serious attention.

But sentimentalism, in itself, had the effect of diminishing the capacity of maritime life to evoke a sense of wonder, the central response of the romantic imagination to the sea and its affairs. Writing at the peak of romanticism in America, Cooper and his contemporaries necessarily viewed the sea from a perspective vastly different from that of their British predecessors. Their aesthetic theory placed its highest premium on the sublime; what was needed was a treatment of the ocean which would not recoil in revulsion from desolation and danger but which would interpret immense power and sweeping distance as positive values, relishing them for the feelings of awe and transcendence they called forth. Their social theory stressed the significance of man's natural environment and emphasized the attainment of freedom and individuality as his highest aims; what was needed was a conception of the ship which, by seizing on the qualities of grace and mobility, would suggest its service as an escape from the corrupting distortions and oppressive restrictions of civilized society or which, by focusing on its responsiveness and treating it as an extension of the will and strength of its crew, would lend it the aura of an epic weapon, another bow of Odysseus with which the seaman could do battle with his elemental antagonist. Obviously, neither the satirized nor the sentimentalized sailor was fitted to the titanic environment in which the romantic imagination placed him. The seaman must be a figure ennobled by his lifelong association and struggle with nature at its most sublime. He must possess courage and intelligence worthy of the stoutly built and delicately tuned ship he sailed. In sum, he must be elevated to heroism.

If the main body of British nautical literature fell short of meeting the requirements of the romantic conception of maritime life, its periphery gave some suggestion of how the fictional treatment of the sea might be infused with wonder, sublimity, and heroism. Until Daniel Defoe turned shipwreck, island survival, and piracy into matters of prosaic reality in *Robinson Crusoe* (1719) and *Captain Singleton* (1720), the sea had long served literature as an

arena of marvels. In the old romances and the imaginary
voyages of the sixteenth and seventeenth centuries, the
ocean, shadowy and unknown, was a setting perfectly
adapted to a blurring of the borderline between probability and pure fantasy. Once embarked, the reader could
expect encounters with diabolical pirates or with females
disguised as sailors in an attempt to elude the attentions of
amorous captains, miraculous escapes from shipwrecks,
remarkable reunions of lovers long separated by wind and
wave, and all the other stock motifs which the Elizabethan
romance had inherited from its classical ancestors. He
could expect to be carried to lands and peoples only
slightly more exotic than those described in the early voyage literature which was to engross the romantic imagination of Coleridge. He could expect, too, in many of the
moral tracts and pious chapbooks of the period, to view
the voyage as a symbolic reflection of and commentary on
man's passage through life.

The imaginative intensity and range of this older approach to nautical materials must have exerted a strong
appeal to those Americans who were familiar with it, as
Cooper's fondness for one embodiment of it, Shakespeare's
The Tempest, testifies. But in the early decades of the
nineteenth century when, as we have seen, American merchant shipping was scouring the globe in search of markets
and commodities, when the American whaling industry
was making even the most remote islands of the South Seas
items of daily report in newspapers, and when exploring
expeditions were probing the mysteries of the polar ends
of the earth, the sea could no longer be taken for granted
as a source of ready-made wonder. The age of romanticism
was also the age of science; if readers wanted marvels, they
wanted them firmly embedded in specific detail, detail that
would be convincing in its fullness, precision, and authenticity. Smollett had given the general public a sense of the

sounds, smells, and sights of shipboard life. Now, when the public appetite for realistic detail was being stimulated still more by the increasing relevance of the sea to American life, it would be impossible to return to the generalized characters and settings of the old romances. The problem for Cooper's age was the finding of means to intensify the impression of immediacy and authenticity that Smollett's technique gave and, at the same time, to establish and maintain a tone of high, heroic seriousness.

By the canons of orthodox eighteenth-century literary theory, the combination of nautical terminology, necessary for accurate and meaningful description, and the exalted tone of serious poetry, the tone demanded by the romantic conception of the sea, was an impermissible violation of decorum. Censuring Dryden's use of nautical terms in *Annus Mirabilis,* Samuel Johnson enunciated the accepted doctrine: "It is a general rule in poetry that all appropriated terms of art should be sunk in general expressions, because poetry is to speak an universal language. This rule is still stronger with regard to arts not liberal or confined to few, and therefore far removed from common knowledge; and of this kind certainly is technical navigation." "Yet," he went on, "Dryden was of opinion that a sea-fight ought to be described in the nautical language." After quoting a passage stippled with words like *oakum, seam,* and *mallet,* Dr. Johnson settled the matter with quiet finality: "I suppose there is not one term which every reader does not wish away."[3]

Indecorous though such terms might be, William Falconer, both a poet and a seaman, had used them freely in his long poetic study of maritime life, *The Shipwreck* (1762), a work that enjoyed great popularity during the late eighteenth and early nineteenth centuries in his own country and in America. If Falconer's blend of neoclassical stock phrases and concrete nautical terminology seems incon-

gruous to the modern ear, contemporary critics were delighted by the innovation, for "who, except a poetical
Sailor, the nursling of Apollo, educated by Neptune,
would ever have thought of versifying his own sea-lan-
guage? what other Poet would ever have dreamt of reef-
tackles, hall-yards, clue-garnets, bunt-lines, lashings, lann-
yards, and fifty other terms equally obnoxious to the soft
sing-song of modern Poetasters?"[4] Falconer's precedent
could well have given Cooper some comfort when, in
writing his first sea novel, *The Pilot* (1824), he was embar-
rassed by the discovery that, although his aim was to "avoid
technicalities, in order to be poetic . . . the subject im-
periously required a minuteness of detail to render it in-
telligible."[5]

But Falconer's innovation had been almost exclusively a
matter of diction. He laid the linguistic groundwork necessary for voicing the romantic concept of the sea, but his
own view of maritime life reflects the eighteenth-century
preoccupation with man as a product of civilization. Although he occasionally gives glimpses of the beauty of the
ship and the sublimity of the ocean, Falconer concentrates
his attention on seamanship as a highly developed and intricate technology, on the crew as the coordinated practi-
tioners of that technology, and on the ship as the complex
system of mechanisms they operate. The ocean, always
something detached and distinct from man, is the object
to which the technology is applied, a kind of raw material
which can be turned to some good use by the efforts of human reason and science. As yet, literature had not taken
the great step prerequisite to the creation of the sea novel
as distinct from the novel which, like *Roderick Random,*
makes extensive use of nautical materials; it had not moved
the sea itself to the center of the stage, finding in it the
focus of interest and significance.

By 1823, when Cooper found himself engaged in the

task of originating just such a novel, the attitudes necessary for the concentration of interest and significance in the sea itself had received full and authoritative expression in the poetry of Lord Byron. The extreme romanticism of Canto IV of *Childe Harold* (1818) offered a startling alternative to the man-centered approach to maritime life that constituted the eighteenth-century norm. Confronted by the ocean, man dwindles to insignificance in Byron's eyes; the sea scorns his feeble strength and sends him, "shivering . . . and howling, to his Gods." But the ocean is more than an embodiment of mere natural force; its vastness and awesome beauty make it the very emblem of divinity:

> Dark-heaving—boundless, endless, and sublime—
> The image of Eternity—the throne
> Of the Invisible.

The only proper response of man to the ocean is transcendental contemplation, a contemplation that permits him to escape from his selfhood and wallow in the infinite, as Harold steals

> From all I may be, or have been before,
> To mingle with the Universe, and feel
> What I can ne'er express—yet can not all conceal.[6]

In England, as we have seen, Byron's voice was to be little heeded by the naval novelists who, encouraged by the success of *The Pilot*, translated their years of service into the materials of fiction. But in America during the first two decades in which Cooper and his contemporaries explored the fictional uses of the sea, in an America surrounded on one side by a virgin continent and, on the other, by the wilderness of the sea, in an America where, long delayed by provincial isolation, the onslaught of romanticism came with especial force and intensity, Byron's note was to set the key.

From a literary point of view, the British interest in the

sea during the eighteenth century, grounded, like that of the American public after 1815, in the excitement engendered by swift commercial and naval expansion, seems premature and abortive. Without the techniques and attitudes of romanticism it could produce only the naval episodes of Smollett, the sailors (salty or sentimental) of the playwrights, and the nautical verse of Falconer and Dibdin. Romanticism, in full flood when American interest in the sea reached its height, permitted a more imaginative, more sensitive, more symbolic, and, at the same time, more realistic conception of maritime life than any that the boundaries of eighteenth-century aesthetics could encompass. It offered a new perception of and response to nature; it manifested a simultaneous concern for the humbly familiar and the strangely exotic; and it invited a union of the awesome and the beautiful in the sublime. By the conclusion of the Napoleonic wars, however, England had turned her attention from the sea. It is significant, perhaps, that the only major British novelist before Conrad to attempt the extensive use of nautical materials was Sir Walter Scott, whose novel *The Pirate* (1822), as Cooper took pains to point out, failed to exploit those materials because of its author's ignorance of their true nature. But in the United States the sea was fresh, meaningful, and above all clearly relevant to the effort to establish a national identity: material fit for the ablest pens. The extraordinary quantity and, at times, high quality of American sea fiction in the first half of the nineteenth century can be accounted for only by the happy coincidence of an extensive and enthusiastic popular interest in maritime life and the availability of the values and perceptions of romanticism.

But appropriate though the time and place may have been for the successful fictional use of nautical materials, the resources of those materials were not to be tested with

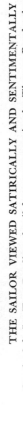

THE SAILOR VIEWED SATIRICALLY AND SENTIMENTALLY

On the left, Lt. Tom Bowling, detail from an engraving by Thomas Rowlandson (1792) for *Roderick Random*; on the right, George Brown, Boatswain's Mate, from the *Naval Magazine* (1836).

MARITIME NATIONALISM AND THE WAR OF 1812

Liberty, America, and Patriotism welcome Columbia's naval heroes to the Temple of Fame; from the title page of *The Naval Temple* (1816).

anything approaching completeness before the appearance of *The Pilot* in 1824. Several forces combined to retard the thorough exploitation of the sea as a literary subject in America: one of the more important was sheer inertia, the general feebleness and timidity of all literary activity in the years immediately following the Revolution. More than that, however, Americans were slow to realize the significance of the sea in their past history, their present condition, and their future prospects. The Jeffersonian emphasis on agrarianism and minimization of commerce for a time diverted the attention of Americans from the ocean; only the steady clamor of maritime growth and naval victory forced the American imagination to look seaward for profit, adventure, and glory. The early experiments that paved the way for the successful literary treatment of the sea by Cooper and his contemporaries rarely attained intrinsic artistic value. Nevertheless, they are significant as gauges of the growth of popular interest in the sea and as attempts to test and refine the means of expressing that interest.

3

The pioneer in the adaptation of American nautical materials to the uses of literature was Philip Freneau, the first in the important line of American writers who combined literary ability with a firm, practical knowledge of maritime life. Freneau, who throughout his life oscillated between the world of words as a journalist and the world of action as the master of a vessel in the West Indian trade, chose the sea as the major subject of his verse, a genre of literature he pursued with persistence, though with uneven results. Freneau's lines, whether of doggerel or of poetry, reflect almost every aspect of American maritime history from 1776 through the War of 1812: the victories of Jones and Barney in the Revolution, the opening of the

China trade in 1784, the attacks on American shipping by England and France during the Napoleonic Wars, and the naval battles of 1812. At least fifty of his compositions focus on the sea, and marine allusions and images enter into many more. Taken as a whole, Freneau's sea verse represents the most substantial use of nautical materials by an American writer before the publication of *The Pilot*.

Unlike his contemporaries, Freneau did not restrict his treatment of maritime life to the reportorial broadside ballad or the sailor's song of the type perfected by Charles Dibdin. Ballads like "Barney's Invitation" and "On the Capture of the Guerrière" testify to Freneau's ability to compose rollicking lines filled with smoke, shot, and hearty oaths, but more important to the evolution of the literary treatment of the sea was his continued effort to utilize nautical subjects in serious poetry. Thus, *The British Prison Ship* (1781) represents the first major attempt since Falconer's *Shipwreck* to conduct a narrative of marine incidents in verse. Time and again in such poems as "The Hurricane," "Lines Written at Sea," and "A Midnight Storm in the Gulph Stream" Freneau tried to capture the sound, smell, appearance, and meaning of the ocean in thoughtful descriptive verse, while in poems like "The Argonaut" and "The Nautical Rendezvous" he explored the motives and nature of men who go to sea.

In adapting maritime materials to serious poetry, Freneau kept close to the path indicated by Falconer. The first canto of *The British Prison Ship* contains the established anomalous mixture of abstract, latinate diction, conventional personifications, and elaborate periphrases with nautical terms that are Anglo-Saxon, colloquial, and specific. Ships are "the train/That fly with wings of canvas o'er the main," as "every sail its various tribute pays." Yet nautical terminology gives precision and flavor to Freneau's description of the onrush of a volley of naval gunfire:

Another blast, as fatal in its aim,
Wing'd by destruction, through our rigging came,
And whistling tunes from hell upon its way,
Shrouds, stays, and braces tore at once away,
Sails, blocks, and oars in scatter'd fragments fly.[7]

The fusion of disparate kinds of diction that runs through all Freneau's serious nautical poetry offers an interesting linguistic parallel to his strangely ambivalent attitude toward seamen and the sea. Only once, in his characterization of Bryan O'Bluster, "a mate of a schooner, bespatter'd with tar," in "Slender's Journey," did he let Smollett's stereotype control his conception of the sailor. Bryan fits the pattern neatly: although "his life was sustained by the virtues of grog," "to see a mean fellow, lord how it would fret him."[8] Like Commodore Trunnion and Tom Pipes, Bryan is less remarkable for his efficiency at sea than for his ludicrousness on land as he stumbles about, bawling nautical commands in a desperate attempt to cope with the alien world of roads and towns and carriages. Freneau's usual characterization is, if less amusing, more thoughtful. At times he views seamen through a captain's eyes as "swearing beasts/Who heaven and hell defy."[9] But more often admiration for this defiant courage of "the nervous race"

Who will support through every blast,
The shatter'd ship, the falling mast[10]

becomes uppermost. The sailors of Freneau's more serious verses are not mere brutes or clowns; their courage redeems them and raises them to a stature that dimly foreshadows the dignity of a Long Tom Coffin or a Jack Chase.

Freneau's admiration for the ship is strong and consistent. To him the ship is the perfect union of utility and beauty, "capacious of the freight," and yet "a stately fabric," "form'd, dispos'd, and order'd" in every part. The beauty of the ship becomes particularly apparent in the interplay of tensions, the dance of color and light, and the momentum of the vessel under sail, images which Freneau's blend of conventional poetic diction and technical terminology can convey with surprising effectiveness:

Too soon the Seaman's glance, extending wide,
Far distant in the east a ship espy'd,
Her lofty masts stood bending to the gale,
Close to the wind was brac'd each shivering sail;
Next from the deck we saw the approaching foe,
Her spangled bottom seem'd in flames to glow
When to the winds she bow'd in dreadful haste
And her lee-guns lay delug'd in the waste.[11]

In Freneau's verse, however, this lively grace and stately symmetry are not unalloyed values, for they serve to tempt man to sea; thus the old sailor Ralph was first lured from the comfort, society, and security of the land:

"With masts so trim, and sails as white as snow,
"The painted barque deceived me from the land,
"Pleased, on her sea-beat decks I wished to go,
"Mingling my labours with her hardy band;
"To reef the sail, to guide the foaming prow
"As far as winds can waft, or oceans flow."[12]

If the beauty of the ship is sinister, then, it is because the sea itself is in some sense evil.

Freneau's conception of the sea is neither clear-cut nor simple. His view is not that of the eighteenth century, which, as we have noticed, saw the ocean as a destructive element that could be exploited for utilitarian purposes by the intelligence and energy of man; nor is it that of the romantics, who reveled in the power and vastness of the sea and viewed it as the emblem of sublimity and freedom. Freneau is fascinated by the sea, but this fascination stems less from its beauty than from its awful power and immensity. Whatever beauty the ocean may have is vitiated

by its loneliness: "the glow of the stars, and the breath of
the wind/Are lost!—for they bring not the scent of the
land!"[13] "Dread Neptune's wild unsocial sea" is not only
lonely but monotonous:

> Seas and skies are scenes that tire
> When nothing more is to admire;
> Soon we wish the land again,
> Nature's variegated scene.[14]

Worse than loneliness, worse than monotony, is the constant threat of death on the ocean, "that inlet to eternity."
Freneau's verse is filled with striking images of death at
sea, where too often beauty serves only as the mask of
horror:

> Though now this vast expanse appear
> With glassy surface, calm and clear;
> Be not deceiv'd—'tis but a show,
> For many a corpse is laid below.[15]

"The Argonaut," Freneau's most successful nautical poem,
stresses the pathos and terror of the seaman's grave, un-
marked and insecure:

> "When conquered by the loud tempestuous main,
> "On him no mourners in procession wait,
> "Nor do the sisters of the harp complain.—
> "On coral beds and deluged sands they sleep,
> "Who sink in storms, and mingle with the deep.
>
> " 'Tis folly all—and who can truly tell
> "What storms disturb the bosom of that main,
> "What ravenous fish in those dark climates dwell
> "That feast on men . . ."[16]

The essential significance of the ocean to man, then, lies
in its capacity to demonstrate human impotence before the
majestic might of nature. In the storm "skill and science
both must fall," for God, not man, controls the sea:

> How feeble are the strongest hands,
> How weak all human efforts prove!—
> He who obeys, and who commands
> Must await a mandate from above.[17]

The reward of maritime life is an awareness of a truth that Freneau's English contemporary George Crabbe phrased succinctly: confronted by the ocean, "Man must endure—let us submit and pray." Yet, at the same time, Freneau derives a kind of stoical delight from the contemplation of an almost inevitably disastrous encounter with superhuman power, for the sea can serve as the supreme proving ground of courage, endurance, and resignation. With Captain Jones he invites man to put himself to the test:

> If thou has courage to despise
> The various changes of the skies,
> To disregard the ocean's rage,
> Unmov'd when hostile ships engage,
> Come from thy forest, and with me
> Learn what it is to go to sea.[18]

In this conception of the voyage as ordeal, Freneau returned to the traditional center of efforts of the human imagination to read the meaning of maritime experience; the voyager becomes the type of all mankind in confrontation with the ultimate realities of life, realities that at once display man's capacity for nobility and lay bare his essential frailty.

4

It is no cause for wonder that Freneau, whose response to the ocean was compounded of this curious mixture of aversion and fascination, expressed an uncertain view of the maritime destiny of America. His subscription to the Jeffersonian doctrine of agrarianism further checked whatever interest he felt in the expansion of American naval and commercial power. In his writings on the subject he consistently minimized the place that the sea was to hold in his country's future; yet, at the same time, he could not restrain his admiration for the men who dare the hardships and terrors of the ocean:

> To every clime, through every sea
> The bold adventurer steers;
> In bounding barque, through each degree
> His country's produce bears.—
> How far more blest to stay at home
> Than thus on Neptune's wastes to roam,
> Where fervors melt, or frosts congeal—
> Ah ye! with toils and hardships worn,
> Condemn'd to face the briny foam;
> Ah! from such fatal projects turn
> The wave dividing keel.

Although the blessings of life at home seem pale indeed in the midst of this song of "the bold adventurer" and his "bounding barque" with its "wave dividing keel," the fact that they are mentioned at all in this context separates Freneau sharply from his Federalist contemporaries.[19]

Even in his verse on the War of 1812, a war which Freneau supported with all his energies, the expression of maritime nationalism is subdued. Freneau is content to preserve the *status quo;* America's aim is "our trade to restore as it stood once before." His most extravagant boast is that the American navy is equal in some respects to that of the British. He assures his readers that "our hearts are as great/As the best in the enemy's fleet." American officers have mastered the techniques of maneuvering fleets; on Lake Erie they "show'd the old brag" that "we, too, could advance in a line."[20] Bravado of this sort seems the epitome of restraint in comparison to the claims and prophecies of Freneau's fellow ballad writers. One of these pictured the heavenly Thrones, Angels, and Principalities assigning the Atlantic to Columbia with these words:

No more shall Albion rule the waves,
For you the broad Atlantic heaves,
    And own[s] your proud control!
For you she visits every shore,
Wafts India's treasures, Afric's ore,
    And wealth from pole to pole![21]

Another envisioned a still wider domain:

Columbia's eagle flag shall fly all fearless o'er the flood,
To every friendly name, a dove—to foes—a bird of blood.
We'll bear the blessings of our land where'er a wave can flow.[22]

To Edwin Holland of Charleston the naval victories of 1812 clearly demonstrated that the ocean was "the region of Glory,/Where Fortune has destin'd Columbia to reign,"[23] and they inspired Benjamin Allen of New York to pen *Columbia's Naval Triumphs*, 1302 lines of heroic couplets in commemoration of Hull, Bainbridge, Perry, and their colleagues. Even the future author of "The Old Oaken Bucket" submerged sentiment in patriotic frenzy and joined the chorus:

Huzza, huzza, huzza, huzza, huzza, boys,
    Free is our soil, and the ocean shall be free;
Our tars, shall Mars, protect beneath our stars,
    And Freedom's Eagle hover o'er the sea.[24]

The popularity of sea ballads in the years following 1812 was nothing new, but their American authorship and nationalistic content were. Before 1812 the overwhelming majority of popular naval songs were of British origin.[25] The author of *A Journal of a Young Man of Massachusetts* deplored this situation and, in issuing a call for the production of American sea songs, summed up neatly both the nationalistic function of such songs and the formula by which they are concocted:

The English naval muse, which I presume must be a Mermaid, half woman and half fish, has, by her simple, and half the time nonsensical songs, done more for the British flag than all her gunnery or naval discipline and tactics. This inspiration of the *tenth* muse, with libations of *grog,* have actually made the English believe that they were invincible on the ocean, and what is still more extraordinary the French and Spaniards were made to believe it also . . . Is not this business of *national songs* a subject of some importance? *Love* and *Patriotism*, daring amplification, with here and there a dash of the supernatural, are all that is requisite in forming this national band of naval music . . . For want of native compositions, we had sung British songs until we had imbibed their spirit, and the feelings and sentiments imbibed in our youth are apt to stick to us through life. It is high time we had new songs put in our mouths.[26]

But by 1816, when it was first published, this complaint was fast becoming obsolete. Although Americans still clung to the comic and sentimental sea songs of Bickerstaffe and Dibdin, their mouths were amply provided with patriotic naval ballads of a thoroughly American character.[27]

5

The drama, as well as verse, reflected the growing hold of the sea on the American imagination in the years before *The Pilot* appeared. English plays containing nautical characters or naval settings had long been popular. Ben Legend first greeted a New York audience in 1750 when Congreve's *Love for Love* was played at the Nassau Street Theater. In 1767 Smollett's nautical farce *The Reprisal* enjoyed four performances on the Philadelphia stage. But the two outstanding successes seem to have been Bickerstaffe's operetta *Thomas and Sally,* which was produced seven times in Philadelphia between 1766 and 1799, and Cross's comedy *The Purse; or, The Benevolent Tar,* which received eight productions in the same city between January 1795 and January 1797.[28]

Although no Freneau arose among American playwrights to challenge English supremacy in the nautical drama, the productions of plays written by Americans and having American marine characters and settings steadily increased in number. As in verse, the connection between American nautical drama and the history of American maritime growth is close and strong. The earliest American nautical drama on record, "The American Citizen," produced in New York on February 3, 1787, celebrated the achievement of the *Empress of China,* the first ship to fly the American flag in Chinese waters.[29] The difficulties with the North African corsairs inspired a spate of plays and musical entertainments that were quick to exploit a situation which afforded a convenient opportunity to combine nautical characters, exotic settings, and nationalistic themes. Although many of these productions are no longer extant, enough survive to provide a clear picture of the genre. James Ellison's *The American Captive* (1812) is a representative example. Ellison stresses his nationalistic intentions, pointing out that "the Drama embraces a subject which is calculated to awaken the feelings of the American reader, as it depicts some of the sufferings to which our sea-faring brethren were exposed prior to the conclusion of the treaties with the Barbary powers," but "as the Drama is of a *national cast,* party reflections are studiously avoided, and such sentiments introduced as will be congenial with the feelings of every lover of his country." Into the setting of palms and palaces bursts Jack Binnacle, an American sailor now enslaved by the Moslems. Jack is a regular-built Dibdin tar; he cheers his comrades with sentiments as bogus as the lingo in which they are phrased: "But never mind, my boys, let the storm blow high or low, the true sons of Neptune never flinch. We'll weather the cape yet, my hearties." This speech is followed, of course, by a rousing sea song. Jack is the perfect vehicle for the author's nationalism, for, like his English prototypes, he is all patriotism: as he assures his captors, "hang me at the yard arm, if I hadn't rather fight 'till my heart-strings snap, than be tributary to any nation." Jack may be a tiger in battle, but, true to the stereotype, he is a lamb in love, for "you must know that the heart of a sailor, though invincible when attack'd by his country's foe, is at once overcome when assail'd by the sparkling eyes of a pretty *girl!*" Jack's patriotic exhortations are capped by the glorious naval spectacle which concludes the play; as two midshipmen sing a duet descriptive of the bombardment of Tripoli, stage directions indicate a scene that must have challenged the ingenuity of any producer:

A distant view of Tripoli by moon-light. The American fleet drawn up in a line of battle before the city . . . On signal from the Commodore's ship several bomb-ketches weigh anchor and stand in for the city . . . Several Tripoline corsairs come out and attack them . . . Several boats blow up . . . Several bastions open fire on the ketches, which is returned by the American frigates.[30]

Meanwhile, other and better playwrights were experimenting with a more realistic portrayal of nautical characters and life. A. B. Lindsley's *Love and Friendship,* written, according to the author's prefatory note, in 1807, is a conventional sentimental comedy that is saved from insipidity by the inclusion of lively and convincing marine elements. It is true that Jack Hardweather, the servant and companion of the hero, resembles closely the traditional old salt of the stage; his speech is heavily interlarded with oaths and nautical metaphors, but at least he neither sings nor falls in love. Like Binnacle, he is a rampant patriot, but he does not studiously avoid partisan politics. Appropriately enough, Hardweather is an enemy of Jefferson's isolationism and jealousy of the navy. And appropriately, too, his nationalism is at its height when he is feeling his liquor: "So to the devil we kick all non-non-importa-tation acts, drydocks, gun boats, Carter's mountain, and protect ourselves like men, by fortifying our har-harbors and building

seventy fours and frigates to keep a look-out ahead for
our enemies and foul weather, my boys!"[31]

But the character of Hardweather is not the only nautical element in *Love and Friendship*. Much of the action
takes place along the waterfront of Charleston, South
Carolina, a major port in the early nineteenth century
and a natural setting for the introduction of Captain
Horner, master of the coasting schooner *Peggy,* and his
hand Jonathan. In the speeches of Jonathan life aboard
"the ole Peggy" is sketched lightly but with rare realism:

I and capun Horner sails in a scheuner . . . Why sometimes I
acts cook, steward, cabin boy, sailor, mate, and bottle washer,
for matter 'f that, for there's on'y four on us aboard on her;
I and the Prentuss, and cousin Bill, and capun Horner; so
when 'e's ashore I plays the skipper.

Informal as this arrangement may seem, Horner's discipline is severe: as Jonathan tells us, "I spose I may's well
go aboard then for sartan for ell be tarnation mad 'f 'e
finds out I on'y been ashore a while, and kick up hell and
leetle Tomy." The *Peggy's* accommodations are limited,
for, as Jonathan frankly informs some prospective passengers, "you won't want for nothen at all on'y what we
aynt got—and that's every thing, that's confurbal."[32] In
these few lines Lindsley thus outlines his portrait of a
humble yet important aspect of American maritime life.
Freneau, at one time the skipper of a coaster plying between New York and Charleston, could have vouched for
its authenticity.

Such experiments in the credible depiction of seamen
and shipboard life on the stage were soon abandoned, as
dramatists rallied to the cause of nationalism at the outbreak of the War of 1812. Like their colleagues the verse
writers, with each naval victory they hammered home to
the American public the importance of the sea to the

national past, present, and future. In plays, pageants, and musical extravaganzas they recounted the prowess of the navy in the Revolution, the Tripolitan War, and the present conflict, and emphasized again and again the doctrine that the sea was the prime source of future national power. The victory of the *Constitution* over the *Guerrière* (August 19, 1812) was hailed in New York by Dunlap's *Yankee Chronology* on September 7, in Philadelphia by "The Constitution; or, American Tars Triumphant" on September 28, and in Boston by "The Constitution and the Guerrière" on October 2.[33] Similar productions commemorated each succeeding naval battle throughout the remainder of the war.

Although the vast majority of these effusions have not survived, sufficient evidence remains to indicate their nature. Most of them were not plays but "olios": hodgepodges of orchestral music, songs, recitations, and pantomimes, all played against elaborate scenery. An advertisement in the Baltimore *Federal Gazette* (October 1, 1813) describes an olio which was presented on the same bill with Goldsmith's *She Stoops to Conquer* and the comic opera "The Heroes of the Lakes" (itself commemorative of the battle of Lake Erie):

On this evening the curtain will rise to a national air and discover (for the first time here) an entire new drop scene representing a splendid temple. In the centre a Rostral Column commemorative of the first seven naval victories achieved by the navy of the United States. The whole painted by Mr. Worrell and assistants, expressly for the occasion. After the play a monody on the late Capt. Lawrence and Lieut. Burroughs, to be spoken by Mrs. Mason. Between the play and the opera will be exhibited a grand naval transparency painted by Mr. Jefferson. The genius of America is seen seated on a rock upon the borders of a lake, presenting to an infant figure of Fame, illustrative of the growing splendor of our naval band a portrait of the youthful hero Commodore Perry. In the perspective a distant view of the enemy's captured fleet at the moment of its being taken possession of by its valiant conqueror and surmounted by our national flag.[34] William Dunlap's *Yankee Chronology,* one of the few of these ephemeral productions that was published, is a less pretentious but equally patriotic piece. This short "musical interlude" opens with a dialogue on a street in New York; Ben Bundle, a young member of the crew of the *Constitution,* which has just returned from her victory over the *Guerrière,* describes the feat to his father Old Bundle and a friend, O'Blunder, with both spirit and technical precision. On the nineteenth of August, as Ben and his shipmates "were cruising in latitude 41, 42 north, longitude 55, 33 west, at 2, P.M. a sail hove in sight to the southward—all hands ahoy to make sail—and before you'd say peas, we had her under top sails, stay-sails, and top ga'nt-sails. Oh! twould have done your heart good to see how she made the sea foam, while every sail swelled like the hearts of her crew at sight of the bragging tyrants of the ocean." Ben, unlike the conventional sailor of eighteenth-century literature, is not treated satirically, nor is he sentimentalized as was Dunlap's earlier sailor Jack Bowlin in *Fraternal Discord,* first performed in 1800. His use of technical terms suggests his professional ability, and his heroic descriptions of his ship and her crew lend him a certain dignity as a participant in the battle. Significantly, too, Dunlap's sailor is not exploited as a source of humor. Rather, by a device that Cooper was to employ in *The Red Rover* and *Jack Tier,* the nautical ignorance of Old Bundle and O'Blunder provides the comedy, feeble though it is:

> *Ben.* We reefed our top-sails, hauled in our courses, and sent down the royals.
> *Bund.* That's right, Ben, down with the royals!—thats an old yankee trick! . . .

Ben. She blazed away like a barn a fire—we stuck to her like true yankee tars—every shot told—
O'Blun. What did they say, Ben?[35]

This hilarious exchange is followed by the rousing title song, which celebrates both the victories of the Revolution and the recent triumph over the *Guerrière.*

The production of reportorial pieces like *Yankee Chronology* naturally declined with the end of the war. But by that time the writers of prose fiction in America were demonstrating their growing interest in maritime subjects and their increasing ability to adopt such subjects to the themes and forms of literature.

6

The earliest American example of the extensive use of nautical elements in prose fiction is a strange little volume entitled *The History of Constantius and Pulchera; or, Constancy Rewarded,* an anonymous chapbook first published in 1794 in Boston. Significantly, in the light of the early sea novels of Cooper, the author of *Constantius and Pulchera* eschewed the pattern of satirical realism established by Smollett and harked back to the still more antique conventions of the romance. Into this tale of the American Revolution he injected nearly the whole catalogue of stock incidents found in classical and Elizabethan romances: abduction aboard ship; shipwreck and miraculous rescue; the assumption of a masculine disguise by the heroine; and a series of sudden separations and remarkable reunions. As several critics have pointed out, the resulting conglomeration of incident is extravagant to the point of absurdity.[36] The hero is snatched from the arms of the heroine by an English press gang on the banks of the Delaware. Forced by her father to embark for France with a wealthy suitor, the heroine rejoins her lover when the British ship in which he is serving captures her vessel.

But shipwreck separates the pair once again. After miraculously floating ashore on a hatch, the heroine is picked up by a privateer from New York. Just before her rescuers are captured by an English sloop of war, the heroine dresses herself as a lieutenant, a disguise which she successfully maintains throughout still another shipwreck, another rescue by an American privateer, another capture by a British cruiser, imprisonment at Halifax, and a final sequence of escape, capture, and rescue which leaves the reader winded and the heroine at Bordeaux, reunited at last with her lover.

But in spite of all this prolonged and violent nautical action, the author of *Constantius and Pulchera* gives almost no sense of the presence of the ship, the sailor, or the sea. He makes little attempt to characterize the hero and heroine, let alone the officers and crews of his vessels. The ships, never named or described, are differentiated only by mention of their nationality and an occasional reference to their general type. The sea itself serves only as a setting that makes possible extravagant adventure, for the author neither indicates any attitude toward it nor attempts to describe it except in storms. Even in those descriptions of storms, he fails to cut through the pattern of convention to the creation of a sense of reality. Rather, the storms of *Constantius and Pulchera* follow a formula as old as the *Aeneid:* "a most beautifully serene day" is suddenly obscured by "a prodigiously black cloud" accompanied by raging winds and mountainous waves; amid the "dreadful peals of thunder" are heard the "fruitless cries and lamentations" of the seamen as the rigging and spars begin to break up; at last the shock of contact with a shoal is felt, and the sea makes its "fatal inroad."[37]

Conventional though the action and description of the book are, the author has made some attempt to particularize his story by embedding it in a historical setting. The threat of the press gang in Philadelphia during the British occupation, the details of the prison at Halifax, and the inclusion of the privateer from Salem in "Essex County, Massachusetts State," all incongrously concrete and specific details in the midst of this stylized and shadowy tale, are tentative efforts of the author to link his romance with the historical reality of an important era in the development of maritime America; as such, they anticipate the method which Cooper, using many of the same conventions, was to follow in his early sea romances.

In sharp contrast to the methods and intent of the author of *Constantius and Pulchera*, Royall Tyler's picaresque novel *The Algerine Captive* (1797) ignores the conventions of romance and, following the precedents of Defoe and Smollett, attempts to cast an aura of credibility over the narration of nautical adventure. Purporting to be the record of the experiences of its narrator, Dr. Updike Underhill, Tyler's novel is characterized by a quantity of reportorial detail and a tone of factual statement that are so convincing that at least one contemporary English reviewer mistook the book for a narrative of actual events.[38] Although most of the peregrinations of Dr. Underhill are by water, maritime material appears infrequently; when it does, however, it is treated with effective realism. Tyler makes good use of his knowledge of nautical technicalities and eye for detail in his descriptions of ships. A certain Moslem vessel, for example, is strangely rigged, "having two masts, a large square main sail, another of equal size, seized by the middle of a mainyard to her foremast, and, what the sailors call, a shoulder of mutton sail abaft." Underhill's ship outruns an Algerine rover by "putting out all her light sails, being well provided with [r]ing sail, scudding sails, water sails, and driver."[39] In its stress on technical precision and authenticity, *The Algerine Captive* emphasizes what was to become a major concern of Cooper, a staunch admirer of Tyler's novel.

Another aspect of *The Algerine Captive* looks forward to Melville, rather than to Cooper. Just as Smollett in *Roderick Random* had emphasized above all the sordidness and brutality of shipboard life, so Tyler reserves his most extensive and compelling treatment of the ship and seamen for the ironically named slaver *Sympathy:*

[The] wretched Africans were transported in herds aboard ship, and immediately precipitated between decks, where a strong chain, attached to a staple in the lower deck, was rivetted to the bar . . . then the men were chained in pairs, and also handcuffed, and two sailors guarded every twenty: while the women and children were tied together in pairs with ropes, and obliged to supply the men with provisions, and the slush bucket; or, if the young were released, it was only to gratify the brutal lust of the sailors . . . The eve after we had received the slaves on board, all hands were piped on deck, and ordered to assist in manufacturing and knotting cat o'nine tails, the application of which, I was informed, was always necessary to bring the slaves to their appetite . . . In vain were the men beaten. They refused to taste one mouthful; and, I believe, would have died under the operation, if the ingenious cruelty of the clerk . . . had not suggested the plan of whipping the women and children in sight of the men; assuring the men they should be tormented until all had eaten.[40]

In this passage and others like it, then, Tyler became the first writer after Smollett to unite the fictional treatment of the sea with the cause of humanitarianism. With the exception of William Leggett and Nathaniel Ames, no American writer of sea fiction before Melville followed Tyler's example.

Like the playwrights who dealt with the North African corsairs, Tyler sounds the trumpet of nationalism in decrying the destruction of American shipping and the enslavement of American citizens. But Tyler was no chau-

vinist; his praises of American liberty are always qualified
by the irony of their conjunction with his description of
the American slave trade. He makes repeated references
to the growth and prosperity of the American merchant
marine, but it is the English "who seem formed for the
command of the sea." Tyler's attitude toward the payment
of tribute to the Barbary States typifies the cautious prac-
ticality of his nationalism. In her present state of weakness America is justified in following the example of the
European maritime countries by "concluding, what some
uninformed men may esteem, a humiliating, and too
dearly purchased peace with these free booters." But
Tyler offers hope for the future assertion of our national
power. In the stirring plea for national unity that concludes the book, the author exhorts his readers to "perceive the necessity for uniting our federal strength to enforce a due respect among other nations."[41] It is apparent
that the history of Dr. Underhill is designed not only to
entertain the reader, but, by appealing to his pride in
the potential physical and moral greatness of his country,
to show him the evils of dissension among factions and
sections and of hypocritical indifference to the national
ideals.

With the publication of *Constantius and Pulchera* and
The Algerine Captive, American novelists had essayed
both of the conventional approaches to the fictional treatment of maritime life: the nautical romance, the heir to
the extravagant devices of classical and Elizabethan fiction, and the pseudovoyage, the offspring of Defoe's concern for verisimilitude. But in the tentative and explora-
tory works of sea fiction that appeared in America before
1823, neither convention established even a temporary
supremacy. Thus the nationalistic spirit of the War of
1812, a major stimulus to the literary use of American
nautical materials, could find expression in both Water-

house's *Journal of a Young Man* (1816), an account so convincing and so full of circumstantial detail that the reader hesitates to accept it as fiction, and *The Champions of Freedom* (1816), Samuel Woodworth's romance of the preposterous career of George Washington Willoughby, a child of nature who is guided along the paths of national duty by the Mysterious Chief, the personification of the American ideal. Although its nautical material is less extensive, *The Champions of Freedom* is the more interesting of the two, because it directly anticipates in its general intent the early historical romances of Cooper. In Woodworth's novel the historical elements of the tale move from the shadowy background of *Constantius and Pulchera* to a position at the front of the stage. That this shift of emphasis was not entirely of Woodworth's volition[42] is reflected in the flabby structure of the book. As the hero, an officer in the American army, dashes from one amatory or military engagement to another, the progress of the war in other quarters is reported to him and the reader by letters from friends who happen to be serving conveniently in the *Constitution* or with Macdonough's squadron on Lake Champlain. Throughout the book, however, Woodworth maintains a steady effort to create a nationalistic frame of heroic proportions within which his characters play out their stories. In Woodworth's eyes the battles of the present war merge with the triumphs of the Revolution to form one continuous pageant of the growing glory and power of America. Not content to let historical events speak for themselves, he tries to symbolize this glory and power in the figure of the Mysterious Chief. Although the Chief, who asks the hero to "think of me as an ALLEGORY," is indeed an absurd and clumsy device, he represents an important attempt to give literary expression to the idea that there is such a thing as an American history and that this history serves to indicate the route by which the nation is to achieve a glorious destiny.

In the adoption of nautical material to the demands of fiction, however, *The Champions of Freedom* represents no significant advance. Although the hero meets Bainbridge, Decatur, and Perry, no report of their conversation is given. A seaman makes an appearance in the person of William O'Hara, an Irishman who, having escaped from the English frigate *Macedonian* in which he was forced to serve, enlists in the American navy. But aside from a good coat of tan and the occasional use of a few conventional nautical metaphors, O'Hara seems totally uninfluenced by his profession. The descriptions of naval battles in the letters of the hero's seagoing friends are chiefly concerned with the statistical detail of numbers involved and casualties. Occasionally, however, a correspondent pauses to comment on the implications of a victory like that of the *Hornet:*

The sinking of the British sloop of war Peacock . . . in fifteen minutes, will fill England with amazement and dismay . . . [It] is a circumstance so extraordinary, that it impresses the minds of our countrymen with an exultation mixed with solemnity! Is it merely our prowess—or is it the finger of Heaven pointing to the path of our future glory?[43]

In response to the stimulus of the victories of 1812, the novel thus had joined with the drama and verse in echoing and strengthening the new awareness of the significance of the sea in the American past and future. But the fiction of the war has little intrinsic worth; its slight and occasional literary values are submerged under the double burden of reportorial detail and jingoistic sentiment.

An event far more remote than the war prompted Charles Lenox Sargent to write *The Life of Alexander Smith* (1819), the most successful extended treatment of nautical subjects in American prose fiction before the appearance of *The Pilot.* The bulk of Sargent's little known pseudovoyage pertains to the theme of island survival, but, unlike *Robinson Crusoe,* it is steadily informed by a concern and admiration for the seaman as such. Based on the history of the mutineers of the *Bounty, The Life of Alexander Smith* is noteworthy in that it gives a full-length portrait of a seaman who is neither a landsman in nautical clothing nor a stereotyped caricature. More than that, the portrait is painted against a vivid and detailed background of American maritime activity in the closing years of the eighteenth century.

The subject of Sargent's novel is Alexander Smith, the mutineer of the *Bounty* who, under the name of Jack Adams, became the patriarch of Pitcairn Island. Purporting to be an autobiography written for the benefit of Smith's descendants, the book is an imaginative extrapolation of the few known facts of Smith's life. Significantly, Sargent converts Smith into an American;[44] he is, in fact, the paragon of Yankee seamanship. Like the author, he is a native of Gloucester, Massachusetts. After receiving his early training in the art of the sailor as a member of the Grand Banks fishing fleet, Smith ships on a Gloucester schooner for Bristol, England, and there joins a brig bound for Bombay. Abandoned on an island near Madagascar, he turns the habitual ingenuity and skill of the Yankee seaman to good advantage: he builds a vessel on the model of the Chebacco boats of his home port and in it manages to reach civilization. Upon his return to the United States he embarks on a ship engaged to hunt seals on the islands off Chile and to trade for furs with the Indians of the Northwest Coast. Left with a sealing party on St. Felix Island for the winter, Smith is forced once again to rely on his own resourcefulness for survival when all but one of his companions are drowned. At last his vessel returns to pick him up and heads for the vicinity of Nootka Sound. Smith, tiring of his shipmates and eager for new adventure, persuades the captain to put him ashore so that he may sojourn with the Indians. When the Indians set him to work constructing a boat for the chief, he decides to seek an easier berth. He steals the vessel he has built, reaches Tinian, journeys to England, and signs on as an able seaman aboard the *Bounty*. From this point on, the plot closely follows the accepted version of the mutiny and of the settlement of Pitcairn, with one important deviation. According to Sargent's story, the settlement is not plunged into a bloodbath of violence; rather, Smith and Christian establish from the start a happy and prosperous community. Sargent accounts for Smith's assertion to later visitors that he is the sole surviving white man as a device to protect Christian and the others, who are hiding in the hills, from punishment by the British authorities.[45]

In attempting to link the *Bounty* incident with America and to portray that most important of all early American maritime ventures, the Northwest trade, Sargent was forced to do violence to the facts of history, for no American vessels were engaged in the Northwest trade before 1788.[46] Although the chronology of Sargent's book is hazy, Smith's service aboard the Northwest trader must have occurred before December 23, 1787, the date the *Bounty* sailed from Spithead. But in spite of this anachronism and the extravagant improbability of the experiences assigned to Smith, Sargent's novel impresses the reader by its quiet, convincing tone of authenticity. In part this effect results from the inclusion of a great amount of accurate detail, detail which makes Smith's exploits credible and their exotic settings real.[47] But the authenticity of *Alexander Smith* springs from more than the verisimilitude produced by a factual background. It is partially the result of Sargent's ability to maintain a diction and syntax appropriate to a literate seaman like Smith; the language of the book is idiomatic and natural, never the impossible jargon of the stage sailor nor the stilted, colorless speech of the typical ideal character. It results, too, from the inclusion of information concerning local customs and habits, information that ties the story to a particular time and place; it is hard to imagine a detail which suggests more richly or economically the Gloucester of the late eighteenth century than Smith's recollection that "as soon as I could haul a brick into the garret window from the ground . . . I was strong enough to haul codfish out of the water." Above all, Sargent's novel is convincing because it is grounded on a perceptive understanding of the motives and nature of man; just as readily as we accept Taji's motives for leaving the *Arcturion* in Melville's *Mardi*, we are satisfied by Smith's reasons for his desire to shake off his shipmates and live with the Indians:

On this voyage we were put on short allowances of every thing. The captain and officers had become soured and morose; and the case was very evident, we had lived too long together, and were heartily tired of the voyage, and each other . . . Sooner than live in hot water continually, with such a quarrelsome and disaffected set, I preferred taking my chance on shore among savages.[48]

Sargent's achievement, then, was twofold. In adapting the materials of American maritime life to the pseudo-voyage, he sketched a panorama of American seamen and their activities that was not surpassed before the appearance of Cooper's *Afloat and Ashore*. Equally important, Sargent was the first novelist, British or American, to treat a nautical character fully and seriously. Smith, unlike Defoe's Crusoe or Captain Singleton, is not only a thorough seaman; he is invested with dignity and a capacity for heroic action. The very nature of Sargent's purpose and material dictated such a characterization. If Smith was to represent the Yankee sailor par excellence, he must not be diminished by satire or softened by sentiment. Moreover, the known facts of Smith's actual accomplishments enforce respect; no stage sailor could become the patriarch of Pitcairn.

As yet, however, American writers apart from Freneau had expressed little of the romantic feeling for the sea and the ship that Cooper was to bring to the novel. The first evidence of the full impact of romanticism on the image of the sea in American literature came in a brief sketch by Washington Irving. "The Voyage," contained in the first number of *The Sketch Book* (1819), is important not only for its priority, but for the dominant influence it was to exert for many years on the tone and content of the American short sea story. In Irving's sketch the sea is no longer entirely divorced from humanity; it is no longer merely an impersonal force against which man pits his courage, strength, and wit to achieve utilitarian ends, nor is it primarily a revelation of the power of a wrathful God. In Irving's eyes, as in Byron's, the sea assumes a new significance through its effect on the human imagination and emotions; it becomes an aesthetic object to be savored for the capacity of its beauty to delight, its immensity to awe, and its danger to excite. Irving's reveries at the maintop, anticipating those of the dreamy romantic at the masthead of Melville's *Pequod,* exemplify the new cultivation of wonder:

There was a delicious sensation of mingled security and awe with which I looked down, from my giddy height, on the monsters of the deep at their uncouth gambols . . . My imagination would conjure up all that I had heard or read of the watery world beneath me: of the finny herds that roam its fathomless valleys; of the shapeless monsters that lurk among the very foundations of the earth, and those wild phantasms that swell the tales of fishermen and sailors.

In his description of a storm, too, Irving's emphasis is

subjective. One ingredient of the formulaic storm of classical and Elizabethan romance is the representation of the
fright of the sailors. But in Irving's account the emotional
effect of the storm is not merely one of several equally
important elements; it dominates the passage. Adjectives
such as "terrible," "awful," and "frightful" receive heavy
stress. The presence of the observer is held before the
reader's consciousness by the reiteration of the verb
"seemed": the clouds "seemed rent asunder" by the lightning, the thunder "seemed echoed and prolonged by the
mountain waves," that the ship remained upright "seemed
miraculous," the waves "seemed ready to overwhelm her."
And in each of these phrases the hyperbolic imagination
of the observer intensifies the force of the storm. The
concluding sentence of the passage illustrates this new
interplay of the human imagination and natural force in
its full development:

As I heard the waves rushing along the side of the ship, and
roaring in my very ear, it seemed as if death were raging
round this floating prison, seeking for its prey: the mere
starting of a nail—the yawning of a seam, might give him
entrance.[49]

The sea is no longer a detached background against which
characters act, a mere natural fact, but a force in which
they are immediately and totally involved.

In retrospect, it seems inevitable that the growing significance of the sea in American life, the availability of
the precedents of British nautical literature, and the gradual accumulation of successful experiments in the literary
use of native nautical materials would lead to the appearance of the fully developed sea novel in the United States
by the end of the nineteenth century. But the combination of interests and abilities that such a work demanded
was a rare one indeed: a love of the sea and an understanding of its importance; a direct acquaintance with maritime

life; an awareness of the unexplored potentialities of the novel as a literary form; and an eagerness to innovate. Perhaps it was less a matter of inevitability than of good fortune that a writer possessing the necessary qualities was at hand in the person of James Fenimore Cooper.

Chapter II

The Tempestuous Ocean for a World

COOPER'S EARLY NAUTICAL ROMANCES

THE SEA NOVEL as we know it owes its inception to the meeting of maritime nationalism and romanticism in the imagination of James Fenimore Cooper.[1] Cooper's experience peculiarly fitted him for his role as innovator of the genre. His voyage before the mast in the merchantman *Sterling* in 1806 and 1807 was crammed with enough excitement to make a deep impression on the mind of any seventeen-year-old boy. English press gangs, Mediterranean pirates, and near collisions were added to the dangers of storm and fog in the crowded and turbulent waters of the Channel and the Mediterranean during the years of the Napoleonic Wars. Upon his return to the United States, Cooper received the naval commission for which his experience aboard the *Sterling* was designed to prepare him.

Though far less exciting than the voyage to England and the Mediterranean, Cooper's three-year service as a midshipman proved still more influential in shaping his literary career, for it made him view the sea not only as the arena of personal adventure but as the locus of national glory. His naval service stimulated that interest in the maritime past of his country that was to culminate in the writing of his *History of the Navy;* it began friendships with officers in the navy that were to sustain his concern with nautical affairs throughout his lifetime; and, most important, it allowed him to experience the glamour of naval service without undergoing the disillusionment of combat. Although the young midshipman chafed at the inactivity of his service and attempted to resign his commission in 1810 because of it, the very frustration of his dreams of naval glory and promotion may be responsible, in part, for his early sea novels, for they can be viewed as fictional fulfillments of his thwarted ambitions.[2] For the nonce, however, Cooper was content, after receiving his discharge from the navy in 1811, to accept the duties of a responsible husband and parent and the prerogatives of a respectable country gentleman.

2

To the former naval officer who, comfortably settled in his new home in Westchester, turned his thoughts "upon ships, and the sea, and farming, and landscape gardening,"[3] the steady clamor of Democratic magazines like the *Port-Folio* on behalf of maritime nationalism and the independence of American literature, must have had a strong appeal. In issue after issue these periodicals called for writers who would challenge the literary supremacy of England as effectively as American seamen had challenged her naval supremacy; for writers who would free themselves from servile imitation of their English masters; for writers who would exploit national materials, among them the maritime victories and heroes of their country.[4] In 1820 a new periodical, *The Literary and Scientific Repository, and Critical Review,* took the field to champion the cause of nationalism, literary and maritime. In the words of William Coleman, one of its sponsors, the *Repository* would be in "no way inferior to the Edinburgh or Quarterly Review; and in one respect, it prefers a superior claim over both, to which no American can be insensible, namely, that instead of insolently reviling and disparaging our laws, learning, habits and nationality, it is our guardian and advocate."[5] Before the *Repository* expired with the publication of its eighth issue in May 1822, it had printed six anonymous contributions of Cooper, four of them on maritime topics, two on literary subjects.

In his two literary articles Cooper reiterated the demand for an independent and national American literature. In reviewing *Bracebridge Hall* he turned the force of his irony on what he judged to be Irving's servile flattery of the English:

It is impossible not to admire the prudence and delicacy, with which our author has touched upon the interesting, but dangerous subject of politics. While he proudly, and no doubt sincerely, declares his increasing attachment to republican principles, he eulogises the aristocracy of Great Britain; descants upon the dignity of descent, and the generous pride of illustrious ancestry! The glorious freedom of the British constitution, is prudently admired, and the great body of the English people are timely and judiciously praised.[6]

Instead of toadying to their English readers, American novelists should chronicle and extol the society and manners of their own country. In his review of Catharine Sedgwick's *A New England Tale* Cooper first stated the nationalistic intention that was to underlie all the novels of his early period with the exception of *Precaution*. The proper theme of American writers should be "our domestic manners, the social and the moral influences, which operate in retirement, and in common intercourse, and the multitude of local peculiarities, which form our distinctive features upon the many peopled earth." Cooper could recall only two novels of any value that had fulfilled this obligation, one of them being "Mr. Tyler's forgotten, and we fear, lost narrative of the Algerine Captive." Historical novels deserve "that place among the memorials of other days, which is due to the early and authentic historians of a country."[7]

In his essays on topics related to the sea, Cooper roughly sketched the outlines of the maritime nationalism that was to become a dominant element in his first three marine romances. Even at this early date Cooper's pronouncements on the subject are set apart from those of his contemporaries by their reflection of his thorough and direct acquaintance with nautical matters and by the restraint and judgment which such a knowledge engendered. He refused to join his fellow maritime nationalists in the claim that already "the trident of Neptune has passed from the grasp of Britannia to that of Columbia." But the very fact that America did not enjoy a monopoly of "the glory of marine warfare" became the basis of his plea for the adoption of practical measures that would fulfill the promise of the young American navy in the War of 1812. Americans "*must* have a navy—powerful, in some measure, as our nation—" for the navy "must and will, at no distant period, become our chief defence against wrongs." The government has the responsibility of enabling the navy to live up to its reputation or letting "that stimulus sleep, which has given it its nobly accomplished renown." Anticipating the method of his early nautical romances, Cooper exhorted the members of the navy to future accomplishments by recalling the glories of the past. He reminded them that "the discipline, subordination, and confidence in each other, which gave them the laurel, can only preserve it to them," and that they must never "lose sight of the words of the departed Lawrence, 'Don't give up the ship.' "[8]

But America's maritime interest was not the exclusive property of the navy. In an essay on tariff policies Cooper stressed the importance of the merchant marine as the keystone of the economy and "the grand engine of Ameri-

can commerce." If Americans possess no natural superiority in naval warfare, the success of their mercantile fleet
seems to be owing to traits peculiar to the American character, traits that have made it "decidedly superior to any
in the world, in skill, in courage, as well as in the knowledge and sagacity by which its operations are guided."[9]
Just as the naval victories of the Revolution and the War
of 1812 give promise of the future naval power of the
United States, so the early achievements of the American
whaling and sealing fleets, the bold commercial exploitation of the Northwest Coast, and the success of American
seamen in competing for the trade with Europe and the
Orient all testify to the eventual domination of commerce
by the American merchant marine. To Cooper at the outset of his literary career, the past was prophecy, and the
stage on which that prophecy was to be enacted was the
sea.

3

The doctrine of maritime nationalism that informs and,
to some extent, accounts for Cooper's early romances of
the sea received full expository expression in his *Notions
of the Americans* (1828), a series of letters in which an
enlightened but fictitious European tourist corrects the
errors and distortions promulgated by foreign commen-
taries on the American scene. To Cooper's Travelling
Bachelor the history of America evinces the strong and
sustained tendency of her people toward the sea. In the
expedition against Louisburg in 1745, in the Revolution,
in the undeclared naval war with France, and in the con-
flicts with the Barbary states, American seamen demonstrated that "the propensity of the nation is . . . decidedly
maritime." The War of 1812 occasioned the most recent
manifestation of this spirit, but it also taught the nation
that naval warfare cannot be waged with spirit alone:

THE SEAMAN AS DEMOCRATIC HERO
Long Tom Coffin on the wreck of the *Ariel*; illustration
by F. O. C. Darley for *The Pilot*.

THE AWESOME SUBLIMITY OF THE SEA

The destruction of the *Ariel*; engraving from a painting by James
Hamilton of a scene from *The Pilot*.

The chief and most lasting effect of the [war] . . . has been to bring a respectable American marine into a sudden existence. . . . The whole nation saw and felt the necessity of protecting their coast, and the friends of the navy have seized the happy moment to interweave the policy [of a powerful naval establishment] with their institutions, in such a manner as to render them henceforth inseparable. That they ought to be inseparable, every man, in the least familiar with the interests of this country, can see.[10]

This policy is as practicable as it is desirable, for America has all that a major maritime power needs. Her seamen have earned a wide reputation for cleverness, responsibility, and activity; above all, "they are not accidents on the surface of society that are willing to float, like most other mariners, whither the current shall carry them, but they are men who can only find the opinions which lie at the root of all their habits, in their native land."[11] America excels not only in the loyalty of her sailors but in the design and construction of her vessels. Cooper's narrator remarks on the durability of the materials used by American shipbuilders, and the speed and economy with which their products are assembled. Most of all, the handsomeness of the vessels impresses the Bachelor. As he enters New York harbor, a panorama of American shipping unrolls before his eyes: the "capacious, beautiful, and excellent" packet ships; a "swift and graceful" fishing smack; the "low, graceful, rakish" pilot schooner; and the spectacle of "the magnitude . . . and beauty of an American steam-boat."[12]

With her long-standing excellence in ships and seamen and with her new consciousness of the importance of the sea to national existence, America will soon be ready, the Bachelor predicts, to acquire the wealth and power that properly belong to her. The vigorous growth of her merchant marine "may much sooner than is now dreamed of, effect a division (if not a transfer) of the commerce, and

consequently of the wealth of the civilized world."
America can anticipate a similar expansion of her naval
might; indeed, "in a very few years this republic will not
be very wary as to its choice of a foe, and in yet a few
more, it will be able to meet fearlessly the greatest power
of the earth in any way that man can elect for the grati-
fication of his lawless propensities." Glorious as the record
of her individual men-of-war has been in the past, the
Bachelor and Cooper look forward to the day when "the
introduction of [America's] fleets into the . . . contests of
Christendom" will "make her a power to be dreaded on
the ocean."[13]

To the discerning and impartial observer, then, the
manifest destiny of the United States is with the sea.
Cooper's traveler grounds his judgment on the nature of
the American character, the history of which demonstrates
"the ability no less than the disposition of the Americans
to continue what they now are—a people more maritime
in their habits and pursuits, compared with their numbers,
than any that exist, or who have ever gone before them."
The opinion that the United States is primarily an agricultural nation is refuted by "the obstinate, glaring, and
long-continued fact, that the American has and does neglect the tillage of his virgin forests, in order to seek more
congenial sources of wealth on the ocean." The very
geography of the country dictates a maritime economy,
for the United States "possesses such an extent of coast,
such rivers, such bays, and such a number of spacious and
commodious havens, as are the property of no other
people." Even the political institutions of America favor
the tendency toward the sea, since a nation "will become
more commercial, and consequently more maritime, precisely as her institutions become more free. The secret of
all enterprise and energy exists in the principle of individuality." Even at the outset of his tour, the Bachelor is

"already deeply impressed with the opinion that America is to be the first maritime nation of the earth."[14]

In the perspective of 1828, Cooper locates the American frontier on the sea. To him the interest in the settlement of the continent seems merely a temporary aberration from the true course of empire, for "the tide of emigration, which has so long been flowing westward, must have its reflux." The promise of opportunity extended by the continental frontier is illusory, and "adventurers in the arts, in manufactures, in commerce, and in short, in every thing else, are already beginning to return from the western to the eastern borders." Discovering that "the great outlet to the rest of the world, the path of adventure, and the only, at least the principal, theatre for military achievements open to the people of this country, is on the ocean," the American imagination is once again turning seaward. The pull of the sea must always be particularly strong in the United States, "where the laboring classes read more . . . of adventure than any where else," a kind of reading that, by stimulating "the restlessness of moral excitement," provides one of the primary "inducements which tempt men to quit the land for the water."[15] An examination of Cooper's literary practice in the years between 1824 and 1830 shows that he conceived it a duty of the patriotic writer to do his utmost to sustain that moral excitement.

4

In attempting to give fictional expression to his conception of the significance of the sea in the life of his nation, Cooper was confronted by awesome difficulties, most of which centered about the problem of tone. Of major importance, of course, was the fact that no precedent existed for what he wished to write: a full-length novel in which the ocean formed the principal setting and in which seamen were the major characters. Among the previous literary treatments of nautical subjects, fragments which conceivably might be combined and ordered to form a useful prototype, few expressed the attitude toward seamen, ships, and the sea that was essential to his meaning. In the original preface to *The Pilot* Cooper paid his respects to Smollett, but he indicated that he was strongly aware of the necessity for a departure from the manner of his great precursor:

It will be seen . . . that, though [the author] has navigated the same sea as Smollet [*sic*], he has steered a different course; or, in other words, that he has considered what Smollet has painted as a picture which is finished, and which is not to be daubed over by every one who may choose to handle a pencil on marine subjects.[16]

Clearly, the democratic seaman, motivated by a yearning for adventure, had very little resemblance to Tom Pipes, nor did the small, swift, and graceful vessels of America have much in common with the ponderous and evil-smelling *Thunder*.

If Smollett's tone of satirical realism was inappropriate, the romanticism of Sir Walter Scott's one attempt at the depiction of nautical materials, *The Pirate*, was scarcely more useful, for, in Cooper's eyes, Scott failed to offer a solution to the crucial literary problem: the fusion of a romantic tone, ideal and exalted, with the technical detail and accuracy that the proper treatment of marine subjects demanded. *The Pirate* is in no sense a sea novel, for the ocean enters into it only as part of the general picturesque setting of Zetland. Occasionally Scott gives a hint of the sublimity of the sea, but his view is always from the shore. Scenes on shipboard are few, incidental, and vague, and, with the exception of the brutal Goffe, sailors are undifferentiated from landsmen. In Cooper's judgment Scott failed to exploit the nautical aspects of his novel because he lacked technical knowledge. The inadequacies of *The*

Pirate became a kind of challenge to Cooper; he determined "to produce a work which, if it had no other merit, might present truer pictures of the ocean and ships than any that are to be found in the Pirate."[17]

Such romantic yet technically accurate pictures must, however, celebrate American maritime activity, and in attempting to select incidents in American history which might serve as suitable frames, Cooper found new difficulties. In his final preface to *The Red Rover* he sums up the problems that face the writer who attempts to combine historical fidelity and the tone of romance:

The history of this country has very little to aid the writer of fiction, whether the scene be laid on the land or on the water. With the exception of the well-known, though meagre incidents connected with the career of Kidd, indeed, it would be very difficult to turn to a single nautical occurrence on this part of the continent in the hope of conferring on a work of the imagination any portion of that peculiar charm which is derived from facts clouded a little by time. The annals of America are surprisingly poor in such events; a circumstance that is doubtless owing to the staid character of the people, and especially to that portion of them which is most addicted to navigation.[18]

The impasse which confronted Cooper was clear: the fictional celebration of his doctrine of maritime nationalism demanded the exalted and ideal tone of romance; the known facts of American maritime history rendered such a tone absurd. The only recourse available to him was to invent appropriate incidents and characters and imbed them in a general historical setting.

This conflict is reflected in the tone of the three nautical romances of the period 1824–1830. Several forces pulled Cooper in the direction of realism. As we have seen, the immediate motivation of the writing of his first sea novel was his seaman-like desire to "present truer pictures of the ocean and ships" than Scott had given, and, indeed, portions of *The Pilot* read like a nautical expert's revision of Scott's pages.[19] Concern for precision and authenticity is continued in the two romances which followed *The Pilot*, for Cooper, who took pride throughout his life in regarding himself as a professional seaman, conceived it to be his obligation as such to preserve the strictest accuracy in all matters involving nautical technicalities. In the first preface to *The Red Rover*, he lays the blame for any errors in his text on the printer and reminds "any keen-eyed critic of the ocean" who should happen "to detect a rope rove through the wrong leading-block" of "the duty of ascribing the circumstances, in charity, to any thing but ignorance on the part of a brother." If accuracy was necessary to preserve Cooper's professional standing among his fellow seamen, it was all the more necessary to serve the best interests of laymen. It behooved the pioneer in maritime fiction to adhere rigidly to the truth of nautical life. Resisting the temptation to cater to the ignorance and credulity of landsmen by entertaining them with extravagant impossibilities, he must, in the words of the first preface to *The Pilot*, make an honest attempt "to paint those scenes which belong only to the ocean, and to exhibit . . . a few traits of a people, who, from the nature of things, can never be much known." Still another limitation on Cooper's freedom to depart from the accurate representation of reality was imposed by the historical framework on which he constructed his early sea novels. The author of *The Pilot* and its successors must be able to assure "curious inquirers into our annals" that they "shall find good poetical authority for every material incident in this veritable legend."[20]

But still more powerful influences demanded the materials and tone of romance. Prime among them, of course, was Cooper's desire to give appropriate fictional expression to his doctrine of maritime nationalism. Important too, however, were purely literary influences. In spite of his admiration for "the inventive talent which employs itself in the province of daily life, which delineates what we have all felt and observed," the early Cooper felt that "the delight of pure imagination, the transportation of ourselves beyond our own bounded vision and existence to the past and the distant, into scenes of splendor, and into conditions which fancy has devised, and fancy alone could sustain or enjoy, are among the rarest pleasures that the reader of fiction tastes."[21] Cooper's penchant for high romance apparently first manifested itself when, at the age of eleven, he was so delighted with "certain old-fashioned heroic romances" that he began the composition of a tale in imitation of his favorite, *Don Belianis of Greece;* "it was to be a great heroic romance, with knights, and squires, and horses, and ladies, and castles, and banners."[22] By the time Cooper reached maturity a far superior, but equally remote and magical work, *The Tempest,* seems to have replaced *Don Belianis* in his literary affections.[23] Clearly, such a taste would find many of the elements of early nineteenth-century romanticism congenial. With the tide of the popularity of Scott and Byron at full flood in America, sublimity, supernaturalism, Satanism, and exoticism must have seemed to Cooper in the 1820's to be inevitable characteristics of romantic fiction.

The resolution of all these intentions and influences achieves its most successful and most typical expression in the second of Cooper's three early romances of the sea, *The Red Rover* (1827). The experimental and tentative nature of *The Pilot* makes it in some ways uncharacteristic of not only the early romances but of Cooper's sea fiction as a whole. To an extent, the author of *The Pilot* shares Scott's reluctance to leave the shore: the majority of the chapters concern action on land, and none of the marine episodes takes place beyond view of the coast.[24] More important, Cooper does not seem to have developed in *The Pilot* the complete and consistent conception of the meaning of the sea that informs its successors, for in its depiction of nautical life the novel places the same emphasis on social order, discipline, and decorum that separates *The Pioneers* from the later Leather-Stocking Tales. *The Water-Witch*, on the other hand, departs from the hypothetical norm represented by *The Red Rover* in that Cooper's concern with the fictional representation of maritime activities is rivalled by his interest in re-creating the supernatural and dream-like mood of *The Tempest* and in rhetorical experimentation.[25] *The Red Rover* is the "purest" sea novel of the three and as such is most nearly in the center of the stream of Cooper's nautical fiction.

5

Early in the summer of 1827, during his first residence in France, Cooper began the composition of his second nautical romance. Even in the pleasant country house in Saint-Ouen on the banks of the Seine, his thoughts apparently turned with ease once again "upon ships, and the sea," for, writing with his usual speed, he had the final chapter ready for shipment to his American publishers by October 15.[26] As he worked on his book, the memory of the passage to England during the preceding summer and the exciting trial of speed between his vessel and a rival packet must have been still fresh in his mind.[27] Equally available, however, was the broad and detailed knowledge of American maritime history that he had first revealed in his authoritative review for the *Repository* of Clark's *Naval History*. From the welter of materials Cooper had to choose those which were adaptable to the tone of romance. A passage from *Notions of the Americans,* published only a few months after *The Red Rover,* indicates and justifies the nature of his choice:

The history of the colonies . . . is not altogether destitute of nautical incidents, that were rather remarkable for skill and enterprise. The privateers of this hemisphere were always conspicuous in the colonial contests; and they were then, as they have always been since, of a character for order and chivalry that ought not to be too confidently expected from a class of adventurers who professedly take up arms for an object so little justifiable, and perhaps so ignoble, as gain. But men of a stamp altogether superior to the privateersman of Europe were induced, by the peculiar situation of their country, to embark in these doubtful military enterprises in America. There was no regular service in which to show their martial qualities; and those among them who felt a longing for the hazards and adventures of naval warfare, were obliged to hoist those semi-chivalrous flags, or to stay at home.[28]

With a little intensification of the chivalry of such nautical adventurers and the dubiousness of their calling, the components of a new maritime romance were ready to Cooper's hand. He had found the perfect historical frame for the ponents of a new maritime romance were ready to Cooper's his experience supplied him.

From the outset *The Red Rover* serves as the vehicle of Cooper's sturdy nationalism. In the opening pages he imbeds his narrative firmly in the historical matrix that he had selected and emphasizes the significance of the era to the destiny of the American nation; the time is 1759, "a period fraught with the deepest interest to the British possessions on this continent":

A bloody and vindictive war, which had been commenced in defeat and disgrace, was about to end in triumph. France was deprived of the last of her possessions on the main, while the immense region which lies between the Bay of Hudson and the territories of Spain submitted to the power of England. The colonists had shared largely in contributing to the success of the mother-country. Losses and contumely, that had been incurred by the besotting prejudices of European commanders, were beginning to be forgotten in the pride of success. The blunders of Braddock, the indolence of Loudon, and the impotency of Abercrombie, were repaired by the vigour of Amherst, and the genius of Wolfe. In every quarter of the globe, the arms of Britain were triumphant.

But the significance of the era resides not only in the vast territorial acquisitions of the English-speaking peoples; the ironic disparity between the enthusiastic loyalty of the colonists, always among "the loudest in their exultations and rejoicings" over British victories, and the "scanty meed of applause" they received in return from the English was preparing the way for rebellion. Yet, for the moment, "the loyalty to the crown of England, which endured so much before the strange principle became extinct, was . . . at its height; and probably the colonist was not to be found who did not, in some measure, identify his own honour with the fancied glory of the house of Brunswick."[29]

Against this background of blind loyalty, Cooper draws the figure of the Red Rover, the outlawed visionary who alone perceives the drift of history. Finding it " 'a disheartening thing to be nothing but a dweller in a colony,' " the Rover conducts a private war of independence. Although he must satisfy his piratical crew by attacking the ships of all nations, he takes particular delight in seeing " 'St. George come drooping to the water.' " for he " 'would rather lower the pride of the minions of King George than possess the power of unlocking his treasury.' " In his moment of triumph over the English sloop *Dart*, this premature rebel strikes a symbolic pose: "one foot was placed, seemingly with supernatural weight, on that national emblem which it had been his pride to lower."[30]

Since he is Cooper's creation, the Rover's dreams of an independent America are closely linked to the doctrine of maritime nationalism. In a conversation with Wilder, the hero of the love-plot and a newcomer to the Rover's ship, he discloses his vision of the glorious destiny of America, a destiny that depends on the exploitation of her maritime resources:

"You have seen my flags, Mr. Wilder: but there was one wanting among them all; ay, and one which, had it existed, it would have been my pride, my glory, to have upheld with my heart's best blood!"

"I know not what you mean."

"I need not tell a seaman like you, how many noble rivers pour their waters into the sea along this coast . . . how many wide and commodious havens abound there—or how many sails whiten the ocean, that are manned by men who first drew breath on that spacious and peaceful soil?"

"Surely I know the advantage of my native country."

"I fear not," quickly returned the Rover. "Were they known as they should be, by you and others like you, the flag I mentioned would soon be found in every sea; nor would the natives of our country have to succumb to the hirelings of a foreign prince."

"I will not affect to misunderstand your meaning; for I have known others as visionary as yourself in fancying that such an event may arrive."

"May!—As certain as that star will set in the ocean, or that day is to succeed to night, it *must*. Had that flag been abroad, Mr. Wilder, no man would have ever heard the name of the Red Rover."[31]

Thus Cooper embodies the theme of nationalism in the Rover's quest for a flag, a quest that, being paralleled by the other major line of action, Wilder's search for familial identity, establishes the primary motif of the narrative. At the close of the novel, both men are freed from their sense of isolation and homelessness, as Wilder's search comes to an end in the discovery of his mother and the Rover finds the nation for which he has longed. In the brilliantly melodramatic scene in which the Rover dies, a death scene rivaled in Cooper only by the account of the death of Bumppo in the nearly contemporaneous *Prairie,* the flag once again functions as a thematic symbol. As the

citizens of Newport celebrate another and more genuine
triumph, the victory at Yorktown, the dying Rover is
carried into Wilder's house:

> With a supernatural effort, his form rose on the litter; and,
> with both hands elevated above his head, he let fall before
> him that blazonry of intermingled stripes, with its blue
> field of rising stars, a glow of high exultation illumining
> every feature of his face, as in his day of pride.
> "Wilder!" he repeated, laughing hysterically, "we have
> triumphed!"—He fell backward, without motion, the exulting
> lineaments settling in the gloom of death, as shadows obscure
> the smiling brightness of the sun.[32]

In one of their many aspects Cooper's first three sea
novels form a trilogy depicting the growth of the separation
between America and England[33] and the slow awakening
of an American national consciousness. In *The Water-
Witch,* designed to show the first stirrings of what was to
become "a nation of singular boldness and originality in
all that relates to navigation," Van Beverout and the crew
of the free-trading brigantine chafe under the restrictions
imposed by their English governors, and their desire for
commercial freedom becomes identified with a yearning
for political independence.[34] As we have seen, a major
theme of *The Red Rover* is the search for national identity,
a search brought to successful completion in *The Pilot,*
which is set in a period "that has a peculiar interest for
every American . . . because it was the birthday of his
nation."[35] In their common celebration of national independence Cooper's first three nautical romances gain a
kind of epic unity. In each the free and daring life of the
sea becomes equated with the promise of political identity
and liberty, as if the values of the seaman's calling neces-
sitated the eventual self-realization of a people so thoroughly maritime as the Americans.

6

Although history provides the frame for *The Red Rover,*
the central panel in Cooper's panorama of independence,
the surprising poverty of the maritime annals of America
in specific events of an appropriately romantic nature
forced him "to invent his legend without looking for the
smallest aids from traditions or facts"; indeed, "there is
no authority whatever for any incident, character, or scene,
of the book . . . unless nature may be thought to furnish
originals, in a greater or less degree, to some of the pictures."[36] But if no historical authority exists for the incidents and characters, there are good literary precedents for
many of them.

Like that much earlier attempt to give fictional expression to the American maritime past, *Constantius and Pulchera, The Red Rover* draws heavily on the stock materials
of romance. Incidents and characters that were already
conventional in the fiction of ancient Greece are dusted
off and set in motion on the shores and waters of the New
World. Gertrude Grayson, the romantic heroine of the
novel, must suffer the hackneyed ordeal of being kid-
napped aboard ship by a pirate, an experience made all
the more titillating for the reader by the fact that her
captor, the Rover, is forced to play the time-honored role
of the amorous captain, over whose better nature "it
might have been fancied that some unholy and licentious
passion was getting the ascendancy." Like Cooper's other
two early nautical romances, *The Red Rover* leans on the
convention of the female character in masculine disguise;
the long implied femininity of Roderick, the Rover's supposed cabin boy, is at last revealed in the final chapter.
Most familiar of the conventional devices employed in
The Red Rover is the remarkable reunion, made all the

more remarkable by Cooper, who substitutes a tattoo and a dog tag for the customary birthmark.[37]

Although, as Marcel Clavel has pointed out,[38] it is highly unlikely that Cooper drew directly on classical literature as a source, the conventions of romance were readily available to him through the medium of his favorite kinds of writing. Such incidents are a stock in trade of the old chapbook romances like *Don Belianis,* and most of them occur in the plays of Shakespeare.[39] In navigating the same sea as Smollett, Cooper found a still more recent precedent for the revival of the classical clichés; *Roderick Random,* for example, employs both a kidnapping aboard ship and a remarkable reunion. And the romantic writers like Scott, Byron, and Hope, at the height of their popularity during the decade in which Cooper was writing his first three sea novels, gave a new and authoritative currency to kidnappings, disguises, reunions, and all the other stock devices of romance.

But the influence of the new romanticism on Cooper was by no means confined to its reiteration of such narrative conventions. In *The Red Rover* and to a lesser extent in *The Pilot* and *The Water-Witch,* he makes free use of the innovations in characterization and setting that his English contemporaries had popularized. In its treatment of the supernatural, *The Red Rover* bears strong resemblance to the romances of Scott. Just as Scott in *The Pirate* uses the Zetlanders' superstitions to increase the intensity and stature of Norna, so Cooper dwells on the superstitious fears of the townspeople of Newport and the crew of the *Royal Caroline* in order to magnify the reader's conception of the Rover and his vessel. In the opening dialogue between the tailor Homespun and Pardon Hopkins, his gullible customer, the Rover is portrayed as ubiquitous and indestructible, like his imagined ally the Devil. Homespun has heard from an eyewitness that the Rover is " 'a man may-be half as big again as the tall preacher over on the main, with hair of the colour of the sun in a fog, and eyes that no man would look upon a second time.' " His ship " 'appears to sail faster than the clouds above, seeming to care little which way the wind blows.' " The ability of the Rover's *Dolphin* to carry sail and her speed make her "the subject of wonder" to the crew of the *Caroline*. One seaman confesses that " 'there is something in the ship to leeward that comes athwart my fancy like a drag,' " and another declares that " 'it is idle to think of outsailing a craft that the devil commands.' " All agree that the *Dolphin* suspiciously resembles the spectral *Flying Dutchman*.[40] Like Scott, Cooper never insists on the supernatural; he makes it clear that it is the product of the ignorance of village gossips and the "untutored faculties" of eighteenth-century sailors, but he nevertheless succeeds in making the Rover seem larger than life by means of these vague but recurring suggestions of preternatural abilities.

A still more important element of the new romanticism in *The Red Rover* is the persistent strain of Byronism that runs through the novel. The clearest manifestation of the influence of Byron on the novel is, of course, in the characterization of the Rover, for Cooper's hero is not only the amorous captain of classical romance, but the noble outcast, the aloof and inscrutable superman, the passionate, guilt-ridden sufferer of Byron and his imitators. In particular, Cooper seems to have been influenced by *The Corsair*, Byron's tale of a nautical outlaw. The Rover and Conrad, the hero of *The Corsair*, resemble each other closely: both men combine great vigor with rather slight statures; the originally fair complexions of both have been dyed red by exposure; both have luxuriant curls, and each reveals his scornful arrogance in the shape of his mouth. The faces of the Rover and Conrad mirror the workings of passion: the Rover's "speaking countenance" betrays "all the sudden and violent changes" that denote "the workings of a busy spirit within"; Conrad's "features' deepening lines and varying hue" indicate the turmoil of "feelings fearful, and yet undefined."[41]

The characters as well as the persons of the Rover and Conrad are nearly identical. Both men are inscrutable but terrifyingly perceptive of the motives and intentions of others.[42] The Rover knows "how to curb" the violence of his "band of desperate marauders," just as Conrad has "learned to curb the crowd" by his commanding manner. Although the pirates of Cooper and Byron are cruel and implacable in their hatreds, neither was born evil. Rather, they are the victims of thwarted ambition: the Rover becomes the enemy of society only after his merits are unrewarded by his British superiors; Conrad, too, has been "warped by the world in Disappointment's school."[43]

Even the trappings and furniture of the Rover are Byronic. Just as Conrad's ship flies a "blood-red signal," the Rover scorns the conventional skull and crossbones for "a deep, blood-red field, without relief or ornament of any sort." The Rover arms himself with typically Byronic weapons, a brace of pistols thrust through a leather belt and "a light and curved yatagan, which, by the chasings of its handle, had probably come from the manufactory of an eastern artisan." The exotic luxuriance with which the Rover's cabin is furnished—the silver lamp and candlesticks, the mahogany table, the velvet couch and blue silk divan with its piles of pillows, the cut-glass mirrors, polished plate and rich hangings—seems modeled on the eastern interiors of the early cantos of *Don Juan*.[44]

Whether the Satanism and exoticism of *The Red Rover* came exclusively from the oriental tales of Byron or whether they were drawn from a wide range of the Gothic and Oriental literature of the late eighteenth and early nineteenth centuries probably never can be established conclusively;[45] it seems clear, however, that *The Red Rover* and, only to a slightly lesser extent, *The Pilot* and *The Water-Witch* are marked by definite characteristics of the new romanticism, characteristics that are most conveniently labeled Byronic. When, in 1838, Cooper again turned to the sea as the subject of his fiction, he abandoned once and for all the psychology and apparatus of the Byronic hero in favor of more realistic characterization. But the influence of the Byronic conception of the sea survived the shift toward realism and continued to distinguish Cooper's sea novels from the work of his English contemporaries.

7

Surveying Cooper's novels for the *North American Review* in 1832, William Hickling Prescott singled out a certain "poetic" feeling as their great virtue; he found that this quality "is particularly apparent in [Cooper's] representations of his own element, the ocean, which he seems, like Byron, to have animated with a living soul." To feel the originality and superiority of Cooper's treatment of the sea, one need only "contrast it with the no less accurate, but comparatively vulgar sketches of another poet sailor, Smollett."[46] This emphasis on Cooper's departure from Smollett and his kinship with Byron is of the utmost relevance to an understanding of the means by which Cooper created a fictional image of maritime life worthy of the grand role that the sea was to play in the destiny of America. The contrast which Prescott suggests between Cooper and Smollett reveals the relative poverty of Smollett's conception of the ocean and the ship, as Marcel Clavel eloquently points out in his brilliant study of *The Pilot*: "Le sublime spectacle de l'océan déchaîné, la grandeur du marin triomphant des éléments par l'intelligence et la manœuvre, la vaillance du navire qui lutte et résiste comme un être vivant, la gloire qui illumine le carnage, Smollett n'avait presque rien vu, rien senti de tout cela."[47]

At the opposite end of the scale from Smollett's anthropocentric view, as we have seen, is the emphasis on the sublimity of the sea in Byron's *Childe Harold.* In *The Corsair,* however, Byron supplies a necessary counterweight to the diminution of man implicit in Harold's conception of the sea, for there the ocean becomes the area of human freedom and achievement. The thoughts and hearts of Selim's crew are boundless and free as " 'the glad waters of the dark blue sea.' " In language reminiscent of that of Captain Jones's inducements to his recruits in Freneau's ballad, Byron's seamen glory in the ocean as a source of delight and an avenue to self-realization:

> "Oh, who can tell, save he whose heart hath tried,
> And danced in triumph o'er the waters wide,
> The exulting sense—the pulse's maddening play,
> That thrills the wanderer of that trackless way?"

And in *The Corsair* the ship, that "walks the waters like a thing of Life,/And seems to dare the elements to strife," becomes the glorious weapon with which man can challenge the sea.[48]

An examination of Cooper's treatment of the sea in *The Red Rover* substantiates Prescott's observation of the resemblance to Byron and the departure from Smollett. In Cooper's book the ocean moves to the foreground of the narrative, rivaling and sometimes displacing the human characters in importance. At the beginning of the marine action of *The Red Rover* the sea performs the function that the natural setting does in Scott's novels; it serves to set the emotional key, to reflect and reinforce the mood of the narrative. As the *Caroline* makes her departure from the coast, the appearance of the ocean belies the hopes that the unusual speed of his vessel had raised in Wilder's heart, for, "in the midst of these encouraging omens, the sun dipped into the sea, illumining, as it fell, a wide reach of the chill and gloomy element. Then the shades of night gathered over the illimitable waste." By constant reference back and forth between his account of the feelings of the characters and his description of the ocean, Cooper intensifies the sense of foreboding and the feeling of isolation from the security of land and civilization; the eyes of the *Caroline's* people "wandered over the expanse of troubled water to leeward, but nowhere could they see more than the tossing element, capped with those ridges of garish foam which served only to make the chilly wastes more dreary and imposing."[49]

As the narrative progresses, however, the sea gradually assumes a new role. No longer merely a mood-setter, the ocean becomes a character in its own right; with the approach of the storm the focus of the reader's attention is shifted from Wilder and his charges to the ship as protagonist and the sea as antagonist. Cooper increasingly treats the ocean as a living being: it "appeared admonished that a quick and violent change was nigh"; the waves lifted "their surly summits"; it was "as if the startled element was recalling into the security of its own vast bosom that portion of its particles which had so lately been permitted to gambol madly over its surface." The storm drives down upon the *Caroline* "with the speed of a race-horse," wrecks her, and then the sea subsides, "though still gently heaving in swells so long and heavy as to resemble the placid respiration of a sleeping infant."[50] The pattern is repeated again and again in the course of the story; in moments of crisis—the sinking of the *Caroline,* the threat of storm to Wilder's open boat, the combat between the *Dolphin* and the *Dart*—the ocean relinquishes its ordinary function of establishing and emphasizing mood to become an antagonist of proportions that dwarf Cooper's men and women.

Although the functional importance of the ocean in Cooper's narrative clearly indicates the extent of his innovation in the fictional treatment of nautical subjects, an understanding of the nature of that innovation requires an analysis of the highly complex and often ambiguous system of meanings and values that he assigns to the sea. In general, it would seem that in Cooper's marine fiction the ocean embodies most of the qualities that the wilderness does in his novels of the frontier. As a modern critic of Cooper has pointed out, "the sea and the wilderness, the water and the forest, were always intimately associated in his mind—witness, in particular, the aqueous quality of *The Pathfinder*."[51] This association is evinced not only in books like *The Pathfinder* and *Oak Openings* in which water and forest are juxtaposed, but in all of the novels of the wilderness, for Cooper habitually uses marine metaphors and analogies in drawing his pictures of the woods and the woodsman's life. Such allusions occur most frequently in descriptions of the appearance of the wilderness, where they emphasize the qualities of vastness and uniformity; they range from such simple near clichés as "the green ocean of woods" to detailed extended comparisons:

From the summit of the swells, the eye became fatigued with the sameness and chilling dreariness of the landscape. The earth was not unlike the ocean, when its restless waters are heaving heavily, after the agitation and fury of the tempest have begun to lessen. There was the same waving and regular surface, the same absence of foreign objects, and the same boundless extent to the view . . . Here and there a tall tree rose out of the bottoms, stretching its naked branches abroad, like some solitary vessel; and, to strengthen the delusion, far in the distance appeared two or three rounded thickets, looming in the misty horizon like islands resting on the waters.[52]

In Cooper's eyes the traveler in the American wilderness

has the lonely majesty of a ship. The aging Leather-Stocking sets out "alone into the waste, like a bold vessel leaving its haven to enter on the trackless field of the ocean."[53] The party of Corny Littlepage leaves "the grave of the hunter, in the depths of that interminable forest, as the ship passes away from the spot on the ocean where she has dropped her dead."[54] And the wilderness, like the sea, demands extraordinary knowledge and skill on the part of those who would live by it. The experienced frontiersman can identify Indian tribes "with the same readiness, and by the same sort of mysterious observation, as that by which the seaman knows the distant sail."[55] He can find his way through the forest as "accurately and as unhesitatingly as the mariner directs his course by the aid of the needle over the waste of waters."[56]

Much as one is tempted to equate the wilderness and the sea under the steady pressure of such comparisons, significant differences separate Cooper's conception of these two aspects of nature. True, they share the common qualities of sublime vastness and loneliness. They both represent what one critic has described as a "refuge from the oppressiveness of a compact society" and another as "the *apeiron* —the area of possibility."[57] Yet the contrast between what Cap in *The Pathfinder* describes as " 'your combing seas, your blue water, your rollers, your breakers, your whales, or your water-spouts, and your endless motion' " of the ocean and "the holy calm and poetical solitude of the forest"[58] is the emblem of a fundamental distinction. In the wilderness the enemy is always human, a Magua, a Captain Sanglier, or a Scalping Peter. But in Cooper's sea novels the destructive capability of man is eclipsed by the power of storm and reef and ice. Time and again human combatants are united by the natural force that threatens both. The violent death of Long Tom Coffin and the peaceful end of Natty Bumppo are the inevitable consequences of their professions, for the skilled and experienced woodsman can cope with his environment; the seaman with an equivalent skill and experience cannot.

The interpretation of the sea that Cooper offers in the early nautical romances reflects this ambivalence. At times, usually in the speeches of female characters, the ocean is portrayed as beautiful, grand, deliciously dangerous. In *The Water-Witch* Alida observes " 'a mingling of the terrific and the beautiful, of the grand and the seducing, in this unquiet profession' " of the seaman. But the angle of vision of the romantic sensibility is not the only one; there is little beauty or grandeur in the death of a seaman who is pulled from his raft when a shark strikes his fishing line:

> The shock was so sudden and violent, that the hapless mariner was drawn from his slippery and precarious footing into the sea. The whole passed with a frightful and alarming rapidity. A common cry of horror was heard, and the last despairing glance of the fallen man was witnessed. The mutilated body floated for an instant in its blood, with the look of agony and terror still imprinted on the conscious countenance. At the next moment, it had become food for the monsters of the sea.
>
> All had passed away, but the deep dye on the surface of the ocean. The gorged fish disappeared: but the dark spot remained near the immovable raft, as if placed there to warn the survivors of their fate.[59]

By compounding multiple points of view, Cooper produces a richly complex definition of the meaning of the ocean. In *The Red Rover* he confronts his characters with a seascape rendered ambiguous by the misty moonlight; the romantic Gertrude, the pious Mrs. Wyllys, and the experienced Wilder respond to different aspects of the scene:

> Gertrude shuddered on reaching the deck, while she murmured an expression of strange delight. Even Mrs. Wyllys

gazed upon the dark waves, that were heaving and setting in the horizon, around which was shed most of that radiance that seemed so supernatural, with a deep conviction that she was now entirely in the hands of the Being who had created the waters and the land. But Wilder looked upon the scene as one fastens his gaze on a placid sky. To him the view possessed neither novelty, nor dread, nor charm.[60]

Thus Cooper's use of the romantic conception of the sea is roughly akin to his use of the supernatural; the double points of view, that of the landsman and that of the sailor, allow him to exploit the effects of the romantic vision without restricting himself to it. He can express the "poetic feeling" his contemporaries so admired without sacrificing the practical realism which his role as a professional seaman demanded.

For the ocean, to the seaman, is not a sublime spectacle but an arena in which he fights for the reward of self-realization. If he is largely insensible to the beauty and majesty of his element, he is not overawed by its dangers. Adrift in an open boat after the foundering of the *Caroline,* Wilder's female charges succumb to their fears:

On every side lay the seemingly illimitable waste of waters. To them, their small and frail tenement was the world. So long as the ship, sinking and dangerous as she was, remained beneath them, there had appeared to be a barrier between their existence and the ocean. A single minute had deprived them of even this failing support, and they now found themselves cast upon the sea in a vessel that might be likened to one of the bubbles of the element. Gertrude felt, at that instant, that she would have given half her hopes in life for the mere sight of the vast and nearly untenanted continent which stretched for so many thousands of miles along the west, and kept the world of waters to their limits.

But Wilder's response to the danger is one of cheerful confidence in his skill and experience: "with a well-trimmed ship, and a fair breeze, . . . we may yet hope to reach the land in one day and another night."[61] As a result of this balance between the romantic and the professional points of view, the sea, vast and wild though it may be, never completely overshadows man as it does in *Childe Harold*. As Joseph Conrad, whose brief but penetrating comments on Cooper's marine novels contain the most thoughtful criticism they have received, has remarked, "in his sea tales the sea inter-penetrates with life; it is in a subtle way a factor in the problem of existence, and, for all its greatness, it is always in touch with the men, who, bound on errands of war or gain, traverse its immense solitudes."[62]

Cooper's seamen delight in the challenge of the ocean as an opportunity to test their strength and skill. Their most articulate representative, the Rover, finds the ocean the perfect outlet for his Byronic restlessness:

"I love suspense; it keeps the faculties from dying, and throws a man upon the better principles of his nature. Perhaps I owe it to a wayward spirit, but, to me, there is sometimes enjoyment in an adverse wind . . . Calms may have their charms for your quiet spirits; but in them there is nothing to be overcome. One cannot stir the elements, though one may counteract their workings."[63]

In all three of the early nautical romances, and in many of the later sea novels, Cooper uses the sea to prove the worth of a hitherto ambiguous character. The skill which Mr. Gray manifests as he cons the frigate through the tortuous straits of the English coast allows the reader to anticipate Griffith in his recognition of the pilot's true nobility. No one who has witnessed the Rover's prodigious feats of seamanship can accept the character which rumor ascribes to him. And, with Ludlow, the reader sheds his contempt for the master of the *Water-Witch* as the brigantine successfully navigates the perilous Hell Gate. By serving in these epiphanal episodes as the major device for revealing character, Cooper's conception of the ordeal as

the central experience in maritime life becomes an integrated and essential part of the structure of his narrative.

To Cooper the ocean is the ideal proving-ground of
human character because, like the wilderness, it is out of
civilization. It offers a way of life unfettered by artificial
restrictions and stripped of the security of an ordered
society. It shatters the decorum of civilization and allows
natural feeling to find expression; indeed, "one hour of
the free intercourse of a ship can do more towards soften-
ing the cold exterior in which the world encrusts the best
of human feelings, than weeks of the unmeaning ceremonies of the land." Yet, seen from another point of view,
the free state of nature is a lawless jungle in which strength
and craft are the only sanctions. The Rover must protect
himself from his savage crew; the extraordinary fortifica-
tion of the after portion of his vessel, his reliance on the
support of the marine guard in any conflict with the seamen, and the systems of informers by which he anticipates
the plans of the crew, all show "how hard it is to uphold
an authority that is not established on the foundation of
legitimate power."[64]

Although it becomes a dominant theme of Cooper's later
novels of social criticism, the notion of legality and social
order never seriously intrudes upon the romantic celebration of wild freedom in *The Red Rover*. If the Rover
resembles a trainer in a cage of lions, he exults in his
danger, viewing it as just one more test of his courage and
ability; to him " 'there is interest even in a mutiny!' "[65]
Throughout the early nautical romances Cooper's stress
is on the positive values of wildness; the Rover's turbulent
spirit and the hazardous, limitless ocean are rendered only
more piquant by their defiance of the standards of civilization. In *The Water-Witch* the celebration of the freedom
offered by the sea reaches its apogee. The brigantine becomes the symbol of escape from the oppression and injus-

tice of organized society. Here the brutal elements of the
outlaw's life disappear, for, unlike the Rover's gang, the
crew of the *Water-Witch* exist in a community of love and
loyalty. Their life is one of change, excitement, and perfect
freedom; indeed, " 'the scud, which floats above the sea,
is not freer than that vessel, and scarcely more swift.' " In
the concluding chapter of the novel Eudora is offered the
love of a father, the security of a wealthy marriage, and
the companionship of a genteel friend: all values of civilization. And all these she rejects in a grandly romantic
gesture for a life at sea with her lover, a life " 'with a ship
for a dwelling—the tempestuous ocean for a world!' "[66]

8

In the early romances Cooper develops a portrayal of
the ship consonant with the romantic tone of his treatment
of the sea. In the convention of nautical writing established
by Smollett in *Roderick Random* and followed by Melville
in *White-Jacket,* the size and mass of the vessel are emphasized; descriptive phrases and metaphors stress ponderous
weight, crushing momentum, and towering height. Such
accounts, usually written from the point of view of a
member of the crew, conceive of the inhabitants of the
vessel as a crowded and richly diverse community, a community that is often viewed as a microcosm of society as
a whole. But for Cooper, wishing to portray man as an
individual, not man in the mass, man confronted by wild
nature, not man in society, Smollett's conception of the
ship was obviously inappropriate. Departing from the convention, Cooper, like Freneau, seized upon grace and swiftness and the identity of seaman and vessel as the focal
points of his image of the ship.

The principal vessels of Cooper's first three sea novels,
like those of most of the later novels, are relatively small
and singularly beautiful and light in their construction.

Barnstable's *Ariel,* which "belonged to the smallest class of sea-vessels," was "a low black schooner, whose hull seemed utterly disproportioned to the raking masts it upheld, which, in their turn, supported a lighter set of spars, that tapered away until their extremities appeared no larger" than the pennant that flew from them.[67] In keeping with its function as a symbol of escape and freedom, the brigantine *Water-Witch* "was airy, fanciful, and full of grace," possessing "a character of unreal lightness and speed."[68] Even the Rover's *Dolphin,* the largest of the three vessels, gives an impression of lightness and grace as Wilder and his party view her from their open boat:

At the distance of a mile there was a ship rolling and pitching gracefully, and without any apparent shock, on those waves through which the launch was struggling with so much difficulty. A solitary sail was set to steady the vessel, and that so reduced by reefs, as to look like a little snowy cloud waving in the air. At times her tapering masts appeared pointing to the zenith, or rolling as if inclining against the wind; and then, again, with slow and graceful sweeps, they seemed to fall towards the ruffled surface of the ocean, as if to seek refuge from their endless motion in the bosom of the agitated element itself. There were moments when the long, low, and black hull was seen distinctly resting on the summit of a sea, and glittering in the sun-beams, with the water washing from her sides; and then, as boat and vessel sank together, all was lost to the eye, even to the attenuated lines of her tallest and most delicate spars.[69]

To convey the ideas of speed and grace, Cooper continually compares his vessels to marine birds. Bearing off, the *Caroline,* "like a bird whose wing has wearied with struggling against the tempest, and which inclines from the gale to choose an easier course, glided swiftly away, quartering the crests of the waves, or sinking gracefully into their troughs, as she yielded to the force of a wind that was now made to be favourable."[70] The *Water-Witch*

floats "on its element like a sea-gull riding the billows,"
and when her rigging is damaged by shot, she changes her
course "like some bird whose wing has been touched by
the fowler."[71] To emphasize the energy and responsiveness
of the ship, Cooper employs the metaphor of the spirited
horse. The *Caroline* strains at her mooring "like a restless
courser, restrained by the grasp of the groom, chafing his
bit, and with difficulty keeping those limbs upon the earth
with which he is shortly to bound around the ring." Under
sail, her crew hold "her in hand, as a skilful rider governs
the action of a fiery and mettled steed."[72] Or the ship becomes a woman, as Cooper stresses her beauty and the
strength of the seaman's attachment to his vessel. Long
Tom Coffin tells Katherine Plowden that the *Ariel* " 'is as
lovely to the eyes of an old seafaring man as any of your
kind can be to human nature.' "[73] To Tom Tiller in *The
Water-Witch* " 'a ship is a seaman's mistress—nay, when
fairly under a pennant, with a war declared, he may be
said to be wedded to her, lawfully or not. He becomes
"bone of her bone, and flesh of her flesh, until death doth
them part." ' "[74]

Under the impact of this continual animizing and personification Cooper's vessels assume the life and volition of
characters. Just as the stormy sea becomes an antagonist of
superhuman proportions, so the seamen and their ship
merge in moments of crisis into an entity, a single animate
being that contains and obscures the identities of the human actors in Cooper's drama. And it is this being, this
unit compounded of vessel and crew, that can meet the
challenge of the ocean. As a storm rushed upon the frigate
in *The Pilot,* the ship bowed and "rose again majestically
to her upright position, as if saluting, like a courteous
champion, the powerful antagonist with which she was
about to contend."[75] Cooper's vessels became characters
not only in combat with the sea, but in their relation to

each other. Thus, in the opening nautical scenes of *The Red Rover* the threat to the *Caroline* comes not so much from the Rover as from the *Dolphin*. Quiescent though she is, the *Dolphin* is like some subtile and savage animal as she rides at her mooring in the outer harbor; just as Hawkeye alone can perceive the real nature of Magua in the opening pages of *The Last of the Mohicans,* so only the experienced seaman can read the true character of the Rover's enigmatic vessel:

So quiet and motionless did she seem, that one who had never been instructed in the matter, might readily have believed her a fixture in the sea, some symmetrical and enormous excrescence, thrown up by the waves, with its mazes of lines and pointed fingers, or one of those fantastic monsters that are believed to exist in the bottom of the ocean, darkened by the fogs and tempests of ages. To the understanding eye of Wilder, however, she exhibited a very different spectacle. He easily saw, through all this apparently drowsy quietude, those signs of readiness which none but a seaman could discover . . . In this state, the vessel, to one who knew her real character, appeared like some beast of prey, or venomous reptile, that lay in an assumed lethargy, to delude the unconscious victim within the limits of its leap, or nigh enough to receive the deadly blow of its fangs.

As Wilder attempts to work the *Caroline* past the anchored *Dolphin,* the muzzles of her guns gape "constantly on his vessel, as the eye of the crouching tiger follows the movement of its prey."[76]

Among Cooper's first three sea novels the characterization of ships reaches its fullest development in *The Water-Witch*. While the *Water-Witch* herself is intensely feminine, everything about her pursuer, the British sloop of war *Coquette,* is masculine, despite the name. The commander of the *Coquette* is the haughty Ludlow, so very much the epitome of manliness that he is nearly absurd. The master is the gruff old seaman Trysail, who boasts that " 'the worst enemy I have will not say I am very womanish.' " The *Coquette,* as a vessel of the King, is the representative of authority and order; her function is to punish the enemies of the Crown, and she is governed by an inflexible system of discipline. The very metaphors that Cooper applies to the *Coquette* are masculine in their connotations. Although the *Water-Witch* is all bird-like grace and beauty, the *Coquette,* as she moves through the water, makes a rushing sound that "might be likened to the deep breathing of some vast animal, that was collecting its physical energies for some unusual exertion." As the sloop maneuvers in the harbor, she appears as "restless as a steed that had broken from its fastenings." Trysail looks forward to the moment when the *Coquette* will prepare for combat with the French, for " 'there is something manly' " about the way a ship strips for action, " 'like a boxer taking off his jacket, with the intention of making a fair stand-up fight for it.' " By contrast, the *Water-Witch* is characterized as intensely feminine. The girl Eudora masquerades as her commander, and her crew is ruled, not by flogging and curses, but by the injunctions of her mysterious figure-head, the sea-green lady. Her seamen regard the brigantine as their mistress and speak of her in sexual terms: " 'Look at those harpings! There is no fall of a shoulder can equal that curve, in grace or richness; this shear surpasses the justness and delicacy of any waist; and there you see the transoms, swelling and rounded like the outlines of a Venus. Ah! she is a bewitching creature.' "[77] Just as the *Coquette* symbolizes masculinity and authority, the *Water-Witch* is the emblem of a freedom that Cooper conceives of as feminine. The brigantine pursues no set purpose but ranges the seas at the whim of her commander, defying the rules and conventions of society. She is resourceful, independent, spir-

ited, daring—everything that orthodox criticism finds
wanting in Cooper's female characters.

9

The relation of the sailor to the ship provides a convenient avenue for the approach to Cooper's portrayal of
the seaman, a portrayal which in many ways constitutes
the most original and profound contribution of his early
marine romances to the literature of the sea. In a remarkable passage from *The Red Rover* Cooper sums up the
values that he assigns to the ship and describes their role
in determining the nature of the seaman. As Wilder approaches the *Dolphin,* he is struck by her appearance:

The perfect symmetry of her spars, the graceful heavings and
settings of the whole fabric, as it rode, like a marine bird, on
the long, regular swells of the trades, and the graceful in-
clinations of the tapering masts, as they waved across the
blue canopy, which was interlaced by all the tracery of her
complicated tackle, was not lost on an eye that knew no less
how to prize the order of the whole than to admire the beauty
of the object itself. There is a high and exquisite taste, which
the seaman attains in the study of a machine that all have
united to commend, which may be likened to the sensibilities
that the artist acquires, by close and long contemplation of
the noblest monuments of antiquity. It teaches him to detect
those imperfections which would escape a less instructed eye;
and it heightens the pleasure with which a ship at sea is
gazed at, by enabling the mind to keep even pace with the
enjoyment of the senses. It is this powerful (and to a landsman
incomprehensible) charm that forms the secret tie which binds
the mariner so closely to his vessel, and which often leads him
to prize her qualities as one would esteem the virtues of a
friend, and almost to be equally enamoured of the fair proportions of his ship and of those of his mistress. Other men
may have their different inanimate subjects of admiration; but
none of their feelings so thoroughly enter into the composition of the being as the affection which the mariner comes,

in time, to feel for his vessel. It is his home, his theme of constant and frequently of painful interest, his tabernacle, and often his source of pride and exultation. As she gratifies or disappoints his high-wrought expectations, in her speed or in the fight, 'mid shoals and hurricane, a character for good or luckless qualities is earned, which are as often in reality due to the skill or ignorance of those who guide her, as to any inherent properties of the fabric. Still does the ship itself, in the eyes of the seaman, bear away the laurel of success, or suffer the ignominy of defeat and misfortune; and, when the reverse arrives, the result is merely regarded as some extraordinary departure from the ordinary character of the vessel, as if the construction possessed the powers of self-command and volition.[78]

Several aspects of this passage warrant comment. There is, of course, the reiteration of the principal elements of Cooper's conception of the ship: her bird-like grace, the nearly sexual attraction that she exerts, her seeming possession of consciousness and will, and the identification of seaman and vessel. There is, too, the familiar suggestion of dual points of view, here employed to combine the landsman's naïve admiration of the beauty of the ship and the seaman's informed appreciation of her ordered efficiency. More important, however, is Cooper's revelation of the effect on the seaman of his association with the ship. Unlike the sailors of eighteenth-century fiction, who are brutalized by the floating prisons which encase them, Cooper's seamen are ennobled by their life-long contact with what he conceives to be an aesthetic object.[79] This association not only engenders "a high and exquisite taste" that can be compared to the sensibilities of an artist, but produces as well an attachment to the vessel that entails, in a very real sense, a separation from the rest of mankind, from the ways and values of the land. The seaman, whose ship is his home and his tabernacle, attains an angle of vision peculiar to his profession; if he is cut off from the comforts and security of civilization, his perspective is not distorted by its artificialities.

Nearly all of the seamen in Cooper's early nautical romances share this quality of landlessness. Long Tom Coffin, who was born in a Chebacco boat, " 'never could see the use of more land than now and then a small island to raise a few vegetables, and to dry your fish—I'm sure the sight of it always makes me feel uncomfortable, unless we have the wind dead off shore.' " His attachment to the schooner *Ariel* is so strong that he has no wish to survive her; he " 'saw the first timber of the Ariel laid, and shall live just long enough to see it turn out of her bottom,' " for Tom is " 'one who has followed the waters since he was an hour old, and one who hopes to die off soundings, and to be buried in the brine.' "[80] Like Long Tom and like Wilder, whose " 'earliest recollections are blended with the sight of the sea,' " and who can hardly say that he is " 'a creature of the land at all,' " the Rover " 'is almost a native of the seas; for more than thirty years he has passed his time on them.' " For Wilder to abandon the ocean " 'would be like quitting the air I breathe,' " just as to the Rover water is " 'an element that has become as necessary to me as the one I breathe.' "[81]

The seaman's "broken and interrupted connexion with the rest of the human family"[82] effects a curious inversion of conventional values and judgments. Again and again, Cooper's use of the double points of view stresses the separation of sailors from landsmen. The sight of certain low blue ridges of land in the Caribbean form, in the Rover's words, " 'the landsman's delight, and the seaman's terror.' " A warm October day with a mild southerly breeze is "just such a time as one, who is fond of strolling in the fields, is apt to seize on with rapture, and which a seaman sets down as a day lost in his reckoning." Unlike Freneau's sailors, who yearn for the scent of the land, the seaman of Cooper's early romances is never truly happy until "he has disengaged his vessel from the land, and has fairly launched her on the trackless and fathomless abyss of the ocean."[83] But although seafaring transposes some values, it confirms others. Cooper's sailors, whatever their moral natures may be, are habitually energetic, resourceful, and daring, qualities which "the constant hazards of a dangerous and delicate profession"[84] necessitate. Possessing these virtues and ennobled by their association with the beauty of the ship and the grandeur of the ocean, they achieve a dignity that had been accorded them in no previous literary treatment of their profession. Even the very correct Mrs. Wyllys acknowledges the new status to which her creator had elevated the seaman when she compliments Wilder on " 'your daring, your hardy, your *noble* profession!' "[85]

The vigor and essential dignity of Cooper's conception of the seaman can readily be seen in the contrast between Wilder, the romantic hero of *The Red Rover*, and Major Duncan Heyward, his counterpart in *The Last of the Mohicans* (1826), or Captain Duncan Uncas Middleton in *The Prairie* (1827). Heyward and Middleton are lay figures that deserve every epithet that over one hundred years of criticism has heaped on them. All uniform and no brain, they are led like children through the forest or across the prairie by Bumppo until the last chapter, when they can return to civilization with their fainting brides. But Wilder is different. He is a seaman, "one who had been nurtured on that element where circumstances . . . exacted of him such constant and unequivocal evidence of his skill."[86] He is brought into the action and allowed to demonstrate his energy and ability under the ordeal of the sea. In spite of the fact that he possesses enough gentility to qualify for the hand of Gertrude, Wilder, thanks to his seamanship, never lapses into woodenness. Although

Barnstable, a romantic hero in *The Pilot* who, as a boy, ran away from school to join the Nantucket whaling fleet, is nearly as credible as Wilder, his fellow officer Griffith and Captain Ludlow of the *Coquette* are comparative failures. Both Griffith and Ludlow stagger under a burden of manly pride and an undue sense of propriety. They are forever choking down their resentment and biting their lips in indignation; " 'fellow,' " says Ludlow to one he deems an inferior, " 'this impudence almost surpasseth patience.' "[87] Griffith and Ludlow fail to achieve the dignity of true seamen because they never completely detach themselves from the forms and values of civilization. The reader is not surprised to learn that at the end of the Revolution Griffith "entirely withdrew from the ocean, and devoted the remainder of his life to the conjoint duties of a husband and a good citizen."[88]

One reason for Wilder's success is that, unlike Barnstable, Griffith, and Ludlow, he receives little competition from the lower ranks, his chief rival for the reader's interest being the equally gentlemanly Rover. The principal common seaman in *The Red Rover* is Wilder's loyal follower Dick Fid. Like many of the minor characters in Cooper's other sea novels, Fid takes after the sailors of Smollett. With Boltrope in *The Pilot* and Trysail in *The Water-Witch* Fid shares the traits of argumentative dogmatism, superstitious ignorance, carefree irresponsibility, and blind obedience to the commands of superiors. His fondness for liquor allows him to be duped by the crew of the *Dolphin*. He is not overscrupulous in handling the property of others, and although his Negro companion S'ip refuses the Rover's offer of money, Fid greedily pockets the handout. When the Rover sends all hands to mischief, Fid joins in the callous horseplay with an ingenuity worthy of Hatchway or Pipes, although "a twinkling of humanity . . . still glimmered through the rough humor of the tar." Fid's physical appearance mirrors this compound of humanity and callousness: his "short, thickset powerful frame" supports a head "in proportion to the more immediate members; the forehead low, and nearly covered with hair; the eyes small, obstinate, sometimes fierce, and often dull; the nose snub, coarse, and vulgar; the mouth large and voracious; the teeth short, clean, and perfectly sound; and the chin broad, manly, and even expressive."[89] Thorough seaman though he is, Dick Fid remains too strictly within the limitations of the eighteenth-century stereotype to distract the reader's attention from Wilder and the Rover; he never transcends his function as a comic foil.

The gentleman-sailors of *The Pilot* and *The Water-Witch,* however, must contend with a third figure in Cooper's gallery of mariners, the ideal seaman. The ideal seaman, unlike Fid, who has spent most of his life in the service of the Royal Navy, or Trysail, the master of an English cruiser, is always closely associated with America; he can be interpreted, in fact, as the outgrowth of Cooper's conviction that democracy improves the character of the lower classes, that the eighteenth-century British stereotype is no longer appropriate for the characterization of the democratic sailor. Long Tom Coffin of *The Pilot* was born in a boat crossing the Nantucket shoals and has served in the Nantucket whale fishery and the American navy ever since. Tom Tiller, the "Skimmer of the Seas" in *The Water-Witch,* is a native of Long Island and has spent his life defying the Royal Navy in his free-trading merchantman. The ideal seaman is not short and thickset, but tall and angular like Long Tom or tall and nicely proportioned like Tiller. He is in, or approaching, middle age; Coffin's black whiskers "began to be grizzled a little with age," and Tiller's brown hair "was already a little grizzled."[90]

Both Coffin and Tiller represent the epitome of seamanship, and both are thoroughly moral men; each
dominates the nautical action of his novel. Coffin is characterized so convincingly that he rivals Bumppo in en-
gendering speculation about his actual prototype[91] and
so forcefully that the structure of *The Pilot* collapses with
his death. Similarly, Tiller dominates the scene whenever
he appears. At the outset of the novel he fixes the reader's
attention just as "the reckless air, the decision, and the
manly attitudes of so fine a specimen of a seaman" attract
the notice of a little knot of admirers on the New York
waterfront. By the sheer glamour of his personality and the
weight of his professional ability, Tiller justifies his claims
to membership in "the aristocracy of nature" and completely eclipses Ludlow in the moment of crisis: "All dis-
tinctions of rank and authority had ceased, except as
deference was paid to natural qualities and the intelligence
of experience. Under such circumstances, the 'Skimmer
of the Seas' took the lead; and though Ludlow caught
his ideas with professional quickness, it was the mind of
the free-trader that controlled, throughout the succeeding
exertions of that fearful night." As he works in the glare
of the fire to save the crew of the *Coquette,* Tiller attains
the ultimate degree of idealization: "Seen by that light,
with his peculiar attire, his firm and certain step, and his
resolute air, the free-trader resembled some fancied sea-
god, who, secure in his immortal immunities, had come
to act his part in that awful but exciting trial of hardihood and skill."[92] In a novel in which the sea becomes
the arena of self-realization and the ship a conscious being,
the seaman attains the stature of a deity.

Chapter III

The Dangers of the Deep

THE WORK OF COOPER'S CONTEMPORARIES,
1820–1835

IN THE PREFACE which he wrote in 1831 for Bentley's new English edition of *The Pilot,* Cooper boasted that his novel had inspired "a tolerably numerous school of nautical romances"; indeed, "sea-tales came into vogue as a consequence."[1] Undoubtedly Cooper had British as well as American nautical fiction in mind. By 1831 the sea novel was well under way in England; Marryat had published *Frank Mildmay* in 1829 and *The King's Own* in 1830. Michael Scott had begun serial publication of *Tom Cringle's Log* in 1829, and William Neale's *Cavendish* appeared in 1831. Although the style of all these books owes more to Smollett than it does to Cooper, the stunning success of *The Pilot* and *The Red Rover* unquestionably accounted for this sudden rush of sea novels by demonstrating to British authors and publishers the readiness of the reading public to accept novels which had the ocean as their principal setting and seamen as their principal characters. In America, however, the popularity of Cooper's early nautical romances stimulated no equivalent production of sea novels before 1835. Only four or five American novels of the period make extensive use of marine elements, and none of them fully satisfies the standard which Cooper's work had set as the criteria of the sea novel. Perhaps the failure of American writers to produce novels which rival *The Pilot* in nature or in excellence can be dismissed with the statement that no novelist having the talent and experience of Marryat or Scott appeared in this country, but a satisfactory explanation of the phenomenon must take into account the vigorous growth of the short sea story in America between 1820 and 1835. For it seems evident that the same creative energy which found expression in the full-length sea novel in England generated an extensive, diverse, and often more than competent body of shorter fiction in America.

The impact of Cooper's success on the writers of these few novels and many short stories is evinced by the two major subjects which engrossed most of them, naval life and piracy. The burgeoning maritime nationalism that had led Cooper to make *The Pilot* the first extensive fictional treatment of the personnel and customs of the American navy also prompted a host of lesser writers to follow in the path he had pioneered.[2] The enthusiasm that the War of 1812 had engendered for the navy as the prime instrument of nationalism continued with only slight fluctuations during the two decades after the war. Even the Republicans finally had been persuaded that the interest of the country demanded a steadily expanding naval service. Both the Whig and Democratic parties which emerged from the Era of Good Feeling encouraged naval construction in spite of the influence of Jeffersonian naval thinking on the Democrats. An ambitious program of shipbuilding, initiated in 1816 by an act authorizing the construction of nine line-of-battle ships and twelve 44-gun frigates, culminated in 1837 with the launching of the *Pennsylvania,* a mammoth ship of 120 guns that had been the object of public attention ever since her keel was laid in 1822. As a result of this program the American fleet more than doubled in size between 1816 and 1842.[3]

The old sailing navy of the first half of the nineteenth century offered a considerable amount of authentic glamour to support the popular imagination in its admiring enthusiasm. The splendor and pomp of its ceremonies, the pageantry of naval balls, the exotic life of its ports of call —Rio, Mahon, Lima—all supplied images that appealed to a public schooled in romanticism. Its senior officers were the national champions of 1812: Hull, Perry, Porter, and John Rodgers, whose figure and face seemed to Thomas H. Benton to be "those of the naval hero—such as we conceive from naval songs and ballads."[4] Its lieutenants and midshipmen had a reputation for hot-blooded gallantry, a reputation sustained by the continual reports in the newspapers of the day of their duels with anyone and everyone who violated their elaborate and extravagant code of personal honor.

The glamorous life of the navy became the subject of a flood of sketches, journals, reminiscences, and narratives, turned out, it seemed, by every midshipman, chaplain, surgeon, schoolmaster, and passenger who had touched the deck of an American man-of-war. In their accounts these travelers interlarded their descriptions of the Levant, South America, or the islands of the South Seas with sketches of the equally picturesque and unfamiliar life of the navy. Even Nathaniel P. Willis, "that squire of dames and poet laureate of the ladies, who dips his dove-quill pen in milk and water and writes upon perfumed paper, made of ladies' cambric handkerchiefs and chemisettes,"[5] paused in his *Pencillings by the Way* (1835) to give his readers an elegant picture of a ball on board the frigate *United States,* the infamous *Neversink* of Melville's *White-Jacket,* in the harbor of Trieste:

The ship has an admirable band of twenty Italians, collected from Naples and other ports, and a fanciful orchestra was raised for them on the larboard side of the mainmast.

They struck up a march as the first boatful of ladies stepped upon the deck, and in the course of half an hour the waltzing commenced with at least two hundred couples, while the ottoman and seats under the hammock-cloths were filled with spectators. The frigate has a lofty poop, and there was room enough upon it for two quadrilles after it had served as a reception-room. It was edged with a temporary balustrade, wreathed with flowers, and studded with lights; and the cabin beneath (on a level with the main ball-room) was set out with card-tables. From the gang-way entrance, the scene was like a brilliant theatrical *ballet* . . .

We went below at midnight to supper, and the ladies came up with renewed spirit to the dance. It was a brilliant scene indeed. The [naval] officers . . . in full uniform; the gentlemen from shore, mostly military, in full dress; the gaiety of the bright-red bunting, laced with white and blue, and studded wherever they would stand, with flowers; and the really uncommon number of beautiful women, with the foreign features and complexions so rich and captivating to our eyes, produced altogether an effect unsurpassed by anything I have ever seen even at the court *fêtes* of Europe.

And, crowded on the forecastle, the sailors, like children exiled to the kitchen, watch the festivities, their "five hundred weatherbeaten and manly faces" providing an interesting backdrop to the scene.[6]

Although the everyday activities of the merchant marine could not compete with the glamour of the navy for a place in the American imagination during the meridian of romanticism, occasional glimpses of life in the packets, whalers, and coasters appear in American fiction before 1835. But one aspect of the life of the American merchant seaman more than met the requirements of early nineteenth-century romanticism. To the modern reader the flood of fiction recounting the hair-raising escapes of merchantmen from the pirates of the West Indies or the dreadful results of a piratical encounter seems to be purely a product of that romantic imagination in its least restrained mood. Yet even the most cursory reading of a record of the times like *Niles' Weekly Register* shows the factual basis of the fictional preoccupation with piracy. Almost every issue of *Niles'* in the early 1820's reported at least one piratical attack on an American merchantman. The account of the fate of the *Aurilla* is typical:

A most horrid act of piracy [was] committed on the 15th of May [1822], on board of the brig Aurilla, of New York, from Baltimore for New Orleans. She was boarded off Key Sal, from two piratical schooners, well fitted with great guns and small arms, and manned by forty or fifty men each. The passengers and crew were beaten in the most shocking manner; and one of them was hung up to the yard arm, and then dropt into the water apparently lifeless. The brig was plundered of every thing that was valuable, at the will of the wretches, the passengers being robbed of their clothing, watches, breast-pins, &c. and they delighted to destroy what they did not please to take away. The villains crowned their crimes, by ravishing the women that were on board, and committing the most brutal excesses on their bodies! After which the pirates released the vessel.[7]

By 1823 *Niles'* could report that 3,002 piratical assaults upon merchant shipping of all nations had taken place in the West Indies since the end of the War of 1812. At least five hundred American vessels in all, valued with their cargoes at $20,000,000, were seized by the pirates of the West Indies.[8]

Truly, as *Niles'* observed in 1821, "the present time seems to be entitled to the appellation of the *age of piracy* —caused chiefly by the spewing out of the late wars, and especially so of the contests between Spain and her late 'American colonies.' "[9] The confusion and turmoil produced by the rebellion of the Spanish colonies provided a convenient outlet for the energies of a race of adventurers, many of them American, that had been bred by the violence and lawlessness of the Napoleonic wars. Writing in

1817, John Quincy Adams pointed out that the fleets of
the South American patriots had been "for the most part
fitted out and officered in our ports and manned from the
sweepings of our streets."[10] In 1820 *Niles'* estimated that
America had supplied the rebel privateers with "not less
than 15 or 20,000 seamen since the conclusion of the war
with Great Britain."[11] To avenge what she deemed American support of attacks on her shipping, Spain made little
effort to suppress the swarm of pirates who preyed on
American merchantmen from the loyal islands of Cuba and
Puerto Rico or to cooperate with American authorities in
putting down such picturesque but piratical upstarts as
"Commodore" Aury, the self-proclaimed governor of Gal-
veston, and Jean Lafitte, his rival at Barataria. With the
help of the British, however, Commodore Porter and an
American fleet, composed almost entirely of small, fast
schooners built on the model of the Baltimore clippers,
waged a vigorous campaign against the West Indian rovers
and sharply curtailed piratical activity by the end of 1823.
With the cessation of hostilities between Spain and her
colonies in 1825 the era of politically sponsored piracy
came to an end, although those pirates who continued
operations on their own remained a serious menace to
American shipping until 1835.

Although the activities of the Mediterranean corsairs
before the War of 1812 had made piracy a familiar element in American maritime life and had early been turned
into literary material by writers like Ellison and Tyler,
the vast extent of the American literature of piracy in the
years between 1820 and 1835 testifies to the success of the
efforts of periodicals like *Niles'* once again "to rouse the
public attention to the subject." The publishers of chapbooks exploited the popular interest by issuing more or
less factual narratives by victims of the pirates, confes-

sions of captured pirates, and accounts of their trials and executions.[12] American printers were quick to reissue Captain Charles Johnson's classic *General History of the Pyrates* (1724), brought up to date by the addition of "a Correct Account of the Late Piracies Committed in the West Indies; and the Expedition of Com. Porter." Again Cooper pioneered in the fictional treatment of a major maritime subject, for just as *The Pilot* had engendered a swarm of naval sketches and stories, so *The Red Rover* inspired many imitations by proving to American prose writers that piracy could be successfully idealized.[13] In the chapbooks the careers of the rovers had been viewed only as lurid records of human depravity and as demonstrations to the young of the fatal consequences of a life of vice. But now it was apparent that by applying the Byronic formulas to piratical characters and by surrounding their life with the sublime connotations which Cooper had attached to the sea, writers could invest piracy with the exotic grandeur and nobility of a romantic subject.

2

Several American novelists joined Cooper in exploiting the popular interest in piracy. Samuel B. Judah's *The Buccaneers* (1827), a historical romance set in colonial New York at the time of Leisler's rebellion, clumsily parades Captain Kidd and his gang in and out of the plot. Although its nautical elements are negligible, Judah's novel is noteworthy for its feeble anticipation of Cooper's characterization of the pirate as Byronic hero and for its rather idealized treatment of Eumet, the only fully drawn seaman in the book.[14] *The Memoirs of Lafitte; or The Barratarian Pirate* (1826), an over-written and cheaply sensational little novel that attempts to unite piracy with sentimentality, also anticipates Cooper in the Byronic treatment of the pirate.[15] The anonymous author of *Blackbeard* (1835), a book described by a contemporary reviewer as "the worst of the last batch of bad novels,"[16] uses Captain Teach and his brawling, looting, murdering, raping crew only as formidable foils to the benevolent ministrations of the Chevalier Oxenstiern, a mysterious alchemist who inhabits an appropriately Gothic mansion in colonial Philadelphia. Although *Blackbeard* owes more to Charles Brockden Brown than it does to Cooper, the novel contains several well-drawn characterizations of American seamen, notably Stephen Lingo, a pilot of Chesapeake Bay, and Jeptha Dobbs, a native of Martha's Vineyard who is clearly modeled on Long Tom Coffin.

The most interesting of this small group of novels is the anonymous *Ramon, the Rover of Cuba* (1829). Although this confession of an imaginary West Indian pirate is almost entirely lacking in intrinsic literary value, it is significant as a prototype of the dime novels of the 1840's and as an early attempt to utilize directly the facts of contemporary piracy for fictional purposes. Nearly all the elements that were to become clichés in the penny dreadfuls of Ingraham, Judson, and Ballou appear in *Ramon*. The plotless succession of lurid episodes, the sniggering tone of the narrator, and the utterly false remorse and pious moralizing at the end are typical of the later flood of subliterary sea fiction. Most characteristic of all is the debasement of the Byronic hero by sensational exaggeration. Ramon is the passionate, proud, and desperate outcast of society raised to the tenth power. Haunted by the miseries of the past, he is at war with all mankind: "I have sought to drown the remembrance of those early passages of my life . . . in the sounds of battle, and to forget myself —the past—every thing, in a life of action and adventure."

In thoroughly stereotyped diction Ramon proclaims his remorse and bares his guilt-ridden heart:

> Ah, bitter, relentless fate! I can never know the joys of domestic bliss. No sweet prattler will ever call me father. No fond, confiding woman will ever lean upon my bosom, or honour me with the title of her protector.
> How many such have I bereaved of husbands and sons! How many hearts have been rendered desolate by this blood-stained hand![17]

If the attempt of the author of *Ramon* to dignify his hero by outfitting him in the trappings of the Byronic soul ends in unintentional caricature, neither does Ramon gather nobility from his association with the sea. For, like many of the dime novelists, the author of *Ramon* simply designates the ocean as the scene of his story; he makes no attempt to equal Cooper's imaginative and knowing revelation of the interaction of sea, ship, and sailor. As a result, the reader suspects that Ramon's admission applies to the author as well: "it is true I was no seaman, and have never become well versed in nautical matters."[18]

Although he failed to benefit from Cooper's achievements in the integration of the nautical milieu with character and action, the author of *Ramon* attained a measure of success in creating a broad panorama of nautical activity in the West Indies during the 1820's and by so doing became the first novelist after Charles Lenox Sargent to deal with an important aspect of the contemporary maritime life of America.[19] The pages of *Ramon* supply a detailed portrait of the personnel and cargoes of the American trade with the West Indies, a trade that thrived in spite of the continual threat of piracy. There is the master of an American merchantman, whose boldness forces Ramon to admit that "there is spirit in some of these Yankees. This fellow, for instance, possessed courage, that, if he had been properly educated, would have fitted him for a first-rate rover." There is Jonathan, the green hand from Vermont, who went " 'to Portland, to get aboard of a vessel and go off to the Stingies [West Indies], where there are mountains of sugar and rivers of molasses.' " And there is Jeremiah Starch, a supercargo who is " 'clerk—head clerk—in the store of Codfish and Clump, down on Long Wharf in Boston.' " The list of Ramon's prizes is a virtual inventory of American exports to the Caribbean: "most of these vessels were loaded with lumber, and came from Portland, Quinebunque [Kennebunk], Socco [Saco], &c. There were two vessels from Rouge Island [Rhode Island] with horses, and another from Neck-to-Cut [Connecticut] with wooden ware, clocks, tin pots, and nutmegs."[20]

A strong current of nationalism runs through this account of the maritime life of the West Indies. An American seaman was, in Ramon's words, "almost the first specimen of a downright honest man I had ever met with." American vessels are equally exceptional:

As we neared the enemy, we made her out to be considerably our inferior in size and weight of metal. She was one of the smallest schooners employed in the service of the United States, and had been fitted out, as I have since learned, expressly for the protection of American trade against our depredations. The vessels in this service, from diminutive size, were called the *Musquito* [*sic*] *fleet*. I observed her narrowly as we came into action. She was a neat affair. Her sails and rigging were in perfect order. She sat like a swan in the water, and under the light breeze which we had, every manoeuvre was executed with an exactness and promptitude that could not but strike one who had been accustomed to the clumsy seamanship of Spanish sailors.

Despite her superiority in size, Ramon's ship is destroyed, whereupon he promptly equips himself with the product of an American shipyard, "a beautiful schooner, Baltimore built, rigged in the most perfect manner."[21]

Much as it violates the point of view of his narrator, the author of *Ramon* cannot resist the temptation to use his piratical hero as the mouthpiece for propaganda in behalf of a firmer American policy in the West Indies. He points out that the United States must not expect the cooperation of the Spanish colonial government in suppressing piracy until Americans stop supplying the South American rebels with the ships and men with which they raid the commerce of Spain:

Is it to be expected that the government of Cuba will be very active in suppressing piracy, when the government of the United States have never moved a finger toward preventing these outrages? I would put the question to any intelligent American, How many South American privateers have been fitted out of one certain port in the United States within the last ten years; and how large a proportion of them have committed depredations, not only on the Spanish, but on all nations?

America, moreover, should vigorously assert her national power. The author deplores the lenient policy of Monroe toward captured pirates and makes Ramon anticipate with fear the time when America will have the sense to elect Jackson to the presidency, for "he will immediately cover the whole Western Archipelago with those scoundrel *mosquito fleets,* manned with long-sided, sinewy Yankees." Knowing that there will be no pardoning of pirates in Jackson's day, Ramon fears that he will have to "give up this business and retire."²² Clumsy and tawdry though it is, *Ramon* thus joins *The Pilot* and *The Red Rover* in linking the sea and American nationalism.

Another novelist even dared to follow Cooper in ranging beyond the subject of piracy in the search for nautical materials suitable to the purposes of fiction. In *Miriam Coffin* (1834) Joseph C. Hart had the temerity to attempt to treat romantically what was generally considered to be the lowliest of maritime subjects, the whale fishery, and in doing so Hart produced the only nautical novel of the period that approaches the early romances of Cooper in literary interest. Yet for all the expressiveness of its style and the striking validity of some of its perceptions, *Miriam Coffin* is by no means a successful novel, for Hart vitiates the force of his romantic conception of the subject by failing to trust in that force. Not content with creating "a just representation of the character and hazardous pursuits of the daring Whale-Fishermen," he seems compelled to placate literary convention by also offering the reader "faithful pictures of a past age," that is, minute accounts of the manners, dress, festivities, and local history of colonial Nantucket, and by "conveying a useful moral, and . . . showing the young female where the true sphere of her duties lies."[23] While these aims are not necessarily incongruent, they fail to come together in Hart's hands. The development of each is generally coherent in itself, but none is convincingly related to the other two. Nevertheless, when the strand of nautical material is separated from the local color and domestic moralizing with which it is entangled, the vigor and sensitivity of Hart's concept of the sea become apparent.

That concept is informed by a strident maritime nationalism. Supremacy on the ocean is America's "great national destiny," for "we are possessed of an immense sea-board of several thousand miles;—of rivers of great depth and extent, which shame the diminutive though boasted rills of Europe. Our river-banks at the north, are lined with forests of the white oak, cedar, and locust; and at the south with the incomparable and undecaying live oak,—all furnishing the most desirable materials for ship-building, within the easy grasp of a people, whose enterprise is proverbial, and whose expansive genius aims at the dominion of the seas." Americans are "the bravest and best seamen in the world," and their vessels, "in combining elegance of model, and swiftness of sailing, with capacity for burthen . . . have outdistanced the floating castles of Europe, and furnished its shipwrights with models for imitation." But unlike the author of *Ramon,* whose nationalism is mirrored in the representation of contemporary nautical life, Hart follows the early Cooper in embedding his doctrine in the maritime past. For, like Cooper, Hart's intention is not to describe and glorify the present but to seize and appropriate the past in order to establish an American tradition, an American heritage which explains the present and justifies his prophecy of the future. For this reason Hart sets his novel not in the contemporary era, the heyday of the sperm-whale fishery, but in an earlier period, a time when Nantucket whalers were first venturing around the Horn into the Pacific in pursuit of their gigantic game. And, although his design becomes obscured in the riot of local color, it is evident that Hart intends his eighteenth-century Nantucket to serve as a microcosm of the nation: "a miniature representation of the vast whole" and a concrete embodiment of the incipient national virtues.[24]

Hart's treatment of maritime material differs from that of all the other early followers of Cooper in that it is firmly grounded in a thorough and thoughtful knowledge of his subject, a knowledge revealed in every aspect of the nautical sections of the novel. The action of the whaling scenes is balanced by richly detailed exposition in which Hart sets forth the uses of the various whaling gear, the appearance and habits of the several species of whales, the methods of flensing and trying out, and the construction and outfit of the whaling vessel. Harts' ships are not the shadowy vessels of *Ramon;* rather, they are sharply sketched in precise, technically accurate phrases. Moreover, like Freneau and Cooper, Hart is capable of describing a ship

from the seaman's point of view, thereby giving the reader
a professional interpretation of the object before him and,
at the same time, defining the relationship of the sailor
to the ship. Hart's account of a whaling master's response
to his new command illustrates the technique:

Macy, on gaining the deck, surveyed her various appoint-
ments with the practised eye of a sailor; and while he stood
upon her ample flushed quarter, casting his looks alternately
from the deck to her taper yards and towering masts, the
novelty and beauty of her proportions filled his eye so satis-
factorily, that a professional feeling of pride and pleasure
was visible in his countenance, as he began to realize the idea
of commanding a vessel, which was by far the largest, and . . .
the most beautiful craft of any he had ever seen in America.[25]

Hart's familiarity with his material finds its best expression, however, in his depiction of the sailor and the sea, a
depiction that in several important aspects foreshadows
Melville's treatment in *Moby-Dick*. Both Hart and Melville were faced with the problem of dignifying their
seamen, Hart's to the level of romance, Melville's to the
level of tragedy. If Melville's blubber-hunters became
knights and squires, Hart's whalemen "are fishermen upon
a grand scale." As they rush to attack an embayed right
whale, they resemble "an army of practised gladiators, in
the arena of the Coliseum." The whaleman is "he that, in
noble daring, challenges the world in emulation, and
braves the dangers of the deep . . . he that outstrips, in
very deed,—in the hazard of grappling with the giant of
the seas,—the vaunted, fabled champions of olden time."
Only once, in the characterization of Bill Smith, an old
English man-of-war's-man, does Hart abandon his exalted
conception of the seaman for the conventional caricature
in the manner of Smollett. But perhaps Old Bill, whose
former association with the Royal Navy is reiterated again
and again, is designed to intensify by contrast the dignity

and rationality of the American sailors. Even Jonathan Coleman, who, like Melville's Stubb, was "a light-hearted, merry fellow, and loved his joke," was "a whaling captain in the very best sense of the word," for "his profession was . . . a passion with him." Like Cooper's sailors, then, Hart's whalemen base their claim to nobility on their vocation. By challenging the sea and its most terrible inhabitant, they achieve the stature of the heroes of romance. The meeting of the Nantucket whalemen and the sperm whales of the Pacific becomes "an exhibition of the noblest of God's creation, both animal and human, waging a war of extermination, and threatening death and destruction by collision."[26]

Hart's attitude toward the sea, however, is the product of no such simple process of idealization. One might expect that, given his buoyant maritime nationalism, he would develop a correspondingly sanguine concept of the ocean, a concept perhaps resembling that of the early Cooper in its emphasis on sublimity and on the capacity both to release and to test the abilities of man. But in the course of his narrative Hart gradually reveals an attitude toward the sea that is disturbingly ambiguous. Although a similar ambiguity in the work of most of Hart's contemporaries could reasonably be dismissed as the result of an inability to control tone, in *Miriam Coffin* the play of incident by which the concept of the sea is constructed is too patterned, too formally arranged, to be accidental. At the beginning of the novel Seth Macy, Hart's ideal seaman, comes home from a long whaling voyage determined to quit forever the hardships of the sea. Within a few weeks, however, Jethro Coffin, a prosperous oil merchant, tempts Macy by offering him command of the fine new whaler *Grampus,* and Macy agrees to go once more to sea: " 'I did not intend to try the sea again, friend Jethro; but it is dull work lounging about shore, and I begin to tire of

inaction already.' " The *Grampus* sails on an auspiciously
bright day; the mood of her crew is typified by Jethro's
son Isaac, who cuts "antic capers" of "unbounded and boy-
ish joy" because Jethro, by permitting the boy to make the
voyage, has gratified "the strong propensity of his son for
the sea." But soon the *Grampus* is intercepted by a French
privateer, and, refusing to surrender his unarmed ship,
Macy determines to ram his enemy. When the crew discover Macy's intention, they utter "a suppressed groan of
horror." The *Grampus* strikes the French schooner, sinks
her, and despite Macy's efforts to save them, all her crew
are drowned. The chapter which began in a mood of ex-
hilaration ends with Hart's gloomy observation: "Thy ship
and cargo were dearly ransomed, Jethro Coffin:—and
Seth!—thou didst sacrifice a hecatomb of human beings
for thy preservation!"[27]

In sharp contrast to the departure of the *Grampus,* her
sister ship the *Leviathan* sails under a prophecy of doom,
for a fortuneteller has warned two of her crew, Henry
Gardner and Thomas Starbuck, that the voyage will end
in calamity. Two years later Seth Macy, who sailed with a
fair breeze in the proud new *Grampus,* returns in the
Leviathan from his "accursed" voyage in the dead of night,
bearing news of the death of Starbuck and of the sinking
of the *Grampus,* and bringing home the body of the
murdered Gardner: "It was thus, sadly and disastrously,
that the voyage of the young men terminated; and thus,
that the high hopes of Jethro Coffin, and his captains, were
blasted. The predictions of Judith, the half-breed fortuneteller, were fearfully realized."[28]

The conflict generated by this alternating pattern of
attraction and revulsion in Hart's treatment of the sea is,
in some measure, resolved in the concluding chapter, for
there it becomes apparent that the ambiguity of the sea
results from the differing points of view of its interpreters.

To characters like the boy Isaac and Jonathan Coleman, the master of the *Leviathan,* the ocean represents only a field for adventurous achievement. Isaac fulfills his ambition of becoming an admiral in the Royal Navy, and Jonathan "again put to sea, and mended his fortunes among the whales. His light heart, and buoyant mind—always looking to the bright side of the future,—carried him happily through the world." But to the more intelligent, more perceptive Macy, a person who sees that the coin of existence has two sides, the ocean seems, if not actually malignant, at least a force that so exceeds the capabilities of man that he should not challenge it. So Macy "would go to sea no more. He was frequently offered the choice of the ships in the harbour; but he could not be tempted." He emigrates to inland New York and becomes "an independent farmer,—the most satisfactory occupation in the world."[29] In *Miriam Coffin,* then, the sea moves vaguely and often clumsily in the direction of symbol. To Hart's characters it becomes a clue to the bias of reality, and to the most understanding of them it defines the limits of man's abilities and teaches him to cultivate his garden. For all its formlessness *Miriam Coffin* may well have given the author of *Moby-Dick* an indication of the potentialities of his material.

3

The impact of Cooper's success in the field of nautical fiction first showed its effect on American writers of short stories in 1827. Although brief character sketches of seamen had appeared earlier in the decade,[30] it was not until that year that extensive nautical elements were joined to a narrative framework. But, once started, a steadily increasing output of short sea stories flowed from the pens of American authors until well into the 1840's. Newly founded periodicals like the *American Monthly Magazine*

(1833–1838), the *New-England Magazine* (1831–1835), the *Knickerbocker Magazine* (1833–1865), and even the *Boston Spectator and Ladies Album* (1826–1827), which was expressly tailored for feminine tastes, provided a ready market for sea stories. Nearly all the popular gift books and annuals like *The Atlantic Souvenir* (1826–1832) and *The Token* (1827–1842) regularly spiced their offerings with one or two tales of the ocean during the late 1820's and the early 1830's. As a result, a substantial body of short sea fiction had come into being by 1835. Although they were often controlled by the example of Cooper in the selection and handling of nautical materials, the contributors to the magazines and gift books also strongly felt the influence of Irving on tone and structure; the best of them, moreover, sought to give expression to their own unique experience of maritime life. If the efforts of American novelists offered no coherent alternative to the image of the sea that Cooper's early nautical romances had reflected, this formidable aggregation of short sea fiction advanced several important modifications of that image.

Since the inception of the true short sea story in American literature coincided with the height of Irving's popularity and with the first appearance of magazines and annuals designed for women, it was perhaps inevitable that one of these modifications should take the direction of sentimentality. At their worst, the sentimental sea stories utilized their nautical settings only as sources for the pathos of long separation and early death. In tales like Catharine Sedgwick's "Modern Chivalry" (1827) the romantic hero, who is supposed to be a prime seaman, is so vaguely drawn and so extravagantly idealized that he bears no traces of his profession, while the common seamen never outgrow the stereotype established by the naval ballads of Charles Dibdin. Although "Modern Chivalry" takes place in the era so effectively portrayed by Cooper in *The Pilot,* the historical context of Miss Sedgwick's narrative remains as indefinite and unconvincing as that of *Constantius and Pulchera.* Nautical details are reduced to the formulas of romance or blithely dismissed with a remark like Miss Sedgwick's confession: "we are too ignorant of such matters, and too peaceably inclined to give any interest to the particulars of a sea-fight."[31] But in the hands of a writer like Nathaniel Ames, who combined a penchant for sentimentality with a thorough knowledge of nautical matters, the sentimental sea story became a means of humanizing the fictional treatment of the sea. In Ames's story "Morton" (1835) the account of the romance between Charles Morton, first mate of the American whaler *Orion,* and Isabella, the ward of the Spanish governor at San Blas, counterbalances the sweep and magnitude of the nautical action, for it provides a point of stability in a narrative that ranges from the west coast of South America to New England, and it supplies in its domesticity a certain relief from the gigantic scale of the descriptions of storms and battles. At its best, then, the sentimental sea story opened the way for a treatment of character and motivation that was more intimate than that of the early Cooper in his emphasis on heroism and sublimity and more perceptive than that of the writers of the eighteenth century in their preoccupation with the seaman's eccentricity.

At the same time that they were developing a new concern for the sailor as a human being, the writers of short sea stories were manifesting a growing interest in the contemporary nautical scene, an interest that presents a sharp contrast to Cooper's efforts to discover and interpret the American maritime past. High on the list of contemporary materials, of course, was the subject of piracy, and in story after story American writers introduced the rovers of the West Indies and the corsairs of the Mediterranean.[32] A still larger group of stories concerned naval life, and here, too, writers focused their attention on the contemporary activities of the navy, not on its past achievements.[33] By 1835 a few venturesome authors even dared to begin the exploration of the more prosaic aspects of the maritime present: in "A Chapter on Whaling" (1835) Horatio Hastings Weld apologized for the mundane nature of his subject and went on to sketch the life of the whale fishery without availing himself of the glamour of the past;[34] the anonymous author of "The Shipwrecked Coaster" (1835) concerned himself with the fate of the schooner *Almira,* bound for Boston from Sandwich in 1827 with a cargo of firewood; and in "Old Cuff" (1835) Nathaniel Ames discovered excitement and variety in the life of a typical Yankee seaman. The interest in the contemporary maritime scene had the effect of directing a large segment of American sea fiction toward the aims and techniques of the pseudovoyage. It put a new premium on the creation of verisimilitude, on documentation, on the inclusion of convincingly realistic detail. It encouraged writers to relate their narratives in the first person, for what could seem more authentic than the account of an eyewitness? With increasing frequency the short sea story took the form of the yarn, a tale told in one sitting by a sailor who had viewed or taken part in the action and whose salty diction furthered the illusion of authenticity.[35]

Still another departure from the concerns and methods of Cooper's first three sea novels was the interest displayed by the short story writers in the supernal and the horrible. Where Cooper had used suggestions of the supernatural only to heighten the stature of certain characters and introduced horror only to set off the courage and skill of his seamen, many of these writers, influenced by English Gothicism and German romanticism and following the

example of Irving, constructed their stories on the theme
of strange and terrible adventure on the ocean. In "A
Mystery of the Sea" (1829), "The Ghost" (1830), and "The
Haunted Brig" (1834), Samuel Hazzard, James Kirke
Paulding, and John Gould took the ghost story to sea,
seconded in their efforts by the anonymous authors who
launched a succession of weird vessels in "The Ice Ship"
(1828), "The Phantom Ship" (1832), and "The Spectre
Fire-Ship" (1834). In other stories the source of terror lay
in the natural disasters to which the mariner was always
exposed. More than ten years before Poe wrote his *Narrative of Arthur Gordon Pym,* Robert Montgomery Bird
explored the horrors of slow starvation and cannibalism
in "The Ice Island" (1827), as did William Leete Stone in
"The Dead of the Wreck" (1830). Both the anonymous
author of "A Night at Sea" (1828) and William Gilmore
Simms in "A Sea-Piece" (1834) described in gruesome detail the sensations of drowning, saving the narrator at the
last possible moment by having him wake up to find that
his frightful experience had been only a dream. Although
the exploitation of terror might seem anything but a
movement toward realism, it had the effect, most clearly
seen in the work of Poe after 1835, of emphasizing the
creation of a realistic surface, for its force depended on the
credibility of the context in which the strange adventure
was embedded. And in their stress on suffering and death,
the tales of horror represented a drastic qualification of
Cooper's conception of the sea, for they signaled the beginning in American fiction of the exploration of the
dark side of maritime life.

Nearly all of these tendencies away from the early romances of Cooper are manifested in the sea stories of
William Leggett. Just as Cooper's romances dominated
the American sea novel in substance and quality before
1835, so Leggett's stories as a group completely over-

shadowed the work of any other contemporary writer of short nautical fiction. Only two other writers, Nathaniel Ames and John Gould, produced a number of sea stories sufficient to warrant publication in book form, and even their work is so inept that the only interest it holds for the modern reader is documentary.[36] The sophistication of Ames's style and his thorough knowledge of nautical matters are vitiated by his inability to construct a plot, while Gould's fantastically improbable characters and situations betray the fact that most of his stories were written before he was twenty-one. Leggett's work, on the other hand, evinces in its growing strength and originality the talent and seriousness of a genuine artist, an artist who, as Fred Lewis Pattee has pointed out, "may be compared to advantage even with Cooper" in the fictional treatment of the sea.[37]

William Leggett was born in New York in 1801. In 1819 his family moved to Illinois, but after three years on the frontier William returned to New York, receiving an appointment as a midshipman in the navy on January 13, 1823. His brief naval career was not a happy one. After a tour of duty in the West Indies, where he contracted yellow fever, Leggett was assigned to the sloop of war *Cyane*, bound for service with the Mediterranean squadron. Aboard the *Cyane* he became the victim of the incessant petty persecutions of his commander, John Orde Creighton, who complained that Leggett had offended him by quoting passages from Shakespeare "of highly inflammatory, rancorous, and threatening import." In 1825 Leggett was court-martialed for having been involved in a duel with another midshipman at Port Mahon. Returning to New York the next year, he resigned his commission and began the brilliant journalistic career that led to his association with Bryant as assistant editor of the *Evening Post* from 1829 to 1836 and to the establishment of his own paper, the *Plaindealer,* in 1837. Between 1828 and 1834 he published a series of ten sea stories in the *New York Mirror,* the *Knickerbocker,* and his own short-lived magazine, the *Critic.* Three of the stories were printed in his first prose collection, *Tales and Sketches by a Country Schoolmaster* (1829), and the remainder were gathered in his *Naval Stories* (1834). Now nearly forgotten, Leggett's stories achieved great popularity in his lifetime,[38] but, in spite of his success, the increasing pressure of his editorial responsibilities after 1834 put an end to his writing of fiction. In 1839, his health weakened by his previous attack of yellow fever, Leggett died.[39]

Leggett's earliest efforts to utilize his naval experience as the material of fiction were tentative indeed. The nautical elements of "The Lie of Benevolence" (1828) are strictly subordinated to a primarily sentimental situation. Set very vaguely in what is presumably the period of the War of 1812, the story concerns Amelia, the young and beautiful wife of John Sanford, an American naval officer. The news of Sanford's death in action is kept from Amelia when she falls ill, but her anxiety for word of her husband forces her attendants to show her a bogus newspaper article reporting him safe. When Amelia sees by accident an authentic account of Sanford's death, she collapses, dead, and Leggett concludes his tale by drawing the reader's attention to the fact that "there is an obvious inference to be drawn from this narration," namely that the divine injunctions against falsehood "are not susceptible of modification according to circumstances, but stand eternally and immutably the same." Fortunately this heavy sentimental moralizing fails to suffocate Leggett's fine description of the departure of Sanford's vessel, but even in this rich account of ritualized confusion, Leggett seems to feel that he must apologize for his nautical details and hurry on to the sentimental business at hand; he breaks off his description of the bustle of preparation with the remark that, "in short, without entering into particulars, the whole ship is in motion," and, sidetracked once more by the process of setting the sails, he rushes back to the suffering Amelia with the question, "But why dwell on particulars?"[40]

By the time he wrote his next story, "A Burial at Sea" (1829), Leggett evidently had found the answer, for in this brief account of the death and burial of Fred Gerard, the ideal naval officer, he manages to exploit particulars—the "deep sepulchral voices" of the boatswain's mates and the tarred hammock that encloses the corpse—as a source of solemn pathos. In "A Watch in the Main-Top" (1829) he abandons sentiment altogether to spin a yarn of violence and terror at sea in the voice of Jack Gunn. Gunn, like Melville's Jack Chase a captain of the maintop in an American frigate, is Leggett's first successful attempt to sketch a common seaman. Tom Spunyarn, an old sea dog who had made a momentary appearance in "The Lie of Benevolence," was little more than a quid of tobacco and a tarpaulin hat, but Gunn breaks out of the eighteenth-century stereotype to become a credible human being, more reckless than responsible, but active, intelligent, and humane. In this story, too, Leggett demonstrates his superiority over his contemporaries in the management of the yarn. While the yarns of writers like John Gould bog down in a morass of salty lingo, Leggett merely suggests the idioms and rhythms of seaman's language, moving gradually and imperceptibly in the course of the narrative toward a more normal and more expressive diction. Thus, Gunn's yarn begins in the language of a Long Tom Coffin: " 'It's now near twelve years,' said he, 'since I shipped the first time in the sarvice; and it was about a year before that I was concarned in a bit of a scrape which I shall never forget, if I live to be as old as the Flying Dutchman.' "

But within a few pages Jack can tell us that "a faint recollection of the occurrences of the night then slowly began to return, which I believe was first prompted by the soreness of my throat, of which every breath made me sensible."[41] Then the colloquial voice returns, and the yarn comes to an end.

Leggett continued to perfect the technique of the yarn in "Merry Terry" (1830) and "The Main-Truck, or A Leap for Life" (1830), but in "A Night at Gibraltar" (1831) and "Fire and Water" (1834) he adopted the form of the dream in order to heighten the mood of horror. The nightmarish sensations of suffocation and vertigo had played important parts in several of his earlier stories. The central incident of "A Watch in the Main-Top" had been a fatal struggle in the water during which the combatants try to throttle or drown each other.[42] Again, in "Merry Terry" the climax of the narrative occurs when Terry strangles his enemy, whose "words died away in a rattling sound, like the gurgling in the throat of a drowning man." As the boy Bob teeters on the very tip of the mainmast in "The Main-Truck," the narrator, watching from the spar-deck, confesses that "I myself had the sensations of one about to fall from great height, and in a sudden effort to recover myself, like that of a dreamer who fancies he is shoved from a precipice, I staggered up against the bulwarks."[43] But now in "A Night at Gibraltar" and "Fire and Water" the narrator's feelings of terror as he falls from a cliff or sinks in the water become the exclusive theme and are pushed to such extremes that only a sudden awakening can explain the survival of the tale. Neatly constructed though they are, the two stories remain mere stunts; in their unconcern for probability of character and circumstance they fail to equal the earlier stories as convincing representations of the danger and brutality of life at sea.

In his last and best sea stories, "The Encounter" (1834) and "Brought to the Gangway" (1834), Leggett returned to the realistic portrayal of naval life. "The Encounter," a tale of storm and collision, displays not only Leggett's established skill in the creation of scenes, but a newly acquired mastery of sustained nautical action. As the story opens, the narrative point of view shifts with kaleidoscopic ease and swiftness from one portion to another of the American sloop of war *Active*. Ranging from the waist to the quarterdeck to the forecastle to the gun room to the steerage, the narrative creates a sense of size, of community, and, above all, of irony as the ship's population goes about its duties, ignorant of the impending catastrophe. A storm strikes, and the narrative suddenly jumps to a new vantage point, from which the vessel and the storm are seen entire. And as they become entities, they become characters, endowed, as Cooper had endowed them, with consciousness and will. The wind "howled and screamed," sounding like the "shrieks and wailings of angry fiends," and the ocean, "as if to revenge itself for its constrained inactivity, roused from its brief repose, and swelled into billows that rolled and chased each other with the wild glee of ransomed demons." The ship first "stood motionless an instant, as if instinct with life, and cowering in conscious fear of the approaching strife," and then "fled before the tempest, like an affrighted thing," "a wild horse foaming and stretching at his utmost speed." Scudding before the gale, the *Active* rams a vessel which is lying to in her path. The two vessels strike, rebound, and close again, "like gladiators, faint and stunned, but still compelled to do battle," and the bowsprit of the strange vessel darts "quivering in over the bulwarks [of the *Active*], as if it were the arrowy tongue of some huge sea monster."[44]

If Leggett's figurative technique is very like that of the

early Cooper, the import of his metaphors is quite different. Cooper's ships are delicate, responsive beings, attuned to and controlled by man, but Leggett's vessels are always massive, dwarfing and dominating their crews; they are "the stately mass," "the driving and ponderous mass," "the vast symmetrical bulk." The sea, too, "measureless, fathomless, unchanging," is essentially alien to man. The Rover might glory in the storm and find a correspondence between his soul and the tempestuous ocean, but Leggett's sailors seem to find only cruelty and violence at sea. In Cooper's novels the removal of the restraints of civilization brings an opportunity for achievement; in Leggett's stories it brings only the threat of brutal oppression. For the one theme that links nearly all of Leggett's stories is their common protest against the inhumanity of shipboard life. In a direct reference to his own naval experience, he names the "tyrannical ignoramus" in command of the frigate in "A Watch in the Main-Top" Crayton, a bully who "was cordially hated, by all who did not despise him too much to allow of the former feeling"; and Jack Gunn's yarn contains a vivid description of nautical brutality in the account of the flogging given Ned, the cabin boy of the merchant schooner *Nancy,* by the drunken seaman Jim Spenser:

"The little unoffending boy, was seized up to the main-rigging, by a piece of ratline stuff, passed so taught [*sic*] around his wrists that the blood was oozing from them in drops; his feet were made fast to the lubber grating, and the great white-livered bully, Jim, was standing over him, his red eyes still redder with passion, and his bloated cheeks pale and quivering from the same cause. In his hand he held a fathom of thirteen thread ratline, which he was drawing off and laying on to poor little Ned's bare back, till his tender white skin was all over streaked with blood."

In "Merry Terry" Leggett curiously anticipates Melville's *Billy Budd* in the use of a situation involving a rosy young man who is the favorite of all the crew except one, that one being a person in a position of authority who hates the boy implacably and apparently inexplicably. Again in "The Mess-Chest" (1833) Leggett's hero "had been the object of a full share of the 'fantastic tricks' which naval commanders sometimes choose to play off upon those beneath them."[45]

The source of evil in Leggett's stories, then, is not the sublimely powerful and sublimely beautiful ship and ocean, but man himself. In "Brought to the Gangway," the clearest statement of his somber conception of maritime life, the story begins with the description of a rare moment when sea, ship, and crew are in perfect harmony, a description which displays the precision and power of Leggett's style at its best:

There was just breeze enough to fill the canvass and crisp the surface of the ocean. The billows swelled gently up into the moonlight, their ridges curling into playful ripples, which glittered for a moment and whirled away, to be succeeded by other shining undulations. The water was of the intensest blue, except where thus checkered by mazy streaks of brightness, or flecked with tuft-like spots of foam, which, here and there, some little wave, saucier than the rest, would fling from it, as in sport. The light streamed on the deck in so strong a flood, that it seemed transmuted into silver by the "heavenly alchemy;" while the shadows of the sails, spars, and rigging, lay so black and well-defined, that the ship had a strange appearance, as if formed of opposite materials, joined in grotesque mosaic. The sails were swelled steadily out by the breeze, and the moonbeams slept in their snowy laps so softly, that they seemed rather to gleam with inherent light, than absorb the lustre of the planet. The signal-halliards were as white and glistening as cords of glossy silk; and the running-rigging, and even the tarred shrouds and backstays, were touched with a thin edge of radiance, like bars of some hard and polished substance.

The ship crept gently and steadily forward, and the slight line of foam which she left sparkled with the brilliancy of frostwork. She was a gallant frigate, and glided on her course under a full spread of canvass. The wind was on her starboard-quarter; and on every mast wide volumes of sails were extended, which rose tapering, one above another, in airy swells, till the loftiest, dwindled almost to a point, looked like a little fleecy cloud. So even and placid was her motion, that she seemed at perfect rest; and her progress was only betrayed by the bank of foam round her bows, and the whitened eddies in her wake. The silence on board was scarcely broken by the low wash of the sea against her sides, which had an indistinct and lulling sound, that harmonized with the faint-heard respiration of the sleeping crew, and heightened the effect of the pervading quiet. Her upper-deck seemed almost deserted. The watch, for the most part, lay hid in the shade of the bulwarks; and such as remained at their posts, preserved a stillness in keeping with the scene. The men at the wheel, on whose white dresses the moonlight streamed, looked like figures carved in marble; while those who stood in shadow resembled statues of bronze.

But the harmony is only a momentary illusion, as unreal as the alchemy of the moonlight, for immediately it is shattered by the contemptuous tones of Lieutenant Parral, as he rouses the watch. When the vain and dissipated Parral, "one of a class of officers happily not numerous," is angered by the slowness of Maurice Seaward, a handsome and educated young sailor, to respond to his kicks and curses, he has Seaward thrown into the brig to await punishment in the morning.[46]

Again and again Leggett reiterates the mood of disenchantment. In contrast to the silvery scene at night, "every thing around, as seen in the dim and smoky light of dawn, had a cheerless and repulsive appearance." Lying in irons, Seaward is surrounded by the litter from the galley and soaked in the spray from the weather port. It is rumored that Seaward had been induced to enlist "by dreams of naval glory": "poor youth! the illusion had been of brief continuance, and was effectually dispelled by the ignominy of his present situation." The ship is ruled by terror and incompetence: the Negro cooks cut short their sympathetic comments about Seaward at the approach of the ship's corporal, for " 'it's not safe talking when there's a ship's cousin within ear-shot.' " The chaplain is an ignorant, flippant coxcomb who was promoted to his present office "as an easy way of requiting him for certain secret services which it was whispered he had rendered" the captain. The bright Sabbath morning and the imposing religious service are disrupted when sail must be shortened and the commander, cursing his men, sends them to their stations, a "strange and startling contrast" to the words of prayer.[47]

Upon the conclusion of the religious exercises, the captain orders Seaward flogged:

It is unnecessary to say that the orders of the naval autocrat were promptly and strictly obeyed. We must take leave to pass hastily over this part of our story; for it is of a nature that no mind can pause upon with pleasure. The white and tender body of the poor boy was laid bare to the lash; his wrists were strongly tied to the gangway, and his ankles to the grating on which he stood. The cats, an instrument of torture the use of which is a disgrace to civilization, were applied to his back with a force that made each stripe leave its mark in blood; and when twelve of these had been given—(the full extent of punishment allowed by the rules of the navy)—an additional "half dozen" were ordered, as if in mockery of the very laws which had just been read, as furnishing the commander's warrant for inflicting corporal punishment at all!

Seaward resumes his duties, but that night, during a gale, he leaps at Parral's throat, and both men, "clasped in a deadly embrace," fall overboard and sink into the sea.[48]

William Leggett was only the first of an important line of young men from genteel backgrounds who went to sea and returned, not to champion the cause of maritime nationalism as Cooper had done, but to expose for the bene-

fit of their countrymen the inhumane system by which
the men-of-war and merchant vessels of America were
governed. Fresh from Harvard College, Nathaniel Ames
served many years in the navy and merchant marine and
came home to write about the cruelty and injustice he
had witnessed.[49] Forced by ill health to abandon his
studies for the ministry, John Gould went to sea in 1833
before the mast and received such brutal treatment at the
hands of Captain Christianson that upon his return he
brought suit against the tyrant, because "I wish sea-cap-
tains to know, from the example of Christianson, that
they cannot with impunity treat their people like dogs;
and because I wish the poor desolate sailor-boy, abroad
and friendless on the ocean, to know from my example
that the majesty of THE LAW will protect even his poor
rights, and punish the scoundrel who tramples on them."[50]
And by 1840, when Richard Henry Dana, another of these
young men, published his *Two Years Before the Mast*,
the American imagination was growing dissatisfied with
the romantic vision of the sea that Cooper's early novels
had expressed.

Chapter IV

The Light and the Dark Together

THE SEA NOVELS OF
COOPER'S MIDDLE PERIOD

THE muffled note of realism that was sounding in the short sea stories of the early 1830's presaged the drastic revision in the next decade of the image of the sea reflected in American literature. In part this revision was a result of the lively spirit of debunking that seized Americans in the 1840's; jaded by a twenty-five year diet of the romanticism of Byron and Scott, they resolved, as Constance Rourke has pointed out, that "the distant must go, the past be forgotten, lofty notions deflated."[1] In part, too, it was a result of the gradual fading of the glorious vision of maritime life called up by the War of 1812. And, perhaps most of all, it was a result of the demand by the American reading public, now thoroughly accustomed to the ocean as a setting for fiction, to know the sea more immediately than Cooper had let them know it, to know the maritime life of the present as it was lived from day to day by the American seaman.

As Cooper's readers took a second look at his early sea novels, they began to qualify the extravagant praise they had at first accorded them. Reviewing the whole of Cooper's work in 1838, the *North American Review* picked *The Pilot* as the most successful of his first three maritime productions because of its "calm and subdued

manner." With considerable restraint the reviewer remarked that *The Red Rover* "borders on romance," while
in *The Water-Witch* "the absurdities of the plot are too
glaring." He advised sea novelists to remember that "the
sublimity is in the subject, and no artificial coloring is
required to heighten the effect."[2] Some of Cooper's fellow
seaman-writers, like Nathaniel Ames and Charles F.
Briggs, raised more outspoken objections. Although his
inveterate jealousy of Cooper undermines one's confidence
in the justice of Ames's criticism, it is nevertheless significant that Ames attacked Cooper for a failure to describe
maritime life as it really is. Ames noted "six or eight very
desperate 'cases' " of blundering in the treatment of matters of seamanship in *The Red Rover* and *The Water-
Witch*. According to Ames, Long Tom Coffin "is a *caricature* (and not a very good one) of an 'old salt' "; indeed,
Cooper's maritime romances can be admired only by "ex-
quisites and boarding school girls, who do not know salt
water from fresh, or at least which end of a ship goes
foremost."[3] In the prologue to a bit of doggerel called "A
Veritable Sea Story," Briggs reiterated the charge that
Cooper had falsified the features of "an ocean life, which
looks so romantic at a distance." Writers like Cooper,
Chamier, and Sue "appear to have gone to sea without
asking leave of their mothers" and to have derived "their
ideas from some naval spectacle at the 'Bowery' "; Briggs
seriously doubted "whether either [*sic*] of them ever saw
blue water."[4] Wearied by the task of reviewing Robert
Burts's *The Scourge of the Ocean,* the most recent repetition of the formula which Cooper had established for the
marine romance, a writer for the *Gentleman's Magazine*
complained in 1837 that "we are tired of nautical tales;
the sea is positively worn out"; surely "novelty is a thing
to be desired, but not expected in maritime delineations."[5]
    The demand for a fresh approach was soon satisfied,

for in 1840 the reviewers of nautical books were unexpectedly confronted with what seemed to them a radically
different treatment of maritime life, Richard Henry Dana's
Two Years Before the Mast. Their response was immediate
and enthusiastic: the *Democratic Review* and the *North
American Review* were startled by the novelty of Dana's
realism; the *Knickerbocker* called the book "one of the
most striking and evidently faithful pictures of the 'real
life' at sea, that has come under our observation"; and the
New York Review described it as "a picture drawn wholly
from nature—from beginning to end, there is not a touch,
or a trait, or a color, of the ideal."[6] Apparently most of
Dana's readers concurred in his opinion that, "with the
single exception, as I am quite confident, of Mr. Ames's
entertaining, but hasty and desultory work, called 'Mariner's Sketches,'" *Two Years Before the Mast* was the first
account of maritime life to be written by a common sailor.[7]
And all the books that naval officers and passengers had
written about life at sea necessarily rendered a false, or at
best incomplete account:

However entertaining and well written these books may be,
and however accurately they may give sea-life as it appears to
their authors, it must still be plain to every one that a naval
officer, who goes to sea as a gentleman, "with his gloves on,"
(as the phrase is,) and who associates only with his fellow
officers, and hardly speaks to a sailor except through a boatswain's mate, must take a very different view of the whole
matter from that which would be taken by a common sailor.

The view from the forecastle was dark indeed; it encom-
passed a life that was "but a mixture of a little good with
much evil, and a little pleasure with much pain." It mud-
died the values that a generation of romanticists had
attached to the sea, because it saw each value fused in-
separably with its converse: "the beautiful is linked with

the revolting, the sublime with the commonplace, and the solemn with the ludicrous."8

Dana's business, then, was to display this life as accurately and completely as he could, "to present the life of a common sailor at sea as it really is,—the light and the dark together." But his realism was not the product of the satirical detachment of a Smollett; rather, Dana's aim was curiously akin to that of the sentimentalists of the 1830's in that he intended to restore the seaman to the human family and make him the object of an understanding compassion. In order to do this, Dana felt that he must strip away the brittle layer of glamour in which the clichés of Dibdin and the idealizations of Byron and Cooper had encased and isolated the sailor:

There is a witchery in the sea, its songs and stories, and in the mere sight of a ship, and the sailor's dress, especially to a young mind, which has done more to man navies, and fill merchantmen, than all the pressgangs of Europe. I have known a young man with such a passion for the sea, that the very creaking of a block stirred up his imagination so that he could hardly keep his feet on dry ground; and many are the boys, in every seaport, who are drawn away, as by an almost irresistible attraction, from their work and schools, and hang about the decks and yards of vessels, with a fondness which, it is plain, will have its way. No sooner, however, has the young sailor begun his new life in earnest, than all this fine drapery falls off, and he learns that it is but work and hardship, after all. This is the true light in which a sailor's life is to be viewed; and if in our books, and anniversary speeches, we would leave out much that is said about "blue water," "blue jackets," "open hearts," "seeing God's hand on the deep," and so forth, and take this up like any other practical subject, I am quite sure we should do full as much for those we wish to benefit. The question is, what can be done for sailors, as they are,—men to be fed, and clothed, and lodged, for whom laws must be made and executed, and who are to be instructed in useful knowledge, and, above all, to be brought under religious influence and restraint?9

Like the muckrakers of the early twentieth century, Dana hoped to reform by exposure. And like the muckrakers, he was more effective in persuading his fellow writers to adopt his realistic techniques than he was in impressing upon them his humanitarian ardor.

In the course of a review of two new nautical books, Herman Melville commented in 1847 on the shift toward the realistic treatment of maritime life that *Two Years Before the Mast* had signaled:

From time immemorial many fine things have been said and sung of the sea. And the days have been, when sailors were considered veritable mermen; and the ocean itself as the peculiar theatre of the romantic and wonderful. But of late years there have been revealed so many plain, matter-of-fact details connected with nautical life, that, at the present day, the poetry of salt water is very much on the wane. The perusal of Dana's "Two Years before the Mast," for instance, somewhat impairs the relish with which we read Byron's spiritual "Address to the Ocean." And when the noble poet raves about laying his hands upon the ocean's mane (in other words manipulating the crest of a wave), the most vivid image suggested is, that of a valetudinarian bather at Rockaway, spluttering and choking in the surf, with his mouth full of brine.[10]

The publishers' lists of the 1840's testify to the point of Melville's remarks. A parade of old tars took up their pens, all putting Dana to shame by the length of their service and the extent of their sufferings. Samuel Leech stepped forward with *Thirty Years from Home, or A Voice from the Main Deck* (1843), the object of which was to give a true picture of the sailor's "life of danger, of toil, of suffering." Nicholas Isaacs could offer only *Twenty Years Before the Mast* (1845), but William Nevens was able to top all his rivals with *Forty Years at Sea* (1845), "a plain, simple, unadorned statement of fact." The young men who, in the early 1830's, had given the public glamorous sketches of a midshipman's life were now replaced by writers like Francis Allyn Olmstead, a recent college graduate, who reported *Incidents of a Whaling Voyage* (1841). Thus in book after book every aspect of the seaman's life was detailed with exhausting thoroughness by those who had experienced that life at first hand. Within five years of its date, Dana's complaint that *"a voice from the forecastle has hardly yet been heard"* was more than satisfied.

2

Cooper had rarely been guilty of the romantic extremes which now disqualified the approach to the sea of a Byron or a "Barry Cornwall" in the eyes of literate Americans, for the romanticism of his first three marine novels had always been tempered by his concern for nautical accuracy. To many of his readers in the 1820's and early 1830's he seemed to be realistic above all. Whittier praised Cooper for "copying direct from nature in his delineations of nautical character" and listed at length the "breathing and wild realities" of *The Pilot* and *The Red Rover*.[11] In 1829 the *Edinburgh Review* attacked Cooper for being too scrupulously faithful to nautical fact: he mistakes "the province of the artist for that of the historian," for, "by considering truth or matter-of-fact as the sole element of popular fiction, our author fails in massing and in impulse."[12] But faithful as Cooper was to his maritime experience, important elements of the three early romances nevertheless conflicted with the interpretation of the sea that Dana had now established. He had chosen settings and subjects which were no longer fashionable, for the deeds of heroic naval officers and glamorous outlaws of the eighteenth century failed to excite the interest of readers bent on discovering the facts of the maritime present. Although he had developed a concept of the voyage as an ordeal, in his portrayal of the ocean Cooper had emphasized beauty, sublimity, and solemnity—the positive halves of Dana's three pairs of values. Moreover, he had slighted the seaman in favor of the ship and the ocean: some of his sailors, like Dick Fid, had fallen too easily into the attitudes of the eighteenth-century stereotype, while his gentleman-seamen had been idealized to such an extent that they became, like Ludlow, clumsy lay figures or, like the Rover, the inhabitants of a gorgeous world which exists only in the Byronic imagination. And always, in characterizing the seaman Cooper had stressed landlessness, the peculiar quality that divorces the sailor from the rest of mankind.

When Cooper returned to the sea novel in 1838 with the publication of *Homeward Bound,* his portrayal of maritime life had moved significantly in the direction of the realism that Dana was soon to popularize. Perhaps this movement reflected the influence of the themes and tone of contemporary short sea fiction, but it also appears to have been the result of a profound change in his conception of the novel. The historical romance, which had served so effectively as a vehicle for his doctrine of maritime nationalism, seemed to Cooper to have failed as a means of expressing the concepts of government and society which he had developed during the latter half of his European residence. Stung by the humiliating American reception of *The Bravo* (1831) and *The Heidenmauer* (1832), he was talking in 1832 of abandoning the romance.[13] In *A Letter to His Countrymen* (1834) he announced his intention to give up the attempt "to illustrate and enforce the peculiar principles of his own country, by the agency of polite literature," and in the same year he proposed that as an alternative he might "return to Europe, and continue to write, for in that quarter of the world I am at least treated with common decency."[14] He neither laid aside his pen nor retreated to Europe, but he did abandon the historical romance for a period of seven years. Seeking new vehicles for his ideas, he tried direct exhortation in *The American Democrat* (1838), satirical allegory in *The Monikins* (1835), and comparison and comment in the five books of travel (1836–1838). When these efforts also resulted in failure,[15] Cooper, still shunning the historical romance, decided to return to the genre with which he had begun his literary career, the novel of manners.

He had intended to open his novel with the arrival of his characters at Sandy Hook from an extended residence in Europe, but "as a vessel was introduced in the first chapter, the cry was for 'more ship,' until the work has become 'all ship;' it actually closing at, or near, the spot where it was originally intended it should commence." Thus the Effinghams were forced to defer their jaundiced appraisal of American institutions and manners, and Cooper found himself writing *Homeward Bound,* his fourth sea novel. If those who cried for more ship expected a repetition of the three previous treatments of maritime life, they must have been surprised by the result of their demand. Certain elements of *Homeward Bound,* it is true, are reminiscent of the early romances. Cooper can still speak of the "magnificent horrors," the "attractive terror," the "solemn and grand enjoyment" in the "sublime sight of a raging sea." The characters are still rivaled by the "surpassingly beautiful" ship which in moments of crisis assumes the identity and volition of a human being: just before a storm strikes, the packet *Montauk* resembles "some sinewy and gigantic gladiator, pacing the arena, in waiting for the conflict at hand." The gentleman-seaman, here represented by Paul Powis, is as glamorously wooden as he had ever been. But there are major differences. The occasional sublimity of a stormy sea is now insufficient relief from the tedium of a long voyage; Eve Effingham is made to rejoice in the fact that her vessel is pursued by a British warship, for " 'how much better is this than dull solitude, and what a zest it gives to the monotony of the ocean!' "[16] The ship, no longer the symbol of freedom from the responsibilities and restrictions of society, becomes a microcosm of that society. Into the *Montauk* is crowded "a congress of nations," and the discipline of the ship serves as a lesson that might well be applied to governments on land. Although vessels in the early romances had been distinguished by their airy grace, the *Montauk* is consistently described in terms of vast bulk and crushing momentum. Even the seaman undergoes a change in *Homeward Bound,* for Captain Truck, the central figure of the book, achieves at once a dignity that is beyond the reach of Dick Fid and a humanity of the sort that never intrudes upon the ideality of the Rover.

This movement away from the romantic treatment of the sea is in some degree the result of the setting and subject imposed on *Homeward Bound* by the social satire for which it is a prelude. That satire called, of course, for a contemporary setting, and for the first time Cooper was forced to deal with the maritime present. Moreover, the plot of the projected novel required that the subject of *Homeward Bound* be the best known and in many ways the most prosaic segment of contemporary nautical life, the packet service between London and New York. Here there was neither the chance to exploit "that peculiar charm which is derived from facts clouded a little by time" nor the freedom to invent a legend "without looking for the smallest aid from traditions or facts";[17] rather, the premium was on verisimilitude. If Cooper was not motivated by Dana's passion for exposing the realities of life at sea, he was at least obliged to pay more attention to those realities than ever before.

On the surface, then, the new tone which Cooper voiced in *Homeward Bound* seems, like so many of his important literary decisions, to have been the product of purely external and fortuitous circumstances rather than the inevitable outcome of a consistent line of artistic development. The fact remains, however, that for a number of years he had been planning and gathering materials for a history of the American navy,[18] a work which, if it was to satisfy his scholarly scruples, must of necessity embody a more soberly realistic attitude toward the sea and the maritime past of the nation than *The Pilot, The Red Rover,* and *The Water-Witch* had expressed. In 1839, when the task was finished, Cooper acknowledged that the tone of the romance was incompatible with truth, "the first, and great desideratum of history":

Some of the greatest writers of the age have impaired the dignity of their works, by permitting the peculiarities of style that have embellished their lighter labours, to lessen the severity of manner that more properly distinguishes narratives of truth. This danger has been foreseen in the present instance, though the nature of the subject, which seldom rises to the level of general history, offers a constant temptation to offend.[19]

In spite of the ardent big-navyism of the *History,* Cooper is never guilty of the romantic chauvinism for which he censured Scott's *Life of Napoleon.*[20] The voice of the *History* is always reasonable, willing to consider both sides of a controversy, able to state frankly errors and failures, and determined to adhere with absolute fidelity to fact. Even the tone of those passages in which he sets forth his doctrine of maritime nationalism evinces a hesitancy, an awareness of the need for qualification, which were never expressed in *Notions of the Americans.* Cooper is just as convinced as he ever was of the material capacity of America for maritime greatness, but, unfortunately, "opinion has not kept pace with the facts of the country." The danger is that, caught between unwarranted jealousy of a large naval establishment and ignorant awe of the power of the Royal Navy, Americans will never make use of that capacity. Thus, in the *Naval History* Cooper abandons his earlier efforts to evoke romantic images of a glamorous and largely fictitious past and concentrates his energies on the task of impressing upon American opinion the facts, the realities of the national experience. If the country is to achieve supremacy, it must "be true to itself and to its predominant principles."[21] Achievement waits upon self-discovery.

After the publication of his *magnum opus,* Cooper returned for the first time in seven years to the historical romance. But the three sea novels, which, with *The Pathfinder* and *The Deerslayer,* constitute his output for the extraordinarily productive years from 1840 to 1842, are set apart from the three early nautical romances by marked differences in tone and substance; indeed, two of them, *Mercedes of Castile* (1840) and *The Two Admirals* (1842) are outgrowths of the *Naval History.* In *Mercedes* Cooper attempts to supplement the *Naval History* by extending his study of American maritime activity back to its origins, the first voyage of Columbus. The subject would seem to offer all the materials of a successful romance: the color and glamour of the Spanish court in the fifteenth century, the high excitement of a voyage which Cooper considers "the greatest adventure of modern times,"[22] and above all the grand and visionary character of Columbus. Yet even with these materials Cooper is unable to recapture the hard brilliance and exalted mood of *The Red Rover,* for his attempts to evoke a romantic atmosphere and to deal in sublimity are continually smothered by his still more urgent concern for historical accuracy and completeness. In no other novel are Cooper's powers of invention so circumscribed by fact, for none is so dominated by the character and deeds of a historical figure. And by 1840

Cooper no longer allowed himself to take the liberties with fact that he had taken in *The Pilot.* The result is that *Mercedes* is source-bound. The narrative is punctuated by discussions of the claims of conflicting authorities, and the descriptions of ships and seamanship turn into disquisitions on the evolution of naval architecture and navigational instruments. To compound the confusion of *Mercedes,* Cooper tosses in a flamboyantly fictitious love story which points up by contrast the unromantic solidity of the rest of the book. Unable to decide whether he is a romancer or a historian, Cooper alternates between one role and the other.

A strong note of didacticism also characterizes *The Two Admirals.* For many years Cooper had been thinking of using an incident from "the teeming and glorious" naval history of England as the subject of a novel. In 1828 he observed that "an American might well enough do it, too, by carrying the time back anterior to the separation, when the two histories were one."[23] But the major impetus for such a work came from the *Naval History,* for *The Two Admirals* is an extension of the campaign waged there on behalf of a navy organized into fleets and commanded by admirals.[24] The book, however, is more than fictionalized propaganda; in it Cooper makes an important advance toward the discovery of an alternative to the purely romantic treatment of the sea. The desire to demonstrate clearly and accurately the nature and uses of fleet maneuvers in itself introduces an element of matter-of-factness in the nautical portions of the book, a quality that only the *Naval History* had previously shown. But brilliantly managed though these extended accounts of naval tactics are, they remain, of necessity, little more than verbal diagrams. To relieve this dryness, this preoccupation with objects, Cooper offers the reader his extraordinarily convincing characterization of the two admirals and of the fine and involved relationship that binds them together. If the sublime sea and the bird-like vessel are lost in the emphasis on the order and discipline of naval strategy, the loss is compensated by the injection into the narrative of the concerns and characters of credible human beings. For the first time, the seaman's claim to the attribute of humanity is consistently stronger than those of the ship and the ocean.

Although *The Wing-and-Wing* (1842) reflects Cooper's concern with naval history in its portrait of Nelson and its description of the execution of Admiral Caraccioli, the novel is, as two of Cooper's ablest critics have pointed out, a reversal of the trend toward a less romantic treatment of maritime life.[25] Like the nearly contemporaneous *Deerslayer* (1841), *Wing-and-Wing* seems to embody a deliberate resolve to retreat from the oppressive reality of here and now. If the annals of America are singularly wanting in suitably romantic incidents and settings, Cooper will abandon America and choose the most breathtakingly romantic scene he knows, the waters of the Mediterranean, and the most stirring period of naval history, the era of the Napoleonic wars; he will make the love story a more important element of the novel than ever before; he will return to the small vessel, the picturesque and graceful lugger *Feu-Follet,* and he will make that vessel "the true hero" of his tale by diminishing and flattening out his human characters in proportion as the ship is magnified and endowed with consciousness and will. One character, however, refuses to give way to the *Feu-Follet;* apparently unintentionally the book is dominated by the figure of Ithuel Bolt, a figure that shatters the mood of romantic escapism. Bolt, an embittered American seaman who aids the French in order to harm the English, perhaps may best be described as a second look, a disenchanted look, at Long Tom Coffin. Like Coffin, he is over six feet tall, stooped, angular, and bony; the coloring and features of the two men are nearly identical, and both are natives of New England. But unlike his counterpart in *The Pilot,* Bolt did not go to sea until he was thirty years old and is still " 'no great matter as a seaman.' "[26] And although both characters respond to similar circumstances in almost precisely the same ways, their motives are diametrically opposed: what is inspired by love of country in Coffin is the result of Bolt's thirst for revenge; Coffin's loyalty is Bolt's selfishness; Coffin's native good sense is Bolt's shrewd craftiness. Bolt is at once the repository of Cooper's well-known prejudices against all things Yankee and, as the victim of oppression, the recipient of his sympathy. Like Ishmael Bush in *The Prairie* and Aaron Thousand-acres in *The Chainbearer,* Bolt emerges from this conflict of attitudes a gigantic figure, so utterly credible in his fullness and complexity that he breaks the spell of witchery that Cooper had sought to cast on his story.

In 1843 Cooper's attention was diverted from the memory that had inspired *Wing-and-Wing,* the leisurely and dreamy excursions he had made in chartered feluccas along the coasts of Tuscany, Romagna, and Naples during his residence in Italy,[27] by a reminder of a vastly different portion of his maritime experience. In January of that year he received a letter asking if he were "the Mr. Cooper who in 1806 or 1807 was on board the ship *Sterling,* Cap. Johnson, bound from New York to London," and if he remembered the writer, Edward R. Myers, who had also made the voyage. Cooper immediately replied in the affirmative, visited his old shipmate in New York, and invited him to Cooperstown for a visit of five months at Otsego Hall.[28] The result of their conversations at Cooperstown was *Ned Myers* (1843), a small volume in which Cooper transcribed and edited Ned's account of his experience as a seaman. Subtitled *A Life Before the Mast,* the book is by far the best of the many nautical reminiscences which were prompted by the success of Dana's work in 1840.

Although it observes perfectly all the conventions of the genre, the richness of Ned's experiences and the expertness of Cooper's transcription of them make one reluctant to classify it with the hackwork of Isaacs, Nevens, and the rest. True to form, *Ned Myers* is designed to expose reality, to give the public "some just notions of the career of a common sailor." Like most of its competitors, the book links its revelations to a pious purpose, that of demonstrating to seamen the evil consequences of their spendthrift and intemperate habits. And in *Ned Myers*, too, an attempt is made to capture the authentic tones of a voice from the forecastle, for Cooper assures the reader that he "has endeavoured to adhere as closely to the very language of his subject, as circumstances will allow."[29] But very few of Ned's rivals had an amanuensis of the skill of Cooper. The style of *Ned Myers* is a minor triumph, for Cooper has indeed succeeded in preserving the idioms and intonation of the seaman and in imposing, at the same time, the order and control which are so conspicuously lacking in the narratives of the other literary tars. But if Cooper had modified Ned's discourse, Ned in turn had apparently modified his; in none of Cooper's previous writings is there the clarity of syntax, the precision of diction, and the racy concreteness of metaphor of *Ned Myers*. To match this superiority of style, Ned's life offers an unparalleled sampling of the whole sweep of American maritime activity in the first half of the nineteenth century. Ned had been a sailor for thirty-six years and had passed an estimated twenty-five years actually beyond sight of land. He had served in nearly a hundred different vessels; three of them had been wrecked, two had foundered, and one had burnt to the water line. He

had once been around the world, twice around Cape
Horn, five times to Canton, and twice to Batavia. He had
seen combat in the American navy on the Great Lakes in
the War of 1812, spent nineteen months as a British prisoner of war, served in the Buenos Ayrean navy, been twice
assaulted by pirates in the West Indies, gone whaling off
the coast of Japan, and smuggled opium in China.

The content of all this experience forms a jolting contrast to the fine, free life of the sea which Cooper had portrayed in the early romances and to which he had sought
to return in *Wing-and-Wing*. "Ned's book," as Cooper
called it, consists of a steady round of floggings, curses, and
delirium tremens, hardships and suffering in every form,
relieved only by an occasional handsome ship, a loyal
friend, or a kind word. There is the Hollander aboard the
Stadtdeel who, crazed by the beatings given him by his
officers, leaps into the sea. There are the appalling scenes
in the hospital for seamen in Batavia where Ned lay for
months "in a distant land, surrounded by disease, death
daily, nay hourly making his appearance, among men
whose language was mostly unknown" to him; it was like
living "on a bloody battle-field . . . a sort of Golgotha, or
place of skulls. More than half who entered the Fever
Hospital, left it only as corpses." And there are those
scenes on board the *Sterling* in 1806 and 1807, scenes
that were as much a part of Cooper's experience as they
were of Ned's: "The assembling of the crew . . . was a
melancholy sight. The men came off, bearing about them
the signs of the excesses of which they had been guilty
while on shore; some listless and stupid, others still labour-
ing under the effects of liquor, and some in that fearful
condition which seamen themselves term having the 'horrors.' "[30] The drenched and crowded forecastle, the cruel
impressment of Philadelphia Bill, the long and arduous
passage home when the *Sterling* could muster only four

hands in a watch, all were a far cry from the delightful
family cruise in the *Divina Providenza* over the blue
waters of the Bay of Naples.

3

In the opening pages of Cooper's next sea novel, *Afloat
and Ashore* (1844), the crew of the ship in which Miles
Wallingford is to make his first voyage join their vessel:
"That afternoon the crew came on board, a motley collection of lately drunken seamen . . . A more unpromising
set of wretches, as to looks, I never saw grouped together.
A few, it is true, appeared well enough; but most of them
had the air of having been dragged through—a place I
will not name, though it is that which sailors usually quote
when describing themselves on such occasions."[31] As the
narrative progresses, it becomes increasingly apparent that
much of Miles's experience is a translation of the incidents
of Cooper's voyage in the *Sterling* as he has recorded
them in *Ned Myers* and in the books of travel. One of his
first duties aboard the *Sterling* had been "to go up and
loose the foretop sail"; Miles's nautical aptitude is first
tested when he is "sent aloft to loose the fore-topsail."
Both Cooper and Miles approach England with feelings of deep reverence and admiration; both are impressed by the quantity of shipping in the crowded
Thames and by the skill of the pilot in threading the
way to the anchorage; both are sadly disillusioned by
their tours through the pubs and brothels of London under the guidance of a corrupt customs official; and both
make trips to the West End with seamen whose unsophis-
ticated comments on English manners and institutions
are at once shrewd and ludicrous.[32] Firsthand experience
with British press gangs shakes the faiths of Miles and
Cooper in English justice. In the course of Miles's fourth
voyage, a British officer boards the vessel which Miles

commands and attempts to impress Thomas Voorhees, a
prime seaman born in New York not ten miles from the
Wallingford home, a man whose family Miles knows;
aboard the *Sterling* the English had impressed the prime
seaman Isaac Gaines, "a native New Yorker, a man whose
father and friends were known to the captain." Similarly,
in both the *Sterling* and Miles's ship an obstinate Swedish
sailor thwarts the press gang by refusing to obey their
orders. And in the *Sterling,* on one occasion "Cooper had
a little row with . . . [a] boarding officer, but was silenced
by the captain," just as Captain Wallingford makes "a
sign for [the mate] Marble to be silent" when the latter
begins to quarrel with a boarding officer.[33]

But personal experience alone was incapable of supplying the extensive factual basis which Cooper sought for
Afloat and Ashore. Apparently he intended the novel to
perform much the same service for the American merchant marine that his *Naval History* had performed for
the United States Navy. If it was to foster a new conception
of the American maritime future by acquainting public
opinion with the facts of the maritime past, the novel
must portray American commercial activity in its most
vigorous era, the period of neutral trading that extended
from the outbreak of the Napoleonic Wars until the im-
position of the Embargo in 1807. But not only must the
action of the novel antedate Cooper's voyage in the *Sterling,* it must take place on a scale far vaster than that of
his own maritime experience, for if, like the *Naval History, Afloat and Ashore* was to recall Americans to a sense
of their national heritage, the action of the novel must
in some way be linked to the larger movement of American history.

To accomplish these ends, Cooper turned to the extensive knowledge of the maritime past that he had displayed in the *Naval History.* He made Miles Wallingford

the virtual embodiment of the national heritage by continually equating Miles's experience with the national experience. Miles, whose father had been wounded during the Revolution in the action between the *Trumbull* and the *Watt*, "the hardest fought naval combat of the war," was born on "the very day that Cornwallis capitulated at Yorktown." He first goes to sea in 1797, a time when the shipping of America "was wonderfully active, and, as a whole, singularly successful." Throughout his nautical career Miles displays a marvelous affinity with events of great national interest: he is present at both the first and last actions of the quasi-war with France; he is on hand to greet the *Ganges,* the first man-of-war to be sent to sea by the American government after the signing of the Constitution; and he is the victim of "the first of the long series of wrongs that were subsequently committed on American commerce [by the British] . . . and which, in the end, terminated by blockading all Europe, and interdicting the high seas on paper."[34]

Like *The Two Admirals,* then, *Afloat and Ashore* is closely related to the concerns and the material of the *Naval History.* Indeed, such a major nautical episode as the series of captures and recaptures of the *Dawn* in *Afloat and Ashore* is patently an expansion of a text furnished by the *Naval History:* "more American ships have been retaken from their prize crews by American seamen left on board them, within the last sixty years, than have been retaken by the seamen of all the remaining captured vessels of Christendom."[35] A deeper connection between the two works exists in their common expression of a peculiarly retrospective kind of nationalism. Both seem intended to memorialize a golden age, an age when national activities coincided with national principles, an age of simple manners and primal virtues. But the distance between the Cooper of 1839 and the Cooper of 1844 can be measured by the uses to which they put that past age. Where the *Naval History* had sought to abstract from it certain principles with which the almost inevitable growth of America to greatness might be guided, *Afloat and Ashore* sees it as the source of not only the principles but the substance of the future: "God alone knows for what we are reserved; but one thing is certain—there must be a serious movement backward, or the nation is lost."[36]

Extensive though the autobiographical and historical elements of *Afloat and Ashore* are, their sum is far outweighed by the amount of material which is drawn from the narratives of travel and exploration of the late eighteenth and early nineteenth centuries. In his previous sea novels Cooper generally stayed within the limits of his own experience; whether the setting was the English Channel, the North Atlantic, the waters of the northeastern coast of America, or the Mediterranean, it was one of which he had direct knowledge. Only once before, in *Homeward Bound*, did he need to supplement that knowledge by drawing from contemporary voyage literature.[37] But as the personification of American maritime enterprise, the hero of *Afloat and Ashore* must sail to every corner of the earth, traversing seas which lay far beyond the compass of Cooper's nautical experience. And if his usual concern for the authenticity of his settings was not enough to send him to the sources of factual material, Cooper had an added incentive in his knowledge that Charles Wilkes, the leader of the United States Exploring Expedition, was about to give the public five huge volumes containing an accurate and detailed description of much of the area over which *Afloat and Ashore* takes place.[38]

Cooper gives very little indication of the identity of the sources for the novel. In the preface to the first volume he obliquely alludes to them by saying that, "on the subject of the nautical incidents of this book, we have endeavored to be as exact as our authorities will allow," but he specifically mentions only one of these authorities, Captain Frederick W. Beechey, whose *Narrative of a Voyage to the Pacific and Bering's Strait* (1831) provided the details of Cooper's account of the coral islands of the Pacific in chapters 15 through 19 of the first volume of *Afloat and Ashore*.[39] In its review of the first volume of the novel, however, the London *Spectator* noticed the general resemblance of Cooper's work to the many recently published narratives of voyages, particularly Dana's *Two Years Before the Mast* and Richard Cleveland's *A Narrative of Voyages and Commercial Enterprises* (1842).[40] Of the two, Cleveland's book bears the closer relation to *Afloat and Ashore*, for it seems to have furnished Cooper both the over-all scheme of his novel and at least one important character. Like *Afloat and Ashore, A Narrative of Voyages* consists of the histories of several far-ranging commercial voyages undertaken in the era of neutral trading, and, like Cooper's novel, it is narrated by a man in his middle sixties who looks back on the exploits of his youth with nostalgic pride. Cleveland's experience, like Miles Wallingford's, encompasses nearly the entire range of American maritime activity from Europe to the Far East. The two Negro characters, George in *A Narrative of Voyages* and Neb in *Afloat and Ashore*, offer a still more specific parallel: both accompany the narrators on several voyages; both, in their speech, appearance, and manner, are described as the Negro epitomized; and both are utterly loyal and superbly courageous. With this one exception, however, the detail of character and incident in *Afloat and Ashore* is drawn from sources other than Cleveland.

A close look at one episode of the novel, the trading visit to the Northwest Coast in chapters 12–14 of Volume I, serves to indicate the extent of Cooper's reliance on these sources. Although the scene of the episode, the coast of what is now British Columbia near the fifty-third parallel, was one with which Cooper had no personal acquaintance, a vast storehouse of information about it was near at hand. From the time of Cook's visit in 1778, the Northwest Coast had become a focal point of many of the great exploring expeditions of the late eighteenth and early nineteenth centuries. Cook's lively description of this area (1784) was supplemented by the official histories of the expeditions of Marchand (1797), La Pérouse (1798), Vancouver (1798), Mackenzie (1801), and Lewis and Clark (1814). A number of less formal but equally accessible books contain information about particular aspects of life on the Northwest Coast. Alsop's *Life and Adventures of John R. Jewitt* (1815), the history of an English seaman who had been captured and enslaved by the natives, is one of the earliest sources of authentic material relating to the Indians in the vicinity of Nootka Sound. Cleveland's *Narrative of Voyages* describes the trade in sea otter skins from the point of view of a Boston shipmaster, while Washington Irving's *Astoria* (1836) chronicles the far grander commercial exploits of John Jacob Astor's American Fur Company. Cooper's familiarity with much of this material undoubtedly accounts for the richness and depth of the scene in *Afloat and Ashore*.[41] At the same time, it tends to obscure his indebtedness to specific sources, for his assimilation of such a mass of diverse information gave him the authority to shape his story according to the dictates of his imagination.

Obscure though they are, traces of Cooper's use of material drawn from two accounts of the Northwest Coast can be discovered. As the *Crisis* nears her destination, she is boarded by an Indian who can speak English and who pilots the ship into a small cove where she is anchored "barely an arrow's flight from the shore." Three more

Indians join the ship at her mooring and exchange furs for the trinkets and hardware of the Americans. The appearance and manner of the Indians inspire nothing but scorn among the crew of the *Crisis;* Moses Marble, the first mate, is especially vociferous in expressing his contempt for their ugliness, their talent for thievery, and, above all, their apparent dull-witted indolence. Although the Americans are put on their guard by their discovery of the remains of a vessel which the Indians had captured and ransacked a few years before, they nevertheless fall victim to a surprise attack during their second night in the cove. The Indians, led by a shrewd, withered old chief whom the sailors call Smudge, overpower Miles Wallingford, the only man on deck, and secure the hatches, thus trapping the rest of the crew below. Only Captain Williams is able to make his way to the deck, and he is quickly struck with a blow which "would have felled an ox" as he gropes through the dark toward Miles. Refusing to surrender, Marble and the other men below determine to ignite the powder magazine and blow up the ship, but they are saved from this last resort when Miles finally succeeds in releasing them so that they may recapture the vessel from the Indians.

In its main outlines this episode closely parallels certain incidents related by Irving in chapter 11 of *Astoria.* Cruising along the Northwest Coast in 1811, the *Tonquin,* a vessel belonging to Astor, was boarded by an English-speaking Indian who offered to serve as a guide and interpreter. Like the *Crisis,* the *Tonquin* entered an apparently peaceful cove where she was cordially greeted by a wily old chief named Nookamis. And like Moses Marble, Captain Thorn of the *Tonquin* was "a plain, straight-forward sailor" who held "the whole savage race in sovereign contempt." During their second day in the cove the crew of the *Tonquin* were attacked by the Indians. In the struggle Captain Thorn was felled by "a blow from behind, with a war-club," but one of the crew, "determined on a terrible revenge," made his way to the magazine after the Indians had won control of the vessel and touched off an explosion which destroyed both the *Tonquin* and her conquerors.

Thus, with the exception of the final outcome, the leading features of Irving's incident are reproduced in *Afloat and Ashore*. Evidently Irving is also the source for some of the details of Cooper's characterizations. Nookamis is obviously the prototype of Smudge, while Captain Thorn contributes elements to the characters of both Captain Williams and Moses Marble. Cooper's narrator pauses after the death of Captain Williams to remark that the Captain's "principal fault was want of caution," just as Irving pauses to notice Thorn's "proud contempt of danger." Thorn's irascibility, on the other hand, is a property of Marble, not of the "mild, well-meaning" Williams; it is Marble who offers to "moisten" the shriveled Smudge a little by throwing him overboard, an offer made in a spirit very like that which prompts Captain Thorn to dismiss Nookamis "over the side of the ship with no very complimentary application to accelerate his exit." But some of the ingredients of Cooper's episode are not in Irving's recipe. Although Irving's Indians come "prying about to gratify their curiosity, for they are said to be impertinently inquisitive," Cooper's Indians are singularly apathetic:

Smudge seemed to be almost without ideas . . . The articles he received in exchange for his skins failed to arouse in his grim, vacant countenance, the smallest signs of pleasure. Emotion and he, if they had been acquainted, now appeared to be utter strangers to each other; nor was this apathy in the least like the well-known stoicism of the American Indian, but had the air of downright insensibility.

One major incident of Cooper's episode also fails to jibe with Irving's narrative. When the Indians attack the *Tonquin*, she is ready to put to sea, but in *Afloat and Ashore* Miles's difficulties are compounded by the fact that the Indians attack at a time when the ship is only partially rigged, for on the previous day Captain Williams had decided to "send down, or rather strip, all three of the topmasts, and pay some attention to their rigging." Emboldened by "the security of the haven, and the extreme beauty of the weather," he thus puts the vessel in "the most unmanageable position."[42]

Cooper's authority for these two departures from *Astoria* is supplied by Captain Cook's account in his *Voyages* of a visit to the Northwest Coast during his third exploring expedition. The outstanding characteristic of Cook's Indians is their utter apathy; with remarkable understatement he describes them as being "destitute, in some measure, of that degree of animation and vivacity that would render them agreeable as social beings. If they are not reserved, they are far from being loquacious." The only emotion of which they seem capable is resentment:

Their other passions, especially their curiosity, appear in some measure to lie dormant. For few expressed any desire to see or examine things wholly unknown to them; and which to those truly possessed of that passion would have appeared astonishing. They were always contented to procure the articles they knew and wanted, regarding everything else with great indifference; nor did our persons, apparel, and manners, so different from their own, or even the extraordinary size and construction of our ships, seem to excite admiration, or even engage attention. One cause of this may be their indolence, which seems considerable.

But indolence was certainly not among Cook's failings. Having found a "convenient snug cove," and the weather being "exceedingly fine," he ordered "the sails to be unbent, the topmasts to be struck, and the foremast of the Resolution to be unrigged, in order to fix a new bib, one of the old ones being decayed"; all this while the vessels were so close to the shore that they could be moored to convenient trees and while the waters of the cove were swarming with native canoes.[43] For more than three weeks Cook's vessels lay crippled as the repairs were made, but by what seems to have been a stroke of pure luck they were left unharmed by the Indians and allowed to proceed on their way up the coast.

Extensive though Cooper's debt to literary sources is, it must not be supposed that the episode or *Afloat and Ashore* as a whole constitutes a relinquishment of those powers of invention that were remarkably displayed in the three early romances. Enough has been said to indicate the ability of Cooper's imagination to combine and transform the raw materials of Irving and Cook into a single coherent narrative. More than that, however, his imagination enabled him to enhance the narrative values of the bare outline provided by his sources by offering him the elements he needed to shape and give meaning to the episode. It is significant that Cooper's one important addition to the external action supplied by Irving and Cook is the hanging of Smudge. From the standpoint of external action alone, this addition seems a shabby and unnecessary denouement to an otherwise exciting account of narrow escape. But viewed in the total context of the episode as Cooper develops it, the hanging of Smudge becomes the crucial incident, capping and pointing up the full meaning of the action.

For Cooper, the central event of the episode is not the escape from physical danger, but rather the revolution that occurs in Miles's judgment of the relative worth of the Indians and the whites. On first encountering the Indians, he is curious about their history and culture:

I did ask some questions of the captain, with a view to obtain a few ideas on this subject, but all he knew was, that these people put a high value on blankets, beads, gunpowder, frying-pans and old hoops, and that they set a remarkably low price on sea-otter skins, as well as on the external coverings of sundry other animals. An application to Mr. Marble was still less successful, being met by the pithy answer that he was "no naturalist, and knew nothing about these critturs, or any wild beasts, in general."

Although he must admit that he has never seen "any beings so low in the scale of the human race, as the northwestern savages appeared to be," Miles struggles against the easy attitudes of the captain and the mate:

I sat looking at the semi-human being who was seated opposite, wondering at the dispensation of divine Providence which could leave one endowed with a portion of the ineffable nature of the Deity, in a situation so degraded. I had seen beasts in cages that appeared to me to be quite as intelligent, and members of the diversified family of human caricatures, or of the baboons and monkeys, that I thought were quite as agreeable objects to the eye . . . Yet this man assuredly had a soul, a spark of the never-dying flame that separates man from all the other beings of earth![44]

With the start of the attack on the *Crisis,* Smudge, the object of Miles's meditation, undergoes an astounding metamorphosis: "from that instant every appearance of stupidity vanished from this fellow's countenance and manner, and he became the moving spirit, and I might say the soul, of all the proceedings of his companions." Using the same technique with which he had resolved the enigmatic character of Mr. Gray in *The Pilot,* Cooper puts Smudge and his followers to the test of action, a test from which they emerge clothed in the attributes and dignity of full humanity. As the narrative continues, Cooper emphasizes the paradoxical transformation of Smudge again and again: Miles is startled to see "Smudge—the stupid, inanimate, senseless Smudge—acting as leader, and manifesting not only authority, but readiness and sagacity," to find that "Smudge, the semi-human, dull, animal-seeming Smudge was at the head"; he is "astonished at seeing the intelligence that gleamed in the baboon-like face of Smudge": "Unpromising as he seemed, this fellow had a spirit that fitted him for great achievements, and which, under other circumstances, might have made him a hero. He taught me the useful lesson of not judging of men merely by their exteriors."[45]

In the ensuing battle for possession of the *Crisis,* only Smudge is taken alive. Marble, elevated to the command of the ship by the death of Captain Williams, determines to avenge the humiliation of the whites by hanging his prisoner in full view of the few Indians who have survived the battle and who are hidden in the cover along the shore. At this moment the intent of the transformation of Smudge becomes apparent, for by that transformation Cooper converts the triumph of the whites into a moral disaster. In the contrast between Marble's shrill anger and the stoical dignity of the Indian, Cooper rounds out the episode by completing the reversal of the initial relationship of white and Indian: now Smudge is the whole man and Marble is something less than human.

Clearly, then, the heart of the episode owes little or nothing to any literary source. Yet even the fate of Smudge evinces the experiential foundation of *Afloat and Ashore.* If the experience of neither Cooper nor the explorers of the Northwest Coast offers any parallel to the hanging of Smudge and the cluster of moral issues it raises, the national experience does. In December of 1842 Alexander Slidell Mackenzie, the commander of the American man-of-war *Somers,* had hanged without formal trial a midshipman and two seamen whom he suspected of plotting a mutiny. In the nation-wide controversy which the incident provoked, Cooper, animated by his characteristic passion for legality and by the fact that he himself had once been a victim of Mackenzie's injustice,[46] vigorously joined. Although Mackenzie was acquitted of all charges brought against him by a naval court-martial, Cooper persisted in his belief that the affair was "one of the darkest spots on the national escutcheon."[47] In the course of an elaborate review which was appended to the published version of Mackenzie's trial, Cooper ascribed Mackenzie's acquittal in part to the influence of commercial interests:

Mercantile cupidity had its share, as usual, in the course of a portion of the city press on this occasion. All mercantile communities are liable to these tortuous views of principles, on such subjects as are supposed to affect the fluctuating and sensitive interests of trade. As a body, men whose entire fortunes are constantly in jeopardy by the extent and hazards of their operations, are not to be trusted in matters that are supposed to conflict with their interests. The magnitude of the last proves too much for poor human nature . . . In the present case, it was supposed that the ships and insurers would possess greater security by an oriental administration of justice, than by giving to the citizen a hearing before he was consigned to the gallows.[48]

One need only compare this passage with the paragraph which concludes the episode in *Afloat and Ashore* to establish the connection between the crimes committed aboard the *Somers* and the *Crisis*:

At a later day, the account of this affair [the hanging of Smudge] found its way into the newspapers at home. A few moralists endeavored to throw some doubts over the legality and necessity of the proceedings, pretending that more evil than good was done to the cause of sacred justice by such disregard of law and principles; but the feeling of trade, and the security of ships when far from home, were motives too powerful to be put down by the still, quiet remonstrances of reason and right. The abuses to which such practices would

be likely to lead, in cases in which one of the parties constituted himself the law, the judge, and the executioner, were
urged in vain against the active and ever-stimulating incentive of a love of gold. Still, I knew that Marble wished the
thing undone when it was too late, it being idle to think of
quieting the suggestions of that monitor God has implanted
within us, by the meretricious and selfish approbation of
those who judge of right and wrong by their own narrow
standard of interest.[49]

Cooper's allusion to his own role in the controversy, his
warning against the undue influence of commercial interests on the public press, his mention of legal principles
identical to those involved in the affair of the *Somers*,
and his occasional echoing of the very language he had
used in reference to Mackenzie's case, all point unmistakably to the factual origin of the fictional incident.

The interweaving of autobiographical, historical, literary, and purely imaginary materials in *Afloat and Ashore*
constitutes a marked departure from the method of the
early romances, which were spun almost entirely out of
Cooper's inventive imagination. It is a departure, too,
from the method of the transitional novels like *Mercedes
of Castile* in which historical and imaginary materials
were not interwoven but stitched together, demarcated by
seams that remain all too visible. If the successful fusion
of fact and fiction in *Afloat and Ashore* represents a new
departure for Cooper, it also represents a curious anticipation of the techniques by which Melville was to construct his sea novels, for, as the last twenty-five years of
Melville scholarship have abundantly demonstrated, Melville's novels are a very similar compound of personal
experience, book-lore, historical fact, and imaginary material.[50] Like Melville, and like all major artists, Cooper
had achieved an integration of the world of experience
and the world of imagination. As Robert E. Spiller has
pointed out, the Cooper of the 1830's offers the spectacle

of "a great romanticist who has suddenly been faced with facts too solid for the dissolving magic of his art."[51] By 1844 the facts were no less solid, but the art no longer required them to melt away.

4

Just as the origins of the episode on the Northwest Coast typify the origins of the novel as a whole, the ambivalent ending of the episode is representative of the tone which Cooper sustains throughout *Afloat and Ashore*. Every aspect of the novel presents a sharp contrast to the glittering ideality and romantic exuberance of *The Pilot*, *The Red Rover*, and *The Water-Witch*. The brilliant and artificial purity of the ship, the seaman, and the sea has become clouded with the complexities of reality; the joyous sense of freedom and attainment has given way to the painful disenchantment of the growth to wisdom.

The most obvious of these changes involves the role of the ship. Among the many durable but often misleading axioms of Cooper criticism is the remark that Cooper's forte is his ability to animate his vessels, to make them more vivid, more vital than the characters who sail them. Such commentary is clear evidence of the disproportionate attention that has been given the early romances, for the whole trend of Cooper's nautical fiction after 1830 is to diminish the personality of the ship and to magnify that of the seaman. In *Afloat and Ashore* that trend reaches its furthest limit. Seen through the eyes of Miles Wallingford, the practical seaman, the ship is merely an object, an object to be described and appraised in terms of its usefulness; his one display of an aesthetic interest is a mark of his naïveté: "I had never seen a square-rigged vessel; and no enthusiast in the arts ever gloated on a fine picture or statue with greater avidity than my soul drank in the wonder and beauty of every ship I passed. I had a large, full-rigged model at Clawbonny; and this I had studied under my father so thoroughly, as to know the name of every rope in it, and to have some pretty distinct notions of their uses." But with experience the sense of wonder and beauty fades, and Miles's descriptions become as matter-of-fact as a builder's specifications: the *Crisis* was "a tight little ship of about four hundred tons, had hoop-pole bulwarks . . . with nettings for hammocks and old junk, principally the latter; and showed ten nine-pounders, carriage-guns, in her batteries." She was "an unusually fast ship . . . coppered to the bends, copper-fastened, and with a live-oak frame. No better craft sailed out of the republic." Even the small vessels in *Afloat and Ashore* are denied the least idealization. To the reader accustomed to Cooper's emphasis on unreal grace and lovely fragility in his descriptions of ships of this order, his treatment of the French privateer *Polisson* comes as a distinct surprise. In the place of the usual extended description of the long, low, dark hull and the airy maze of rigging one brief phrase appears: "a stout, but active craft of sixteen guns." Gone, too, are the oriental splendor of the *Rover*'s cabin and the fanciful décor of the *Water-Witch*: the cabin of the *Polisson* is "a crowded, dark and dirty hole."[52]

The shift in Cooper's attitude toward the ship is reflected with equal distinctness in his metaphors. The abbreviated descriptions in *Afloat and Ashore,* of course, offer far fewer opportunities for metaphorical statement than do the elaborate ship portraits in the early romances; as a result, the sheer weight of the conception of the vessel as an animate being is considerably diminished. More than that, however, the nature of the metaphors in *Afloat and Ashore* is significantly different from that of Cooper's earlier figures. Although the substance of these metaphors is approximately the same as that of their predecessors, their meaning has been vastly qualified, even reversed. Cooper still compares the ship to a woman, but the complex system of meanings which such comparisons conveyed in *The Water-Witch* has been reduced to the mere idea of responsiveness: the *John* "minded her helm, as a light-footed girl turns in a lively dance." He still compares the ship to a marine bird, but now the bird is a duck, not a gull, and it is no longer in flight but at rest on the water. He still compares the combat between ships to a battle between human beings, but the vessels no longer meet like sinewy gladiators in the arena; rather, they clash " 'scratching out each other's eyes, like two fish-women, whose dictionaries have given out.' "[53]

One class of metaphors, the cluster of equine images, resists the movement from the ennobling to the homely. In the early romances these metaphors had been used to connote a sense of restrained power, of energy controlled and directed by an intelligence; they had served to reinforce Cooper's conception of the interplay of ship and seaman and to emphasize that relationship as the means by which the seaman can meet the challenge of the sea. In *Afloat and Ashore,* however, the horse is no longer held in check. As the *Dawn* runs yawing before the storm, she is "like a gay horse that breaks his bridle." She joins another vessel, and the two ships resemble "two vehicles dashing along a highway, with frightened and runaway teams." When the *Dawn* luffs up into the wind, she is like "a steed that had suddenly thrown his rider, diverging from his course, and shooting athwart the field at right angles to his former track, scenting and snuffing the air." The ship snaps her cables and falls off before the wind "like the steed that has slipped his bridle, before he commences his furious and headlong career."[54] The equine images still connote power, but it is now a power beyond the control of man.

In *Afloat and Ashore* Cooper returns to something very like the eighteenth-century conception of the ship. The emphasis is not on grace, speed, and lightness but on bulk and momentum; he speaks of "the vast machine," "the great mass." If the vessels of the early romances represented individual freedom and achievement, the ship is now a microcosm of the world, an *"omnium gatherum of human employments,"* a huge vehicle ever moving "like the earth moving in its orbit, indifferent to the struggles of the nations that are contending on its bosom." The focus of attention shifts from the ship and her single guiding spirit to the community of human beings which inhabits her. No single passage better illustrates Cooper's new conception of the ship than Miles's description of the gun deck of the English frigate *Briton* in action:

Although the season had well advanced into the autumn, the weather was so warm, that half the men had stripped for the toil—and toil it is, to work heavy guns, for hours at a time, under the excitement of battle; a toil that may not be felt at the time, perhaps, but which leaves a weariness like that of disease behind it. Many of the seamen fought in their trowsers alone; their long, hard cues lying on their naked backs, which resembled those of so many athletae, prepared for the arena. The gun-deck was full of smoke, the priming burned in-board producing that effect, though the powder which exploded in the guns was sent, with its flames and sulphurous wreaths, in long lines from the ports toward the enemy. The place appeared a sort of pandemonium to me. I could perceive men moving about in the smoke, rammers and sponges whirling in their hands, guns reeling inward, ay, even leaping from the deck, under the violence of the recoils, officers signing with their swords to add emphasis to their orders, boys running to and fro on their way to and from the magazines, shot tossed from hand to hand, and to give its fiercest character to all, the dead and dying weltering in their blood, amidships.[55]

In this inferno it is the crew, not the ship, that is important. For the usual panoramic view of the battle, a view which dwarfs the human actors, Cooper substitutes the field of vision of a narrator who is himself an actor. Significantly, too, the men rather than the vessel receive the ennobling comparison. Still more important, however, is the emphasis on collective labor and suffering, on coordination and discipline. The ship in the early romances is a refuge from society; here she is an epitome of society.

If the ship in *Afloat and Ashore* is in some degree stripped of the qualities of an animate creature, the seaman assumes the dimensions of a complete human being. The sailors of the early romances, whether idealized like Long Tom Coffin or caricatured like Dick Fid, are essentially abstractions, mere embodiments of their profession. They exist only within their special environment; they are separated from the family of man by their values, their habits, even their speech. Thus their significance stems from their function as symbolic reflections of the meaning of the ship and the ocean. But the better they serve as vehicles for abstract meaning, the less useful they become as mediators between the fictional world and the world of the reader's experience; the more landless they are, the less recognizable they become as human beings. In *Afloat and Ashore,* however, Cooper's aim seems to be not to portray maritime life as a discrete entity but to emphasize its continuity with the rest of human experience. As a result, the sailor, who had been little more than an appendage of the ship, now attains the status of a character.

The prime seaman in the novel, the professional equivalent of Coffin and Fid, is Moses Marble. Marble, who indoctrinates Miles in the ways of the sea and who accompanies him first as superior and then as subordinate throughout his nautical career, seems on the surface to be as landless as his predecessors. Raised as an orphan,

Marble had gone to sea at the age of eight: " 'I never had father or mother, to my knowledge; nor house, nor home of any sort, but a ship.' " Like Coffin and Captain Truck, he is awkward and uneasy on land. For him " 'there is little amusement in a sailor's walking on the levellest 'arth and handsomest highways, on account of the bloody ups and downs a fellow meets with.' " And like his predecessors, Marble is thoroughly at home on the water. According to Miles, Marble is "a very good navigator, one of the best I have ever sailed with"; Miles has never known "a more in-and-in-bred seaman." It is Marble's habit "to consider himself a timber of the ship, that was to sink or swim with the craft"; he loves the *Crisis* " 'as much as some folks love their parents.' "[56]

Marble's isolation, however, is neither romantic or humorous, for, unlike Coffin or Fid, he is not content in his landlessness. His life consists not in the enjoyment of a carefree freedom but in a restless search for roots. Humiliated by the loss of his vessel to the French, he decides to spend the rest of his days alone on a desert island that he has discovered in the middle of the Pacific; in justifying his decision to Miles, he reveals the pathos of that search:

"I am without a friend on earth—I mean nat'ral friend—I know what sort of friend you are, and parting with you will be the toughest of all—but I have not a relation on the wide earth—no property, no home, no one to wish to see me return, not even a cellar to lay my head in. To me all places are alike, with the exception of this, which, having discovered, I look upon as my own."

But Marble soon abandons the experiment and eventually rejoins his friend:

"I soon discovered, Miles, that if I had neither father nor mother, brother nor sister, that I had a country and friends. The bit of marble on which I was found in the stonecutter's yard, then seemed as dear to me as a gold cradle is to a king's son; and I thought of you, and all the rest of you—nay, I yearned after you, as a mother would yearn for her children . . . I had consaited that I could pass the rest of my days in the bosom of my own family, like any other man who had made his fortune and retired, but I found my household too small for such a life as that. My great mistake was in supposing that the Marble family could be happy in its own circle."

The quest for roots ends when Marble discovers his long-lost mother and his niece Kitty. Although Cooper cheapens the resolution of Marble's plight by gilding it with sentiment, the fact that the values of the early romances are overturned remains clear: for Marble, "'next thing to being a bloody hermit . . . is to belong to nobody in a crowded world; and I would not part with one kiss from little Kitty, or one wrinkle of my mother's, for all the desert islands in the ocean.' "[57] Solitude and wildness have been exchanged for domesticity.

The sailor, then, is a human being and partakes of the complexities of a human being. In his complexity Marble becomes an amalgam of all his predecessors in Cooper's sea fiction. Like Coffin, he displays an instinctive wisdom in his philosophic moments. Like Fid, he is often crude in his behavior and callous in his attitudes. With Tom Tiller he shares a certain recklessness and a capacity for sudden growth to heroic stature at times of crisis. He can become comic like Captain Truck as he bumbles through the forms of society, evil like Ithuel Bolt in his sullen pride and blind vengeance, or sentimental like Oakes and Bluewater when a poignant situation reduces him to tears.

But for all its many facets Marble's character has a depth and richness of motivation that, with the exception of Bolt, no other of Cooper's sailors possesses. When they are not merely toys of the plot, characters like Coffin, Fid, and Tiller are governed exclusively by their role as sea-

men: their decisions and responses are conditioned by
their profession. Marble's character, however, seems to stem
less from Cooper's abstract notion of seamen as a type
than from his knowledge of certain specific seamen. Thus
Marble reacts to the Indians in the way that he does, not
because all seamen do, but because Captain Thorn of the
Tonquin did. But if Marble is in part Captain Thorn,
he is much more Ned Myers. Like Marble, Ned in 1843
was middle-aged, "a man of quick apprehension, considerable knowledge, and of singularly shrewd comments."
Ned, too, was of obscure and dubious parentage and was
"completely alone in the world . . . 'If I tumbled overboard,' I said to myself, 'there is none to cry over me.' "
It is apparent, moreover, that Ned was the source for the
crisis in Marble's career, the decision to remain on the
desert island. Like Marble, Ned was the victim of self-
destructive impulses: he confessed to his readers that
"nature has so formed me, that any disgust, or disappointment, makes me reckless, and awakens a desire to
revenge myself, on myself, as I may say." And when faced
with frustration, Ned, like Marble, sought to bury himself in the most remote quarters of the globe: "It was
my intention to double Good Hope, and never to return
. . . I could find enough to do between Bombay and Canton; and, if I could not, there were the islands and all
the Pacific before me."[58] Moses Marble, then, takes on
some of the individuality of a real man. If he lacks
the attractiveness and glamour, the special nobility of the
seamen of the early romances, he comports with the soberly matter-of-fact tone in which *Afloat and Ashore* is
keyed.

No single aspect of *Afloat and Ashore* indicates more
definitively the distance which separates the methods and
attitudes of that novel from those of the early romances
than the treatment of the sea. The "graphic" descriptions

of the holy beauty and sublime power of the ocean, so admired by the readers of Cooper's early fiction, have nearly vanished, diminished and muffled by the new emphasis on characterization. Like the ship, the sea makes less frequent and less extensive appearances in *Afloat and Ashore* than it had before; like the ship, too, the sea assumes a significance vastly different from the one assigned to it in the early romances.

In part this difference in significance stems from the fact that the ocean in *Afloat and Ashore* no longer is used to mirror the passing moods and feelings of the characters. Where a kind of harmony or correspondence had existed between the seamen of the early romances and their environment, now the sea has become something external, alien, and inimical. The word *angry* echoes through nearly all of Miles's marine descriptions: he speaks of "the vast and angry Atlantic," the "cauldron of angry waters," the "chaos of waters . . . looking green and angry," "the angry billows"; he is appalled by "the manner in which the elements can play with such a mass of wood and iron as a ship, when in an angry mood." The ocean is as wild as ever, but wildness now connotes violence and death, not freedom and attainment. It evokes the nightmarish images that had haunted Leggett: as the waves threaten to swamp his small boat within sight of the shore, Miles "can only liken our situation at that fearful moment to the danger of a man who is clinging to a cliff, its summit and safety almost in reach of his hand, with the consciousness that his powers are fast failing him, and that he must shortly go down." The one departure from this stress on the hostility of the ocean occurs as Miles's last command, the *Dawn,* gradually sinks beneath him. With what seems to be a startlingly abrupt and incongruous shift in his attitude toward the sea, Cooper has Miles tell us that "the ocean beamed gloriously that eventide, and I fancied that it was faintly reflecting the divine Creator, in a smile of beneficent love."[59] But the shift is less in the conception of the sea within the novel than in the moral outlook of Miles, for at this late stage of the narrative, as we shall see, he has lost his sense of dislocation and abandoned his attempt to run from the hardships and responsibilities of life. Whereas the hostile sea of the greater part of the book seems to betoken Miles's failure to assume the role God has ordained for man, the beaming ocean in this passage suggests that Miles's new attitude is in harmony with the order of the universe and its Creator.

If the ocean is inimical throughout most of Miles Wallingford's contact with it, it is not without a certain lure in its promise of adventure and release from the cruelties and obligations of life ashore. Impelled by this lure, Miles runs away from home in order to go to sea, but even this moment of high excitement is qualified by feelings of fear and foreboding: when he discovers that he has made good his escape from home, he does not know whether he feels "the most relieved or pained by the certainty of this fact." Throughout much of the novel Miles's attitude toward the ocean displays the same ambivalence. At times he conceives of himself as a person who pursues "his adventures for the love of the sea"; on other occasions he classes himself with "the victims of fate." He is never able to explain fully the attraction he feels for the sea: "there was a strange pleasure to me, nothwithstanding all I had suffered previously, all the risks I had run, and all I had left behind me, in finding myself once more on the broad ocean."[60] The image of the sea in *Afloat and Ashore*, then, shows a marked resemblance to Freneau's: a maritime life is at once attractive and fatal; beneath its inexplicable lure lies the suggestion that its promises will never be fulfilled, that its values are illusory.

As the examination of Cooper's handling of the ship

and the seaman in *Afloat and Ashore* indicates, this refusal to idealize, distort, or simplify informs all the marine elements of the novel. None of Cooper's other sea fiction more precisely accords with Dana's observation that maritime life represents a fusion of the beautiful and the revolting, the sublime and the commonplace, the solemn and the ludicrous. Cooper's insistence on displaying the entire spectrum of maritime life seems to be partly the result of the didactic, even documentary, intention with which he wrote. In his preface to the first volume he set forth the rationale of the novel:

Every thing which can convey to the human mind distinct and accurate impressions of events, social facts, professional peculiarities, or past history, whether of the higher or more familiar character, is of use. All that is necessary is, that the pictures should be true to nature, if not absolutely drawn from living sitters . . . It may aid those who can never be placed in positions to judge for themselves of certain phases of men and things, to get pictures of the same, drawn in a way to give them nearer views than they might otherwise obtain. This is the greatest benefit of all light literature in general, it beng possible to render that which is purely fictitious even more useful than that which is strictly true, by avoiding extravagances, by portraying with fidelity, and as our friend Marble might say, by "generalizing" with discretion.[61]

If the *Naval History* was an attempt to delineate with scrupulous accuracy past history of the higher character, *Afloat and Ashore* was an attempt to represent familiar history with equal precision and comprehensiveness.

5

Because of Cooper's documentary intention in *Afloat and Ashore* and because of the generous measure of social commentary with which Miles laces his narrative, critics have been reluctant to read the book as a novel. When they have noticed it at all, they have usually refused to grant it the integrity that is the criterion of a work of art. Those who have praised the book have concerned themselves with a single aspect: the broad panorama of American maritime activity in its golden age, the nostalgic portrait of life in middle New York state at the end of the eighteenth century, the interesting glimpses of Cooper's early life, or the caustic criticism of contemporary manners and values. Although they applaud Cooper's handling of any one of these elements, they often join with those who condemn the book in the judgment that *Afloat and Ashore* as a whole fails to cohere, that its already episodic structure is further disjointed by the multiple and conflicting purposes with which Cooper wrote.[62] Yet in spite of the tendency of the narrative to break off in self-contained chunks, in spite of the constant oscillation between sea and society, in spite of the digressive commentary of Cooper's aging narrator, the appearance of discontinuity in *Afloat and Ashore* is a result not of Cooper's failure as a novelist, but of the reader's failure to perceive the techniques which shape the narrative and the themes which give it meaning.

Most obvious of the devices that unify the novel, and the only one that has received critical attention of any kind, is the consistently and richly characterized voice in which the novel is narrated. Cooper brought to the writing of *Afloat and Ashore* a wide experience in the use of narration in the first person. He had experimented with it in the epistolary *Notions of the Americans* and the books of travel; he had spoken through a satiric persona in *The Monikins* and *The Autobiography of a Pocket-Handkerchief* (1843); and in *Ned Myers* he had had the opportunity to reconstruct in the first person the career of a retired sailor. The last book, of course, offers the closest parallel to the design of *Afloat and Ashore,* for in it

Cooper had attempted to capture the discursive structure of the spoken yarn, the perspective of recollection, and the homely idiom of the practical seaman. And more than any previous work, *Ned Myers* is written from the point of view of a concretely characterized narrator, a man in "every way entitled to speak for himself."[63]

But Miles Wallingford and Ned Myers have little more in common than that they are both seamen of long and varied experience. To a large extent, Miles seems to owe his authentic vitality to the fact that he is an imaginative projection of Cooper's own personality. As James Grossman has pointed out, Miles's history may be regarded as a continuation in fantasy of the career that Cooper began before the mast of the *Sterling*. Significantly, the image of the seaman's life of action and isolation seems to have long served him as a refuge from the pressures of reality. As late as 1833, when he was talking of abandoning his literary career, Cooper entertained the possibility of earning his livelihood at sea. Only half jokingly he wrote to Horatio Greenough of his intention to "turn sailor again," warning Greenough "not [to] be surprised if you hear of my sailing a sloop between Cape Cod and New-York ere long."[64] But Miles is more than the fulfillment of a youthful dream; in his nostalgia for the days of personal and national vigor, in his dogmatic rejection of all things purely modern, in his pessimistic view of the future, he is the Cooper of actuality. If the figure, "an old fellow, whose thoughts revert to the happier scenes of youth with a species of dotage," is a little distorted by caricature, it is still recognizable as that of the man who, eight years earlier, had viewed the last twenty-five years as the slow deterioration of "the little national pride and national character created by the war of 1812."[65]

Through this sharply defined personality, the action and characters of *Afloat and Ashore* are seen. Being strictly in character, the asides, the digressions, the caustic running commentary serve as signals of the unifying point of view. The assault by the Northwest Indians on the *Crisis,* the foundering of the *Dawn* in the Irish Sea, and the loss of Clawbonny, the Wallingford farm, to a grasping creditor are linked not only because they all belong to one man's experience but because they all evoke the same kind of interpretive extension.

Just as the episodes are linked by their common manner of narration, so are they united by a common motif, the repeated pattern of capture and liberation. Although capture and liberation provide the basic plot of many of Cooper's earlier novels, here these seemingly simple actions manifest themselves in a newly complex and subtle fashion. In a narrative like *The Last of the Mohicans* capture and liberation are merely a plot mechanism, a mechanism that serves no other function than providing a framework from which the chain of incident may be suspended. In *Afloat and Ashore,* however, capture and liberation are so reiterated, so intricately ramified and convoluted, that they become a unifying motif and slowly gather to themselves thematic significance. Afloat Miles Wallingford is involved in one series of captures and escapes after another. During his first voyage he is nearly captured twice, once by Malayan pirates in the Straits of Sunda and once by a French privateer off Guadaloupe. During his second voyage Miles is captured or threatened with capture once by Indians, once by Malays, and twice by French privateers. Although his third voyage takes place in time of peace, Miles is not permitted to return without enduring two threats of capture by British men-of-war. A crescendo of capture and liberation marks Miles's final voyage. At the outset his vessel narrowly escapes capture by one British cruiser off Block Island, only to be captured by another in the English Channel.

Although the Americans overpower the British prize crew, they are almost immediately recaptured by a French privateer. Miles and his men once again liberate themselves, but he is soon made a prisoner, this time by the British, when an English frigate saves him from the wreck of his own vessel. After five months of imprisonment Miles manages to make his escape and returns to America where, now nearly twenty-three years of age, he steps ashore, "a ruined and disappointed man."[66]

Although at times it is expressed in psychological rather than physical action or submerged in metaphor and symbol, the pattern of capture and escape is sustained throughout the shore sequences of the novel. Miles's adventures begin when he runs away to sea to escape the legal career that his guardian, Mr. Hardinge, has planned for him. Ominously, the boy's first glimpse of the city where he plans to find a ship is of the state prison, a sight that he is unable to regard "altogether without dread." The notion of entrapment and liberation reappears in London, where Miles aids the Mertons, who are trapped in a coach that is about to plunge into the waters of a canal, "to escape." In New York Miles fears that the girl he loves, Lucy Hardinge, has been "caught" in the "trap" of a rival whom he suspects of being a fortune hunter. His sister Grace, whose affections have been ensnared by the unscrupulous Rupert Hardinge, finds "release" in death, which allows her to "shake off the ties" of love. Another kind of release occurs when Miles helps Marble to free his mother's farm from the "grasp" of the usurer Van Tassel.[67]

But if the family property of Marble is liberated from the hold of an outsider, Miles jeopardizes his possession of his own farm, Clawbonny, by mortgaging it to finance his final voyage. On returning from that voyage, he learns that Clawbonny is in the hands of a stranger named

Daggett, the supposed heir of Miles's creditor, who had died while Miles was at sea. He hears rumors, moreover, that Lucy Hardinge is about to marry his rival. As a climax to his misfortune, he is imprisoned for a debt to Daggett of sixty thousand dollars. With the resolution of these difficulties, the cycle of capture and redemption and the novel itself come to a close. At the same time that Lucy secures his release from prison on bail, Miles discovers that he has been mistaken in believing her to be engaged: "it was comparatively little to me to learn I was free myself, after so unexpectedly learning that Lucy was also free."[68] Not only are the lovers free to marry, but Clawbonny is once more in Miles's possession, for it turns out that he, not the villainous Daggett, is the true heir of his deceased creditor.

Thus sustained and stressed, the motif of capture and redemption serves to unify the seemingly heterogeneous episodes of *Afloat and Ashore* on the level of action. The farm on the banks of the Hudson and the island in the mid-Pacific become the locale for the same kind of act; the apparent discontinuity of the novel is only geographical. To fail to perceive this fundamental unity is to miss the meaning of *Afloat and Ashore;* it is to be deceived, as Miles is, by false appearances.

Afloat and Ashore and its near contemporaries *The Pathfinder* (1840) and *The Deerslayer* (1841) are the first of Cooper's novels in which the protagonists undergo a major development. In the earlier novels the heroes are static characters; like the Rover or Tom Tiller, they gradually disclose their true natures as the plot unfolds, but their awareness and their attitudes remain a constant. In *Afloat and Ashore,* however, the growth of Miles Wallingford to maturity becomes the central theme. The mechanism of this growth, the process by which it is accomplished, consists in the movement from delusion to enlightenment, a process intimately associated with the motif of capture and liberation, for the endless round of captures and escapes is paralleled by an equally extensive series of deceptions and illuminations. Miles is deceived by the sophistication of Rupert, by the friendliness of Sweeny, by the gentility of the Mertons; he is mistaken in his reliance on the stupidity of the Indians, on the justice of the English, on the amity of the French. As each error is corrected, Miles is freed from the prison of an illusion. But not only is the progress from delusion to enlightenment analogous to liberation from physical imprisonment; in the most successful of the episodes it is the cause of that liberation. Thus, because he is deceived by the appearance of Smudge, Miles becomes the Indian's captive, but because he eventually achieves a true understanding of the character of Smudge, he is able to liberate himself. For the individual as well as the state, then, maturity can be reached only by the alignment of opinion and fact, idea and reality. " 'Make-believe is much made use of in this world,' " says Marble, " 'but it won't hold out to the last.' "[69]

If the progress from delusion to enlightenment is the process by which maturity is reached, maturity itself consists in the attainment of a modus vivendi that effects a compromise between desire and possibility, between the ideal and the actual. The world which Miles leaves when he first goes to sea is the pastoral unreality of Clawbonny, a world composed of the idyllic relationship of the four children, the lovely landscape of the Hudson valley, and the security and comfort provided by a prosperous farm and the labors of a willing, genial body of slaves, all presided over by the benevolent Mr. Hardinge. The sea gives Miles his first contact with suffering and hardship, with responsibility and accomplishment; if the true meaning of the sea remains in doubt, his nautical experience does provide him with a vantage point from which he can see the values and relationships of society for what they are.

At this point the novel assumes the character of a debate between wildness and civilization. From Clawbonny to the wild ocean, from London and New York to the Northwest Coast and the coral island, the narrative ranges, pitting one life against the other and giving unqualified approval to neither. The comfort and companionship of life on shore are counterbalanced by its deceit and tameness; the excitement and opportunity of life at sea are counterbalanced by its loneliness and violence. Rupert Hardinge, Miles's companion on his first voyage, rejects the sea, gives himself over to society, and is destroyed as a man. Marble rejects society, adopts a life of utter solitude and wildness, and finds that the experience would " 'fit a man for Bedlam.' " But Miles, unwilling to sacrifice either freedom or companionship, vacillates between his disparate worlds. Afloat, isolation and danger drive him back to his home, his family, and his friends. Ashore, frustration and artificiality make him "all impatience to get to sea." The only avenue of escape, a return to the world of his childhood, is, as Lucy tells him, closed forever: " 'Our lives cannot be lived over again; we cannot return to childhood; feel as children; love as children; live as children; and grow up together, as it might be, with one heart, with the same views, the same wishes, the same opinion.' " Indeed, to Miles " 'Clawbonny will never again be the Clawbonny it was.' "[70]

Shuttled between land and sea, Miles leads a schizophrenic existence. He has been " 'in London, and on a desert island in the South Seas—the very extremes of human habits,' " and to him the two experiences are utterly discontinuous. He finds himself to be a "different personage in command of the Crisis and in the pit of the

Park theatre in New York." He assumes that " 'it is true, Clawbonny is not the Pacific, and one may be pardoned for seeing things a little differently *here,* from what they appeared *there,*' " for, viewed from Clawbonny, his nautical experiences " 'possess the colors of a dream.' " From all sides characters confirm him in his feeling of discontinuity by reiterating the contrast between land and sea; even the cook Dido points out to him that " 'dere great difference . . . atween Clawbonny and a ship.' "⁷¹

In the course of his last voyage, Miles's worlds begin to coalesce, and with the coalescence comes maturity. Just as the *Crisis,* the name of his old ship, suggests tension and indecision, the *Dawn,* the name of the vessel in which he makes this voyage, appropriately connotes *éclaircissement* and resolution, for Miles attains maturity by his realization that all his experience is of one piece, that no one portion of life offers a refuge from another, that existence must be met on its own terms. During the voyage Miles discovers that iniquity and injustice are not the exclusive property of civilization; as Marble phrases it, " 'these are onmoralizing times, and the sea is getting to be sprinkled with so many Van Tassels, that I'm afeard you and I'll be just that dear, good old soul, my mother, and little Kitty, to be frightened, or, if not exactly frightened, to be wronged out of our just rights.' " Whether on land or sea, "there is no question that man, at the bottom, has a good deal of the wild beast in him." Thus the ocean offers no escape from human rapacity, nor does it fulfill its promise of unfettered self-attainment. If man cannot escape the conditions of existence, neither can he alter them; alone on the deck of the sinking *Dawn,* Miles learns that "we must all yield up our lives once; and though my hour came rather early, it should be met as a man meets every thing, even to death itself."⁷²

Knowing now that the attempt to run away to sea is

futile, Miles returns from the voyage equipped to face reality. In the hurried final chapter, which traces out the careers of all the major characters, Cooper briefly indicates the kind of compromise the mature man achieves. Refusing either to abandon the world, as Marble had tried to do, or to surrender himself to it, as Rupert had done, Miles surrounds himself with his family and tested friends and remains in the semiseclusion of Clawbonny; although he occasionally makes sorties into the wider world, he never travels without his family, and he always returns to " 'dear Clawbonny, . . . the true home of a Wallingford.' " He has attained the understanding and self-discipline that are needed to confront and resolve the dilemma which Cooper had first defined in *The American Democrat:* "An entire distinct individuality, in the social state, is neither possible nor desirable. Our happiness is so connected with the social and family ties as to prevent it; but, if it be possible to render ourselves miserable by aspiring to an independence that nature forbids, it is also possible to be made unhappy by a too obtrusive interference with our individuality." More than that, he has come to the realization that, as Cooper had indicated in *The Heidenmauer* (1832), "the task assigned to man is to move among his fellows doing good, filling his part in the scale of creation, and escaping from none of the high duties which God has allotted to his being."[73]

In *Afloat and Ashore,* then, Cooper finally abandons the novel of mere nautical incident, the novel that is focused primarily on the sea as the epitome of wild nature and that depends for its interest and meaning on the representation of the ocean as the antithesis of human society. In the new emphasis on the seaman as man, the voyage becomes a shaping force; if maritime crisis in the earlier novels had at best served only to reveal character, now it influences and determines character. The voyager returns with a fresh vision, a new set of values; not merely disenchanted, he is a better man, a man who can perceive reality and appraise it accurately. This theme, it is true, is muted in *Afloat and Ashore* by Cooper's documentary concerns, but it nevertheless establishes a link between the sea novel and the traditional conception of the voyage as the allegorical counterpart of the progress of the soul through experience. Maritime life is now interesting not because it is far removed from common experience but because it offers meaningful parallels to the lives of all men.[74]

Chapter V

An Ocean Unapproachable and Unknown

THE WORK OF
COOPER'S CONTEMPORARIES, 1835–1850

THE HISTORY of the nautical novel in America from 1835 to 1850 is the record of the gradual disintegration of the idealized conception of maritime life established by Cooper in his early romances and the attempt to construct a more meaningful alternative to that conception. Following the lead of the short story writers of the previous decade, some novelists focused their attention on the depiction of the contemporary maritime scene. *Maritime Scraps* (1838) by a "Man-of-War's-Man" and *Life in a Man-of-War* (1841) by a "Fore-Top-Man" offered nearly identical, half-auto-biographical, half-fictional accounts of life aboard an American frigate, accounts which closely parallel Melville's *White-Jacket* (1850) in structure and content. Melville's *Redburn* (1849) was similarly anticipated by another work consisting of a blend of personal experience and fiction, Charles F. Briggs's *Working a Passage* (1844).[1] In his brief narrative of a passage before the mast in a trans-Atlantic packet ship, Briggs remained faithful both to his model, Dana, and to his own conviction that Cooper's romanticism had falsified maritime life. The tone of Briggs's description of the merchantman *Scattergood* is typical of that of the book and of the whole effort to revise in realistic terms the early Cooper's exalted image of the sea:

[She] was a very shabby disorderly looking craft: her rigging all hanging in bights, points and gaskets flying from her yards, and her side and bulwarks stained with iron rust, she looked as though she had been fitted out by the parish. Her decks were in confusion, and her mates looked like any thing but sailors. I stepped on board and asked for the Captain; the cook, a Chinaman, pointed him out to me standing upon the poop. He was a feeble little old man, dressed in a long snuff-colored surtout; his hands were encased in a pair of buckskin mittens, and he was trying to screen himself from the penetrating mist by holding a faded green cotton umbrella over his head. The ship, her master, and her crew, seemed made for each other.[2]

A far cry, indeed, from the graceful *Dolphin* and the Red Rover, enshrouded in glamour and mystery.

When romanticism did manifest itself in the nautical fiction of the late 1830's and 1840's, it usually took a form quite different from that of Cooper's first three sea novels. Heavily costumed historical melodramas like *Nix's Mate* (1839) by Rufus Dawes, the anonymous *The Brigantine* (1839), and *The Matricide* (1845–1846) by John K. Duer relegated the sea to the subordinate position it had held in Scott's *The Pirate* and treated it in the Gothic manner perfected fifteen years before in the short tales of terror on the ocean. A few tentative experiments in the substitution of the geographically remote for the romance of the distant past were made, but by and large this field was left fallow by American novelists until the appearance of Melville's *Typee* (1846). When novelists carried their readers to unknown seas, as Cooper did in *Afloat and Ashore*, they generally did so less to exploit the romantic appeal of the exotic than to document the expansion of the American maritime frontier. Those writers who persisted in following the romantic conventions which *The*

Pilot, The Red Rover, and *The Water-Witch* had established found themselves faced with a drastic loss of literary status. By the mid-1840's the only market for idealized stories of the pirates and naval heroes of the American past was provided by the publishers of story papers and dime novels. Their demand was clearly for romance: "Domestic stories, so-called, are not exactly of the class we desire; but tales of the sea and land—of the stirring times of the Revolution—or of dates still farther back, are more in accordance with our wishes."[3] But it was a demand so insatiable, so uncritical, that no writer who responded to it could maintain his integrity.

In the three most interesting novels of the period, Edgar Allan Poe's *Narrative of Arthur Gordon Pym* (1837–1838), Robert Montgomery Bird's *Adventures of Robin Day* (1839), and Charles J. Peterson's *Cruising in the Last War* (1839–1840) many of these fluctuations in the fictional expression of maritime life can be traced in detail. Whatever its failings as a work of art or as a coherent study of the meaning of the sea may be, Poe's short novel, the best known of the three, occupies a pivotal place in the development of American nautical fiction. From one point of view, *Pym* is the final outcome of the Gothic tendency of many of the short sea stories published before 1835. The nightmarish situations with which Bird, Stone, Simms, and Leggett had experimented are exploited to their furthest limits by Poe, who, at least on the level of explicit narrative, regards the ocean simply as a credible setting for the evocation of terror and horror. Such an attitude must not be confused with the neoclassical conception of maritime life. To a writer like Smollett, the sea is sordid and brutal, not ghastly and thrilling. And if Smollett dwells on the less pleasant aspects of nautical experience, he condemns as he describes. But to Poe, the value of the sea lies in its capacity to stimulate the delicious shudder of terror, to provide scenes of pain and death. While the mariners of Freneau and Cooper are lured to the ocean by its beauty, its freedom, its promise of achievement, Gordon Pym goes to sea in search of "suffering and despair": "For the bright side of the painting I had a limited sympathy. My visions were of shipwreck and famine; of death or captivity among barbarian hordes; of a lifetime dragged out in sorrow and tears, upon some gray and desolate rock, in an ocean unapproachable and unknown."[4]

Gordon's expectations are amply fulfilled. After enduring days of near starvation and suffocation in the hold of the whaler in which he has stowed away, he comes on deck to find that the officers and many of the crew have been savagely butchered by a gang of mutineers. Allying himself with his young friend Augustus Barnard and with Dirk Peters, a grotesque and immensely powerful seaman who has befriended the boys, Gordon waits for the chance to escape from the mutineers. By a ruse the three at last gain control of the ship, but they, together with Richard Parker, their only prisoner, are again placed in great peril when the vessel founders in a storm. Their hopes of rescue are raised by the sight of a brigantine bearing down upon them, but as the ship sweeps by just beyond reach, they see that all her people are dead, the victims of some sudden and mysterious plague. Tortured by hunger and thirst as they cling to their drifting hulk, the four men determine to sacrifice one of their number so that the others may survive. The lot falls to Parker; he submits quietly to his execution, and his companions devour his corpse. Before the sufferers are finally picked up by the English sealer *Jane Guy,* Augustus dies of a wound he had received in the struggle for mastery of the whaler. Gordon and Peters accompany the *Jane Guy* on a sealing expedition to Kerguelen's Land and Tristan da Cunha and then on an exploring voyage to Antarctica. The little schooner pierces the barrier of ice that rings the Pole and enters an area of open waters and moderate temperatures. The first land she makes is a group of strange islands on which the people, the animals, the rocks, and even the streams are black. Deceived by the friendly behavior of the natives, the crew of the sealer are caught in an ambush from which Gordon and Peters alone escape alive. After weeks of hiding in an elaborate system of caves on the black island, the two men escape in a canoe. Knowing that they could never make their way through the ice in the frail craft, they head southward toward the Pole. As the canoe is drawn by a current toward an immense white curtain of ashy vapor, Gordon's tale comes to an end:

And now we rushed into the embraces of the cataract, where a chasm threw itself open to receive us. But there arose in our pathway a shrouded human figure, very far larger in its proportions than any dweller among men. And the hue of the skin of the figure was of the perfect whiteness of snow.[5]

Poe surpasses his predecessors not only in the accumulation of horror but in the vividness of its presentation. Not content, as most of them were, with stressing the response of the characters to the horrifying situation, Poe also supplies his reader with a vivid description of whatever it is that evokes the response. Through brilliant manipulation of detail, he thus creates some of the most grisly scenes in any literature. One example will suffice; as the brigantine sails past the wreck of the whaler, Gordon discovers that he was mistaken in believing the seaman on the forecastle to be alive:

We saw the tall stout figure still leaning on the bulwark, and still nodding his head to and fro, but his face was now turned from us so that we could not behold it. His arms were extended over the rail, and the palms of his hands fell outward. His knees were lodged upon a stout rope, tightly stretched, and reaching from the heel of the bowsprit to a cathead. On his back, from which a portion of the shirt had been torn, leaving it bare, there sat a huge seagull, busily gorging itself with the horrible flesh, its bill and talons deep buried, and its white plumage spattered all over with blood. As the brig moved further round so as to bring us close in view, the bird, with much apparent difficulty, drew out its crimsoned head, and, after eying us for a moment as if stupefied, arose lazily from the body upon which it had been feasting, and, flying directly above our deck, hovered there a while with a portion of clotted and liver-like substance in its beak. The horrid morsel dropped at length with a sullen splash immediately at the feet of Parker.[6]

The effect of this technique is to force one to the conclusion that Poe, as one of his critics has suggested, "did not fully recognize the distinction between terror and horror as a motive in art."[7] Even the shock value of Poe's procession of nightmarish images and gratuitous horrors gradually diminishes, for in the world of *Pym* living inhumation, slow starvation, and cannibalism become matters of course.

In his Gothicism Poe worked a vein which other writers of sea fiction had largely abandoned by the late 1830's, but his stress on documentation and *vraisemblance* relates *Pym* closely to other works which immediately preceded and followed the publication of Dana's *Two Years Before the Mast*. Poe spared no pains to give his novel the appearance of fact. The preface performs a double reverse by having Gordon Pym explain that he had allowed Mr. Poe to publish the first few chapters *"under the garb of fiction."* Encouraged by the credence which the readers of the *Southern Literary Messenger* lent this fictionalized fact, Mr. Pym has decided to continue the narrative in his own words; readers, however, will find it easy to establish where Poe's work ends and his own begins, for "the difference in point of style will be readily perceived." Actually, the only stylistic difference separating the rest of the novel from the early portions which Poe first published in the *Messenger* is an increased use of the devices of the pseudo-voyage. Poe can imitate perfectly the diction and pious tone of *Robinson Crusoe:* after describing the storm which wrecks the whaler, Gordon observes that "by the mercy of God, however, we were preserved from these imminent dangers, and about midday were cheered by the light of the blessed sun."[8] He can rival Cooper in interlarding his narrative with long expository digressions on the principles of seamanship. And, like the authentic narratives of Delano, Cleveland, or Morrell, *Pym* seems to manifest its author's conscientious desire to acquaint his readers with topography, climate, and fauna of the remote and unfamiliar islands on which the action takes place.

To make this wealth of circumstantial detail as authentic as possible, Poe drew heavily from a wide variety of sources; his own maritime experience was limited to that of any fairly well-traveled resident of the Atlantic seaboard in his time. For the technical details of ship-handling that are strewn throughout the novel and for the extended discussions of stowage and lying-to, he apparently relied on a manual of seamanship, but his authority did not save him from several glaring nautical anomalies of the kind that would make Cooper snort with contempt. The fact that most of Gordon's experiences aboard the whaler were drawn from one or more of the many nautical anthologies published in the period seems to account for the disproportionately heavy burden of horror in that portion of the novel, for compilations like *Remarkable Events and Remarkable Shipwrecks* (1836), designed for distribution on the waterfront and along the peddlers' routes, consisted of accounts of only the most sensationally disastrous incidents of maritime life: founderings, wrecks, explosions of steamboats, piratical atrocities, mutinies, maroonings, mas-

sacres of sailors by the South Sea islanders—the whole
inventory of suffering at sea. For his geographical descriptions and for his summary of the history of Antarctic exploration, Poe both plagiarized and quoted with citations
from Benjamin Morrell's *Narrative of Four Voyages to the
South Seas and Pacific* (1832) and Jeremiah N. Reynolds'
*Address on the Subject of a Surveying Exploration to the
Pacific Ocean and South Seas* (1836). There is some evidence, moreover, that, like Cooper, Poe made use of
Irving's *Astoria* and Cook's *Voyages*.[9]

The realism produced by Poe's attempt to capture the
style and authority of authentic narratives is entirely super-
ficial. Although its verisimilitude was sufficient to gull
many of his readers and some of his reviewers,[10] the novel
fails to render a full and truthful account of maritime life.
Like Cooper's early romances, *Pym* presents only one half
of the spectrum of reality; but if Cooper's image of the sea
is idealized, Poe's is warped in the direction of the grotesque. And like the early Cooper's, Poe's intentions apparently lie beyond the scope of realism; but where Cooper
constructs a meaningful, internally consistent statement of
the values of wildness, Poe seems concerned only with the
evocation of horror and terror, the stimuli of which are
chosen arbitrarily, even capriciously. One feels that, in
Poe's skillful hands, any material is a potential source of
horror and terror. That these emotions stem from the
materials of maritime life is essentially irrelevant; the
reader's response has no necessary bearing on the meaning
and value of the sea.

Several attempts have been made to discover a deeper
purpose and achievement in *Pym*. Acknowledging that the
novel fails when judged by the conventional standards of
realistic fiction, Patrick F. Quinn proposes that we read it
as a psychological drama, an internal journey into the
world of dreams.[11] One such reading is that of Marie Bo-

naparte, who contends that "the whole content of this story —as it was of Poe's life—is the ardent and frenzied search —ever frustrated, ever renewed—for the lost mother: a mother always hidden, always present and made manifest here in those vast and universal symbols whose significance is unconsciously sensed by man."[12] But useful though Mme Bonaparte's analysis is to the student of Poe's psyche, it fails to explain how the novel, as a work of art, differs in technique and value from a dream, and it fails to bring us closer to an understanding of the nature of "those vast and universal symbols" with which Poe works; the capacity of the sea to serve as a maternal symbol seems somehow less significant when one learns that, according to Mme Bonaparte, the whaling ship, the black island, the South Pole, and even a large Newfoundland dog also function in *Pym* as emblems of the lost mother. Gaston Bachelard, too, has discerned the presence in *Pym* of a stratum of meaning beneath the surface of the narrative; for him the action is symbolic of man in conflict with "the elemental world itself," a conflict between man and "a universe of monstrous forces."[13] But Gordon's enemies are as often internal forces (like his own self-destructive impuse to go to sea) as external; as often human antagonists (like the mutineers and the natives of the black island) as elemental. Another interpretation of *Pym,* perhaps a more accurate rendering of the modern temper than of Poe's meaning, is that of Edward Davidson, who reads the book as a "parable of how the mind moves from an assumed coherence and reality of things to a recognition that everything, even the most logically substantial, is an illusion; the mind makes its own reality." Thus Gordon's narrative records his growth to the realization that "existence is a flux and an aimless war because there is no other procedural or definable rationale to the universe itself."[14]

Whether the apparent aimlessness and inconsistency of

THE BYRONIC PIRATE
Illustration by F. O. C. Darley for *The Red Rover*.

NAUTICAL ROMANCE AT THE END OF THE LINE
From the title page of the cheap novel *Fanny Campbell, the Female Pirate Captain* (1845).

Pym are the symbolic reflection of such a profoundly pessimistic *Weltanschauung,* or whether they are merely the symptoms of Poe's loss of control over his narrative, there is good reason for the feeling that the novel is more than the recital of terrifying adventures afloat. The recurrent pattern of deception and revolt in the action of the tale hints at some larger meaning. The heavy stress placed on the colors black and white creates an aura of significance.[15] And, of course, the tantalizingly enigmatic ending of the novel invites the reader to frame some more satisfying conclusion in symbolic terms. It seems clear that Poe designed *Pym* to have the effect, if not the content, of a symbolic narrative, and in linking the suggestion of metaphysical significance to a remote and exotic maritime setting, he pointed the way to the greatest achievement of American sea fiction.[16]

The setting of *Pym* is in itself indicative of the increasing interest displayed by the writers of American nautical novels and stories in the maritime frontier. *Pym* was one of the first works to capitalize on the popular excitement which the preparations for the United States Exploring Expedition had stirred; it was no accident that the novel appeared during the summer in which Wilkes's little flotilla first set sail, or that the latter half of Gordon's adventure takes place in the very quarter of the world that the expedition was to explore. But Poe's interest in Antarctic exploration lay deeper than a desire to exploit a topical subject. He had long been interested in the views of Jeremiah N. Reynolds, who for over twenty years had urged the exploration of the South Pole and who, more than any other individual, was responsible for the formation of Wilkes's expedition. With many other theorists, Reynolds shared the belief that Antarctica consisted of more than a vast expanse of ice. At first he endorsed Symmes's theory of concentric spheres, the hypothesis that an aperture at the Pole gives access to a series of inner worlds, but in the 1830's he adopted the more modest notion that beyond a barrier of ice exists a temperate, habitable area.[17]

If Poe's early story "MS. Found in a Bottle" (1831), in which the narrator plunges into an immense gap in the sea at the South Pole, reflects Reynolds' early acceptance of Symmes's theory, *Pym* derives from Reynolds' later notions. With a salute to "Mr. J. N. Reynolds, whose great exertions and perseverance have at last succeeded in getting set on foot a national expedition, partly for the purpose of exploring these regions," Gordon pushes on beyond the sixty-fifth degree of southern latitude and finds that the climate grows steadily milder the farther south he goes. As Reynolds speculated, the region is habitable, being warmed apparently by a volcanic eruption from the interior of the earth. But before Gordon can give a full account of his discoveries, discoveries which the exploring expedition might soon confirm, his narrative breaks off, and the reader must be content with the knowledge that Poe's hero has been instrumental in "solving the great problem in regard to an Antarctic continent," in "opening to the eye of science one of the most intensely exciting secrets which has ever engrossed its attention."[18]

For all its inadequacies, *The Narrative of Arthur Gordon Pym* serves as a useful index to American attitudes toward the sea at the mid-point between *The Pilot* and *Moby-Dick*. The mere fact that a writer so versatile and so sensitive to the vagaries of popular taste as Poe should choose to produce a sea novel at this time indicates the intensity of the public demand for nautical literature. And in its very confusion of aims and concerns, its attempt to combine Gothic romanticism and documentary realism, scientific discovery and mystic revelation, *Pym* reflects the multifarious values that Americans in the late 1830's attached to their image of the sea, a range of values which Cooper's early romances did not encompass.

2

Robert Montgomery Bird's neglected novel *The Adventures of Robin Day* represents an important variant of the treatment accorded maritime life in American fiction during the third and fourth decades of the nineteenth century. Like so many of its contemporaries, *Robin Day* was an attempt to find a satisfactory alternative to the glowing idealization of Cooper's early romances, but the answer it proposed was not the one which Cooper himself was exploring, the blending of sentiment and documentary realism. Rather, Bird was one of the few Americans to follow the path indicated by Captain Marryat, a return to the tone and substance of Smollett's novels.[19]

Like its English models, *Robin Day* is more antiromantic than realistic. By setting the highly improbable stock incidents and characters of the romance in the milieu of American low life and by maintaining a heavily ironic tone, Bird conducts a running satirical attack on romanticism in most of its manifestations. He takes pains to point out that the sadistic little savages who are Robin's boyhood companions are "neither Cupids nor cherubs, such as the poets delight to picture them." As the brutal schoolmaster M'Goggin and his Negro servant dangle from the noose in which the boys have ensnared them, they "wage a battle which could only be compared to the aerial fray of the Genie and the Lady of Beauty, in the Arabian story." And when Robin protects a girl from the advances of his drunken companion, he feels himself "transformed into a hero of romance whom a wondrous destiny had thrown into contact with my star-ordained heroine, for whom I was to dare all perils and achieve all exploits that had ever been recorded of a Belmour or Lord Mortimer."

Bird even manages to turn his satire on the latest tendency of American romanticism, the revival of interest in the War of 1812. If other writers regarded the war as the golden age of American glory, he sees it as the perfect setting for the mock-heroic. He pictures "the ferment into which the people of the Middle States were thrown by the visitations of sundry British fleets to their waters; Admiral Cockburn being at the moment employed with all his forces in the Chesapeake, robbing farmers' hen-roosts, and Admiral Beresford attempting the same thing, though with no great luck, at the mouth of the Delaware." But the local patriots are equal to the emergency:

The news of these gallant forays had just reached our town, which was kept in a furious commotion by the passage through it of sailors and soldiers on their way to the scene of action; and still more by the patriotic efforts of its citizens, who, having no better way to show their zeal, mustered three or four companies of volunteers, who killed the British without stirring from home, and kept the town in a terrible tumult, day and night . . . by firing off cannons, and sometimes arms and legs.[20]

Caught up in the excitement and fired with dreams of martial triumph by his quixotic friend Dicky Dare, Robin rushes off to war, only to find himself fighting on the wrong side, since in his enthusiasm he has enlisted with a band of marauding British sailors whom he mistook for American militiamen. At sea the battle rages no more gloriously; the only Yankee ship which Robin encounters is not a gallant frigate of the United States Navy but a merchantman in which the shrewd Captain Galley drives a brisk trade in contraband goods, a schooner smugly named the *Fair American*.

The result of this return to Smollett is the resuscitation of many of Smollett's strengths and all of his weaknesses. Bird nearly matches Smollett in sheer narrative energy,

the ability to maintain a steady flow of vivid and boisterous action. His picaresque design enables him to exploit materials overlooked by his more romantic contemporaries, the life of the tavern and the road, of the
beachcomber's shack in New Jersey and the slave quarters
in Virginia. His satire is rich and various, comprehensive
in its scope and neatly adjusted to the nature of each of
its specific targets. But like *Roderick Random,* Bird's
novel moves only under the steady pressure of incident;
Robin, its narrator and central character, is not only static,
but passive. Badgered by ill-fortune and shuttled from
one domineering companion to another, he is always the
victim, never the agent. And, like Smollett, Bird too
often violates the moral tendency of his satire in straining
for a comic effect. Thus, after waging a vigorous satirical
campaign against cruelty, he has Robin's nemesis, Captain Brown, savagely flog a Negro who is writhing by the
side of the road in what are apparently the last throes of
a fatal illness. But it is all right, for the Negro has only
been faking, and Brown's blows send him hopping off,
loudly affirming his sudden recovery. By undercutting the
ethical basis of his irony, Bird tends to reduce the world
of *Robin Day* to a valueless chaos, a world in which malice
and brutality are as likely to be the occasion of laughter
as of pity or protest.

But laughter rarely intrudes upon the most important
element of *Robin Day,* its treatment of maritime life. With
the exception of Robin's brief excursion with the marauding party of the Royal Navy, the nautical episodes of the
novel are confined to its beginning, the history of Robin's
early life with a colony of wreckers on the New Jersey
coast, and the end, the account of his unwilling participa-
tion in the piratical voyage of Captain Brown. In these
portions of *Robin Day* Bird presents his most effective
statement of the theme that runs through the entire book,

the refutation of the romantic concept of the virtues of wildness and the nobility of the natural man. In a very real sense, Robin's early environment is a natural one, removed from the influences of civilization and closely associated with the sea. Robin's master, Stephen Duck, is the natural man, an ignorant and brutal seaman who employs Robin as cook and punching bag aboard the oyster shallop *Jumping Jenny*. As a result of this environment and this tutelage, Robin, at the age of thirteen, has become "a kind of Orson, or Wild-boy Peter":

[My] grovelling disposition there were some who considered an inborn one, a characteristic of a naturally low and vulgar spirit; though I am very well convinced it was all owing to Skipper Duck and his villainous treatment; and certain it is, had any nobler feelings ever existed in my bosom, they could not have survived the long course of debasing cruelty to which I had been subjected. The truth is, it had resulted in quenching every spark of intellect and spirit I ever possessed, in stultifying, in reducing me to a condition very little above that of a mere animal.

The natural life not only stunts development; it has the power to erase the effects of a previous contact with civilization. When Robin's successor aboard the *Jumping Jenny* first fell under Duck's influence, he was a bright, spirited boy from a comfortable and cultivated home, but "five years of slavery in the hands of such a man as Skipper Duck, were enough to . . . rob him of every faculty of mind, and every acquisition of manners, feeling and knowledge: the only wonder was that he should have retained any thing, that he should have recollected any thing, that he should not have been wholly brutalized."[21]

Imbued by his boyhood with "an inveterate horror of salt water," Robin nevertheless determines to test the virtues of another kind of wildness, that of "the great West, whose name associated the most agreeable ideas of

freedom and independence."²² From his experience in the
Creek War in Tennessee, he soon learns that the associations are illusory, for the western wilderness offers him
only famine, exposure, and another opportunity to study
at close hand the natural man, this time in the person of
the Indians, whose savage cruelty makes even Captain
Brown seem humane. But Robin, always the victim, stumbles out of the forest only to be snatched off to sea by
Brown.

As an early reviewer of *Robin Day* pointed out, "the
conception of incidents at sea, towards the close of the
story, is marked with power of a different and higher
kind" than that which characterizes the handling of Robin's adventures ashore.²³ With Robin's embarkation in the
piratical schooner *Viper*, the mood of the novel suddenly
darkens as Bird drives home his thrust at the romantic
glorification of wildness. The comic connotations of physical violence are stripped away, and its horror receives a
new stress. This change is largely the result of the transformation of Captain Brown from a malicious scoundrel
to a bloodthirsty, inhuman brute, fully worthy of the
name by which he is known afloat, "Hellcat." To his sorrow Robin discovers "that Captain Brown on land, and
Captain Hellcat at sea, were two very different persons;
and that, however much I might have detested the one,
there remained for me nothing but to fear the other."²⁴
If Brown ashore had flogged the Negro back to health,
Brown at sea flays a man alive with five hundred lashes
of the cat. If Brown ashore took delight in administering
quack medicines to the village yokels, Brown at sea finds
satisfaction in suspending a recalcitrant seaman from the
bowsprit, there to be devoured by sharks in full view of
the rest of the crew. Although he offers Robin no bodily
harm, Brown thus keeps him in a state of constant terror.
And to Robin, Brown represents the sea, for he is a superb

seaman, active, skillful, experienced; he is the one man aboard the *Viper* who maintains his courage in the face of the storm that wrecks her.

The power of Bird's dark conception of the sea seems to stem from the fact that in this portion of the novel he drew less from his English prototypes than from his own feelings and experience. Slight though it was, his acquaintance with the ocean was apparently sufficient to produce a lifelong antipathy to all things nautical. As a boy in New Castle he had spent many hours swimming in the Delaware and watching the life of the river and the port, but even the recollection of this experience was linked with tragedy; two of his best friends were drowned in the river, an event which, his wife tells us, "made an impression never to be effaced from the youthful heart."[25] Whatever the effect of this disaster may have been, one of his earliest writings, "The Ice-Island," reflects his conception of the sea as the locale of suffering and horror. From his brother Thomas, who had early gone to sea and who eventually commanded a packet ship which plied between American ports and Liverpool, Bird undoubtedly learned much about maritime life, but that he never shared his brother's love for the ocean is revealed in his account of his own trans-Atlantic passage in 1834:

How tired I got of the sea, and all its concerns in the . . . short term of sixteen days, words can't express; and yet there was never a greater variety of sea rarities displayed in so few days . . . The first twelve or thirteen days, it blew in almost incessant gales, which twice waxed into tempests, and once became an absolute hurricane, which was not at all to my liking, though marvellously magnificent. This rage was preluded by a brace of waterspouts, one of which I saw from the forming to the fading thereof, and so near that I could trace the spiral motion of the spray—by a morning rainbow—very rare—and by other such wonders, of which I haven't time to make a page or two of sentiment. All that I have to say of the sea particularly, is that it is an awfully disagreeable place, and that I wish I could get home without recrossing it.[26]

At one point in *Robin Day* Bird takes out an insurance policy against the censure of nautical critics and shows the similarity of his own attitude toward the sea and that of his hero:

I may as well confess a greater ignorance of all naval and nautical matters than would seem becoming in one who drew his first breath on the sea, spent his childhood in an oyster-boat, fought—or served—six weeks as a volunteer in the British Navy, and who smelt powder in—but I must not anticipate my story. The truth is, as I suspect, my early experience gave me a disgust to the sea and its affairs; and, although I have since tried to dive a little into their mysteries, it was all labour lost, and I find myself as ignorant as ever. This will explain, and, I hope, excuse, the errors into which I may fall, in treating these passages and branches of my existence.[27]

It is little wonder that a mind so nearly antithetical to that of the early Cooper should produce novels which seem to be direct rebuttals of the attitudes that underlie Cooper's romances of the forest and the sea. If *Nick of the Woods* (1837), based on the premise that the Indian "in his natural barbaric state . . . is a barbarian," was designed to counter Cooper's heroic portraits of Chingachgook and Hard-Heart,[28] *Robin Day* is no less a challenge to the representation in *The Red Rover* and *The Water-Witch* of the fine, free life of the nautical outlaw. Indeed, one can scarcely avoid reading Captain Brown's speech to the crew of the *Viper* as an ironical commentary on the philosophy of Tom Tiller: " 'Now, my jolly dogs, the sea is before you and the gallows behind you—the gallows or the yardarm, d'ye see, blast me; whereof, on one or the other there's not a man of you but must swing the moment he turns his face backward. So a free life is the word for all, because, shiver me, my hearties, you can't help it; a free life and a jolly one.' "[29]

The significance of *Robin Day*, then, lies in the fact that it is the one full and consistent expression of the neoclassical conception of the sea in American fiction. It is allied with neither Poe's exploitation of maritime life as a source of morbid but thrilling horror nor Dana's attempt to reproduce the full spectrum of the sailor's experience, from the romantic to the sordid. Rather, it constitutes a rejection of the sea. To Bird, the life of the ocean is a denial of all the values which the civilized man cherishes; in releasing man from society, the wilderness of the sea and the forest returns him to the condition of an animal, for the qualities which make him human depend for their creation and survival on the order and restraint that society alone can provide.

3

Charles J. Peterson's novel *Cruising in the Last War*, first published in monthly installments in *Graham's Magazine* during 1838 and 1840, is in many respects the antithesis of *Robin Day*, since it represents one of the last attempts by a fairly serious and competent writer to return to the themes and tone of Cooper's early romances. Peterson's one important departure from Cooper was the adoption of a narrative structure expressly designed to meet the problems of serial publication, a structure perfected in England by Michael Scott in *Tom Cringle's Log* (1829–1833) and *The Cruise of the Midge* (1834–1835), both of which first appeared in the pages of *Blackwood's Magazine*.[30] Scott's novels, an outgrowth of the pseudovoyage, take the form of an extended yarn in which the narrator recounts his adventures in the course of a voyage, or "cruise." Within the frame provided by the departure and arrival of the narrator's ship, the form affords the writer almost infinite flexibility: he can add or delete material in accordance with his editor's needs; he can shape his accounts of storm and battle in neat, install-ment-sized units; and he can release himself and his reader from the necessity of following intricate subplots. But like Scott, Peterson too often abuses the freedom provided by his linear structure. In the constant rush of action char-acters make their appearance with a flourish and then vanish, never to reappear; incidents succeed each other so rapidly that they must be repeated if the narrative is to be sustained; setting follows setting with the bewildering speed of a travelogue.

Some degree of order and coherence is imposed on the first half of *Cruising* by the source from which Peterson drew his material. His prefatory boast that "the main in-cidents of the cruise are strictly true"[31] is more than the customary attempt at verisimilitude, for the first half of his narrator's adventures is based on the manuscript "Journal of the Private Armed Brig Yankee." The *Yankee,* owned by James De Wolfe and John Smith of Bristol, Rhode Island, was one of the most successful privateers of the War of 1812. Her second cruise, which provided the incidents used by Peterson in his novel, lasted from October 17, 1812 to March 12, 1813. From Newport the *Yankee* sailed to her cruising station off the west coast of Africa, where she began her raids on British shipping. Before she returned to Rhode Island, she had made prizes of eight English vessels having a total cash value of more than $200,000.[32] Although he elaborated extensively on the bare facts of the "Journal," Peterson followed the main outlines of his source closely. His hero, Harry Dan-forth, sails from Newport in the fall of 1812 as third officer of the privateer *Yankee.* After more than a week of stormy weather, the brig puts in at the Cape Verde Is-lands, obtains provisions, and then takes up her station off the African coast. Harry is put in charge of the second vessel captured by the *Yankee,* the English schooner *Alder.* He makes a brief trading expedition up the Gabon River in Africa and then sails for home, arriving on the American coast in early spring. Although Peterson felt free to spice the incident of the "Journal" with invented material, notably Harry's rescue of the beautiful Isabel Thornton from the cabin of a burning East Indiaman and his battle with cannibals on the Gabon, his source does serve to impose an order, if only the order of probability, on the tempo and sweep of the narrative.[33]

No such restraint curbed Peterson's powers of invention in the second half of *Cruising.* Within the space of a little more than a hundred pages, Harry undertakes three more cruises, one in the *Yankee* off the Grand Banks, another in the *Yankee* in the Caribbean, and a third in a United States frigate in the Mediterranean. A brief look at Harry's experiences in the Caribbean will illustrate Peterson's prodigal use of incident, for into this single episode he crammed almost the entire action of *The Red Rover.* Like Cooper's hero, Harry Wilder, Danforth and his party are rescued from a hastily constructed raft by the enigmatic captain of a lovely, but very war-like vessel. Danforth's rescuer, like Wilder's, proves to be a renegade British naval officer turned pirate, a man who governs his savage crew by the sheer dominance of his personality. When Danforth aids the enemies of the outlaws, the pirate captain protects him from the vengeance of the crew in the same way that the Rover saves Wilder from the wrath of the sailors after they learn that he is a British agent. Danforth, like Wilder, feels a mysterious kinship with his guardian, and just as Wilder learns from the dying Rover that he is in reality Wilder's uncle, so Danforth learns that the captain is the cousin of Isabel Thornton, the girl Danforth loves.[34]

But Peterson's debt to Cooper extends far beyond the borrowing of incident. Like *The Pilot* and, in a lesser degree, *The Red Rover* and *The Water-Witch, Cruising* is designed to evoke a glorious tradition of American naval accomplishment, a tradition that forms the basis of Peterson's buoyant faith in the future maritime supremacy of America:

England is in the decline of advancing age; the United States is in the first flush of youth. With a mercantile marine already approaching that of our mother country, though our vast resources are as yet only beginning to be developed, what will be our position, as a naval power, when we have attained to manhood, and when our ships will be counted by hundreds where they are now computed by tens![35]

Although the novel alludes to the daring exploits of John Paul Jones and to the achievements of the navy in the war with the Barbary pirates, it is set in the period of the War 1812, the era in which "we . . . taught [the British] our superiority." Peterson's nationalism is far more belligerent than the early Cooper's: to the seaman Taffrail, the English are a "hereditary foe"; American sailors are animated by "a deep, unflinching detestation of their tyrants," the British. Peterson cannot sing the praises of American naval architecture without disparaging English shipbuilders: upon seeing a particularly graceful vessel, Harry Danforth knows " that craft . . . was never built in England,' " for " 'there's not a naval architect in the whole three kingdoms . . . who could turn out such a beautiful model.' " Peterson has all the heated enthusiasm of the author of *Notions of the Americans,* but it is an enthusiasm untempered by Cooper's concern for factual accuracy and his sense of historical proportion. As a result, Peterson's expression of maritime nationalism often slips into mere chauvinistic rodomontade, the kind of irresponsible bombast which pictures the battle of the *Constitution* and the

Guerrière as forming "an epoch in the history of the world."[36]

The same extension of the techniques of Cooper's early romances occurs in Peterson's treatment of the seaman, the ship, and the ocean. If Cooper's sailors are diminished by his emphasis on their environment, Peterson's are nearly annihilated. Harry Danforth, infinitely brave and infinitely active, is idealized to the point that he loses all traits of individuality, including whatever may have been the effect on his character of his long maritime experience. Thornton, the pirate captain, is the stereotyped outcast of the world, "returning that world's proscription with undying hate"; it is inevitable that "the smiles that marked that face were only assumed to mask the mighty passions slumbering at the heart." But unlike the Rover, Thornton undergoes no sea change in his translation from the pages of Byron; apparently his association with the ocean is only accidental, for Peterson makes no attempt to explore the correspondence between the Byronic temper and the marine environment. The one representative from the ranks of the common seamen, Taffrail, remains nothing but a purveyor of salty phrases, and we must take Peterson's word for it that "there is something noble in the character of a sailor, wherever he is found."[37]

Just as Peterson adopts Cooper's triad of characters, the idealized gentleman-sailor, the mysterious Byronic outcast, and the homely old salt, so he appropriates Cooper's conception of the ship. The vessels in *Cruising* are as idealized as its hero. Without exception they are surpassingly beautiful; in their airy delicacy they are more like things of "magic than of human ingenuity."[38] The devices by which Cooper animates his ships and emphasizes their grace and speed become formulas in Peterson's hands. No matter what the context, his vessels are invariably introduced with one of two metaphors: either that of "a high-mettled courser" or that of "a sea-bird on the wing."[39] The effect of this mechanical technique is to reduce Cooper's figures, always meaningful, always functional, to the level of the conventional epithet.

Peterson's forte unquestionably lies in his ability to paint huge, sweeping seascapes. Like Cooper's early romances, *Cruising* is focused less on the activities and concerns of human beings than on the play of natural forces; but while Cooper's descriptions of the ocean ultimately form an integral part of the novel in that the sea serves either as the antagonist of the characters or as the mirror of their mood, Peterson's marine scenes are usually gratuitous, coming at close regular intervals regardless of the needs of the narrative. And while Cooper's descriptions grow out of a rich and consistent conception of the meaning of the sea, Peterson's exist only to produce an effect, the evocation of sublimity. As a result, *Cruising* has a curiously pictorial quality. In each brief chapter or installment, the narrative pauses at least once to make way for an extended description of a scene so striking that it conveniently halts the characters in the midst of action. A lunar rainbow compels the whole crew of the *Yankee* to stare "spell-bound." The spectacle of a tropical moonrise makes them "pause for a moment in involuntary admiration." A blustery night off Cape Hatteras offers so grand a sight that Harry Danforth must abandon his efforts to save his vessel in order to gaze "in mute delight." Even amid the perils of an encounter with a British convoy on a dark and squally night in the North Atlantic, Harry stops a moment, his eye "attracted by the sublimity of the scene."[40]

The strange detachment occasioned by these scenes does more than provide a rough kind of justification for their inclusion; it stresses their sublime quality by supplementing objective descriptions with the intense response of the characters. The appearance of a white squall gives Peterson's narrator a chance to explain the rationale of the technique:

How often has the attempt been made to describe a hurricane at sea!—how often has the pen failed to picture its terrible sublimity? The scowling heaven; the wild tumultuous deep; the awful roaring of the wind; and the no less fearful moaning of the sea beneath can never be adequately understood unless by those who have once beheld them. But if a tempest alone is terrific, how much more so does it become, when night adds its horrors to the scene, and the impenetrable darkness around is only relieved by the blaze of the lightning, or the lurid radiance of the heavens to windward. At such times the grandeur of the scene rivals all description. The mind even becomes momentarily regardless of the dangers that surround it; a crowd of high and lofty feelings throng the bosom; we seem to rise above ourselves; and swelling with prouder, more exalted emotions we take part in the elemental war, and mingle amid the strife of nature.[41]

Sublimity, then, is all; the importance of the sea is not its value as the emblem of freedom and achievement or as the image of inhuman chaos or as the symbolic setting for an allegory of spiritual experience. For Peterson, the sea exists to inspire awe and delight.

4

In its distorted imitation of the themes and attitudes of Cooper's early romances, its stress on action at the expense of characterization, its linear plot, and its florid and slipshod style, Peterson's novel set the pattern for the flood of cheap nautical novels which inundated the American book market in the 1840's. These precursors of the dime novel are readily distinguishable by their format: the vast majority of them are slim, octavo volumes that are bound in paper covers and printed in double columns relieved only occasionally by a crude and usually irrelevant illustration. Though nearly as uniform as their appearance, their contents are far from drab. The manufacturers of these productions, Tom Sawyer's "favorite literature," drew their raw materials largely from *The Pilot, The Red Rover,* and *The Water-Witch,* but, unhampered by any concern for nautical or historical authenticity and possessed of no restraint or taste, they warped Cooper's characters and incidents in the direction of either the absurdly ideal or the sensationally grotesque. The result is a parody of the early Cooper: Byronic outcasts with names like Melvyn, the Monster of the Main, stalk the pages of the cheap novels in pursuit of lovely females with a penchant for fainting and masculine disguise; handsome gentleman-sailors invariably go to sea with a faithful old salt whose name is usually Long Tom and who speaks in a dialect so briny that it is nearly unintelligible; the sea is always sublime; the vessel is always a long, low, black schooner.[42]

An adequate notion of the style of this hackwork may be gained from a description of the methods of composition employed by E. Z. C. Judson, the notorious "Ned Buntline," who, in the course of two years, supplied his publishers with five sea novels and a volume of short stories:

A friend once inquired how he managed to do such an amount of literary work, and asked if his plots were carefully prepared in advance. He replied, "I once wrote a book of 610 pages in sixty-two hours, but during that time I scarcely ate or slept. As to my method—I never lay out a plot in advance. I shouldn't know how to do it, for how can I know what my people will take it into their heads to do? First I invent a title, and when I hit on a good one I consider the story about half finished. It is the thing of prime importance. Then I take a bound book of blank paper, set my title at the head of it, and begin to write about the fictitious character who is to be the hero of it. I push ahead as fast as I can write, never blotting out anything I have once written, and never making a correction or modification. If you will examine the leaves of manuscript you will see that the pages are clean, with no erasures—no interlineations. If a book does not suit me when I have finished it, or at any stage of its progress, I simply throw it in the fire, and begin again without any reference to the discarded text."[43]

Worthless though the cheap sea novels of the 1840's are as literature, they nevertheless serve to indicate the force which maritime life exerted on the popular imagination. Designed for the barely literate, they show that the image of the glamorous, adventurous life of the sea was as widely held, as deeply rooted in the American myth, as was the equally false image of the life of the frontier during the next half century. The arrival of the cheap novels also serves to mark the literary bankruptcy of the romantic conventions which Cooper had established in his first three sea novels, for after 1842 no respectable publisher would issue a novel written in the manner of *The Red Rover*. Joseph Holt Ingraham, whose romantic novels *Lafitte* and *Captain Kyd* had enjoyed publication by Harper's in 1836 and 1839, was forced to find an outlet for his work during the next decade in the story papers and shilling shockers of Gleason and the Williamses. Similarly, the romantic nautical tales that had appeared serially in the magazines were issued in book form only by the publishers of cheap fiction.[44] It was fitting that Cooper, who had introduced the idealized treatment of maritime life to American fiction in *The Pilot*, should be the last to gain a serious hearing for it in *Wing-and-Wing*.

5

Like the subliterary output of the publishers of cheap novels, the shorter nautical fiction of the period between 1835 and 1850 is more impressive for its quantity than for its quality. No writer of the stature of William Leggett appeared among the authors of the hundreds of short sea stories that found their way into the pages of the periodicals and gift books of the era. At its best, their work offers an honest and adequate image of some segment of maritime life; at its worst, it is as sensational and trashy as the most lurid of the cheap novels. But the very fact that they are not shaped and colored by the artistry of a powerful and original talent makes these stories all the more reliable as samples of notions and attitudes that were generally held. If they have little intrinsic value, they do, at least, help to illuminate the context from which the achievements of Cooper and Melville emerged.

Many of the types of sea stories that had engrossed the interest of readers in the previous decade now suffered a sharp decline in popularity. Very few writers continued to use nautical settings and characters for tales of sentiment; such tales were now written almost entirely by and for women and were usually set in a thoroughly domestic *milieu*. A similar decrease about 1840 in the number of stories of pirates seems to be the result of historical circumstances, as well as of changes in literary taste. One writer, who offered his readers a "real—meaning thereby an actual, veritable pirate, in contradistinction to your ideal Red Rovers, and all such fanciful craft," pointed out that piracy, with all its "pleasant and poetical associations"—"black flags, and bloody, emblazoned with death's heads, scuttled ships, with projecting planks nicely balanced over their quarter rails, and low, black schooners, with masts stepped at an angle of forty-five degrees"—had ended with the execution of the infamous Gibbs in 1831; "then and there, on Bedlow's Island, was hanged until it was dead, the romance of the seas."[45]

But the real damage to the romantic conception of the sea seems to have come less from any change in the nature

of maritime life than from Dana's new interpretation of
that nature. Thus the publication of *Two Years Before the
Mast* coincided not only with a great reduction in the
number of piratical tales, but with the virtual extinction
of the once popular supernatural treatment of the sea.
Even before 1840 nautical Gothicism had shown signs of
disintegration, for the serious stories of phantom ships and
ghostly mariners were beginning to be displaced by comic
yarns telling of a shrewd Yankee seaman's encounter with
the Devil or the Flying Dutchman or a bevy of mermaids.[46] Undoubtedly, these yarns were influenced by
Irving's comic use of the supernatural, but their structure
and diction suggest that their authors often drew directly
from the folklore of the sea. Further evidence of the increasing literary exploitation of folk materials is supplied
by the appearance in the late 1830's of a new and very
specialized kind of tale, the account of an unsuccessful
hunt for some huge and dangerous marine creature. Jeremiah N. Reynolds' story "Mocha Dick; or the White
Whale of the Pacific" (1839), which has attracted much
attention in recent years as a source for *Moby-Dick,* is the
best known but by no means the only representative of
this category.[47] "A Chapter on Sharking" (1836) recounts
a vain attempt to capture an immense albino shark in
Long Island Sound. "Hunting a Devil Fish" (1836) describes the escape of a giant manta from a midshipman's
harpoon. In "A Midsummer Night's Watch" (1837), a
nursing sperm whale crushes the whaleboat that has attacked her, and in John Sherburne Sleeper's story "A
Whale Adventure in the Pacific" (1841), a Gay Head Indian's dream presages another disastrous encounter with
a gigantic sperm whale. A related group of stories concerns
more pleasant but equally wonderful experiences with
strange beasts. "Mess-Table Chat" (1840) by A. A. Harwood tells how an omnivorous seaman reverses the usual

course of affairs by trapping and devouring an enormous boa constrictor and an alligator. In Sleeper's "Dick Trysail's Solitary Cruise" (1841), a sailor who has fallen overboard is carried to land on the back of a sea turtle, while in "Charley Brail's True Story" (1847) by John Codman, a large merchantman is towed from Borneo to Madura in record time by a whale. Like the tall tales of the backwoods, the legends and myths of the forecastle were at last finding a place in the vehicles of respectable literature and bringing with them a sense of wonder far more vivid and compelling than that produced by the mechanisms of Gothic supernaturalism.

The clearest manifestation of the impact of Dana on American short sea fiction is the appearance in the 1840's of a substantial body of tales concerned with the life of the merchant seaman. For all his realism, Dana had demonstrated that the heroism, pathos, humor, and beauty which the writers of short stories had hitherto sought in the annals of piracy and the naval service could also be found in the prosaic routine of the merchant marine. With the success of *Two Years Before the Mast* as encouragement, John Sherburne Sleeper published under the pseudonym of "Hawser Martingale" *Tales of the Ocean and Essays of the Forecastle* (1841), a collection of short pieces he had written for his paper, the *Boston Mercantile Journal*. In 1847 he was followed by his friend John Codman, who, writing as "Captain Ringbolt," brought out *Sailors' Life and Sailors' Yarns,* a similar compound of stories and essays published originally in the *Mercantile Journal*. Codman's book is the more interesting of the two. Like Sleeper, he is heavily didactic, interspersing his narratives with digressive little lectures on naval architecture, the duties and prerogatives of captains and shipowners, and the pitfalls and rewards of a sailor's life. But unlike *Tales of the Ocean, Sailors' Life* is designed to counteract a specific evil, the false impression of maritime life given currency by "books which have had too extensive a circulation, and which, purporting to be narratives of personal experience, have obtained a great deal more credit than they deserve." Codman's account of maritime life is "not the result of 'one cruise,' or of 'two years before the mast;' but of thirteen years in various stations from the hawse-hole to the quarter-deck." He is perfectly willing to acknowledge and condemn the hardships imposed on seamen by penny-pinching owners and cruel or incompetent officers, but he also is obliged to point out that sailors are not the innocent victims that writers like Dana have pictured them to be:

> They tell you of the nobleness and generosity of the sailor; but go among them in the forecastle to learn of their depravity. Believe not the plausible stories of those whose little experience, strong prejudices, and interested motives, would lead you to believe that all the sailor's misery at sea is the consequence of brutal treatment of their officers. Such things are not so, nor would the captain of the Pilgrim [Dana's vessel] have been thus abused, had not death rendered him powerless in his own defence. No, there is depravity in the sailor's heart as well as in that of the landsman.[48]

Notwithstanding the breadth of Codman's maritime experience, the field of vision in his stories is limited to the view from the quarterdeck. "Nathan Smith," for example, traces the career of a nautical Horatio Alger who, by diligence, loyalty to his officers, and utter devotion to his profession, rises to the command of an Indiaman; "The Old Sailor," on the other hand, describes a seaman's degradation by the agency of rum, whores, landlords, and lawyers.

But in spite of their bias and their heavy moral freight, Codman's tales are, as Melville pointed out with great generosity to a writer whose point of view he could not tolerate, "simply and pleasantly told, and withal entertaining."[49] They offer convincing glimpses of the Boston trade with the East Indies, of the trim and taut Indiaman "slashing along under a press of canvass," of the green hand from Vermont, wretched with seasickness, of Captain Dodge, the parsimonious down-Easter who commands the bark *Jared Spriggins* of Portland, of the joy of a crew homeward bound in their first view of Boston light. And they suggest, too, the wonder and beauty of the sea, a suggestion that is not altogether obscured by the romantic clichés into which Codman too often lapses:

For who, however timid he may be from natural disposition, can look upon the ocean in a time of its rage, and hear the mad roar of the crested billows, without losing all thoughts but those awakened by the majesty of nature displayed above and beneath him? Lakes, rivers, forests and mountains are beautiful, and indeed sublime. But are they animated beings like the waves of the ocean, whose hoarse and hollow voices are ever speaking in the sailor's ear—not only showing him, but *telling* him in tones louder and more distinct than all the homilies ever delivered, "The Lord God Omnipotent reigneth?"[50]

Sleeper and Codman were not the only writers of short nautical fiction to exploit the new interest in the life of the merchant seaman. In a tale of the merchant marine written for the *Ladies' Companion,* a magazine which had hitherto restricted its use of nautical materials to ultra-romantic stories of pirates, William Starbuck Mayo issued a manifesto in justification of his subject:

The deeds of our naval officers are emblazoned in the page of history—the memory of their triumphs preserved in the hearts of their countrymen, but the feats of our commercial marine, the gallantry, courage, and skill of its officers, however strikingly evinced, pass unrecorded and unknown. We will relate one authentic fact, which, if it had occurred in the public service, would have rendered the names of the actors famous in the annals of the sea.[51]

Forgetting the teachings of Dana, some writers applied the extravagant and sensational manner of the cheap novelists to the new subject,[52] but the ablest of them preserved the realistic and humanitarian intentions of *Two Years Before the Mast*. In "The Captain's Story" (1846), Mayo spins a yarn of a trading voyage in the little brig *Moresco* from Baltimore to Liverpool to the Cape Verde Islands and back to Baltimore. The interest of the story grows out of the conflict between two lazy seamen and a bucko mate who is a firm believer in the "Hell-afloat system," a discipline that operates on the assumption that the common sailor " 'is the incarnation of human depravity,' " and that " 'it is necessary to continually work him, and curse him, and flog him, to make him earn the salt-junk and rusty pork upon which he is half-starved.' " The seamen respond to the mate's program as might be expected, and " 'in this way, cursing and grumbling, and flogging, as thousands of vessels have done since, we made our course across the Atlantic.' " Mayo's narrator, the master of the brig, would like to delight his auditors with descriptions of the ocean like those supplied by " 'the flights of our great American poets' " or of " 'a seasick girl on her first voyage,' " but he must admit that " 'such a perfect marine pandemonium as the Moresco' " was hardly conducive to romantic reverie. In the ironical accents that were to echo through *White-Jacket*, the narrator exposes the discrepancy between democratic ideals and nautical realities:

"You believe . . . in the progress of humanity; in the march of the mind; in the development of the genius of American civilization, don't you? Well, it is a comfortable belief, but if you want to keep it, never go to sea before the mast—if you do, ten chances to one you will have it knocked out of you with a marling-spike or a belaying-pin, as soon as your officers get you into blue water.[53]

A similar antiromantic note is sounded in the few tales

of contemporary naval life that were published between 1835 and 1850. Very little of the color and glamour that characterize the earlier sketches of naval service finds its way into stories like "An Execution at Sea" (1836), a sober account of the detection and hanging of a murderer aboard a United States frigate, or "Ashore and Afloat" (1841) by "Jack Swifter," which hinges on the exposure of the incompetent captain of an American sloop of war. The one stronghold of the romantic treatment of contemporary naval life lay in the preposterous stories of E. Z. C. Judson. Judson's boast that his tales first appeared in "that excellent and well-known periodical, Lewis Gaylord Clark's Knickerbocker Magazine," is less a recommendation of his work than evidence of the deterioration of the standards of the *Knickerbocker,* for the style of his stories is as tasteless and slipshod as that of his novels.[54] But whatever their stylistic weaknesses may be, Judson's stories are unflinching in their resistance to the trend toward realism; their flamboyant and utterly false representation of naval life conceals with perfect success the fact that their author had served five years in the navy.

Despite Judson's efforts, the romantic conception of maritime life found its principal outlet in stories of nautical exploit in the War of 1812, a subject that had received very little attention in the first era of American short sea fiction. A close relationship exists between this group of stories and the tales of buccaneers that had been popular before 1840. The war, of course, took place well before the demise of piracy, and few writers could resist the temptation to inject a long, low black schooner and a Byronic pirate or two into their narratives. And like the tales of piracy, these stories constitute a return to the substance and manner of *The Red Rover.* They are in no sense concerned with the disciplined and ordered existence of the regular service, as are the naval novels of Marryat and

Chamier; rather, the great majority of them deal with privateering, a subject which, unlike the regular service, releases the writer from the obligation of following the outlines of historical fact and permits him to capitalize on the romantic aspects of maritime life: the grace of the small, swift vessel and the freedom and glory of independent achievement.[55]

Unfortunately the attempt to revivify the idealized treatment of the ocean in American short fiction fell into the cockney romanticism which too often spoiled the novels that were patterned after Cooper's early romances. Henry A. Clark's story "The Cruise of the Raker" (1848) illustrates the major characteristics of the genre. The hero, First Lieutenant Morris of the American privateer *Raker,* is as animate as the wooden figurehead of his vessel: "as he stood with his left arm resting on the mainboom, and his gracefully turned little tarpaulin thrown back from a broad, high forehead, surrounded by dark and clustering curls, and with his black, brilliant eyes lighted up with the enthusiasm of thought, he presented a splendid specimen of the American sailor." The other nautical characters consist of the identical comic tars Jack Marlinspike and Dick Halyard and a pirate chieftain who is an incredible amalgam of the Byronic outlaw and the amorous captain of conventional romance: " 'I have not for years,' " he assures the heroine, " 'spared an Englishman in my deep hatred, or an Englishwoman in my lust.' " The vessels are as stereotyped as the characters: it is inevitable that the *Raker* should scud "like the fearless bird which spreads its long wings amid the fury of the storm and the darkness of the cloud" or plunge through the night "like a blind and unbridled war-horse."[56]

In spite of his addiction to purple language, Clark is more convincing in his treatment of the sea than in his characterization. He has a forceful, if by now conventional, conception of the significance of maritime experience:

[The sea produces] a sense of exultation mingled with awe. It is upon the ocean that man learns his own weakness, and his own strength—he feels the light vessel trembling beneath him, as if it feared dissolution—he hears the strained sheets moaning in almost conscious agony—he sees the great waves dashing from stem to stern in relentless glee, and he feels that he is a sport and a plaything in the grasp of a mightier power; he learns his own insignificance. Yet the firm deck remains—the taut sheets and twisted halliards give not away; and he learns a proud reliance on his own skill and might, when he finds that with but a narrow hold between him and death, he can outride the storm, and o'ermaster the wave.

But if the reader is told that this is the meaning of the ocean to man, he is never shown that meaning in terms of action and character, for Morris and the rest pursue their wooden way through the narrative untouched by their awesome and ennobling environment. The only use that Clark makes of his conception of the sea is in his descriptive passages. Like *Cruising in the Last War,* Clark's story is dominated by its extensive and gorgeous marine scenes, scenes which, in their stress on sublimity and their fierce chiaroscuro, recall the engravings in contemporary gift books of the paintings of Cole and Turner. Clark offers his readers a thunderstorm at sea, "perhaps the sublimest sight in nature, especially when attended with the darkness and mystery of night," and a ship on fire at night in midocean, a "magnificent spectacle—the grandest, the most terrific, perhaps, it is possible to conceive." He revels in "the glorious feelings engendered by the storm," "the dread—the vast sublimity of the breathless moment" when "mighty thoughts and tumultuous conceptions are striving for form and order within our throbbing breasts." "Is not the scene," he asks, "is not the hour, truly sublime?"[57]

If it is sublime, it is an irrelevant sublimity, extrinsic to the narrative and forced on the reader only by the shrill insistence of the writer. Like the cheap novels, the group of stories which "The Cruise of the Raker" represents testifies to the dissolution of the early Cooper's vision of maritime life. What had once been an integrated and coherent representation of one segment of human experience now became a device for the titillation of the romantic sensibility.

Chapter VI

The Voyage of Life

COOPER'S LAST SEA FICTION

No more bitter rejection of the idealized treatment of maritime life exists in American literature than Cooper's penultimate sea novel, *Jack Tier* (1846–1848). In large measure, the special quality of the book is an effect of the circumstances of its publication, for it was designed to appear in *Graham's Magazine,* the outlet for such latter-day nautical romances as Peterson's *Cruising in the Last War* and Clark's "Cruise of the Raker."[1] *Jack Tier* demonstrates Cooper's ability to adapt his narrative to the formal requirements of serial publication; in it he abandons the intricate structure of many of his later sea novels for a simple, linear plot, and he shapes his chapters, nearly twice the usual length, in neatly turned episodes or ends them tantalizingly on a note of high suspense.[2] But these structural modifications are the only concessions that he makes to the formulas followed by Peterson and Clark, for the whole meaning of *Jack Tier* resides in its savage destruction of the values which they attached to the sea. It is as if Cooper had embraced the opportunity to subvert the idealization of maritime life within one of its most powerful strongholds, the pages of *Graham's.*

As James Grossman has pointed out, Cooper's method in *Jack Tier* is to immerse the materials of his early romances in a corrosive bath of realism.[3] Like the work of the cheap romancers of the 1840's, the novel is a grab bag of characters and incidents gathered from *The Red Rover* and *The Water-Witch*. Under a cloak of ambiguity and mystery, Captain Stephen Spike, like Tom Tiller, conducts an illicit trade in a swift and beautiful brigantine manned by a sober, middle-aged crew. A superb seaman, he duplicates Tiller's feat of passing through Hell Gate without a pilot. Spike is pursued by a woman in masculine disguise who calls herself Jack Tier and whose freedom with the romantic heroine, Rose Budd, arouses the jealousy of the romantic hero, Harry Mulford, just as Ludlow mistrusts Alida's relationship with the disguised Eudora in *The Water-Witch*. But Spike's attraction to Rose Budd and Jack Tier's consequent jealousy come from *The Red Rover*, where the Rover's disguised mistress fears that she is to be displaced by Gertrude. And like Harry Wilder, Harry Mulford, Spike's second-in-command, finally resolves the conflicting claims of loyalty to his chief and vessel and obedience to the law by deciding to aid the enemies of his captain. By far the most striking of Cooper's borrowings from his earlier novels is the character of Rose's aunt and guardian, Mrs. Budd, whose derivation from Mrs. de Lacey in *The Red Rover* is unmistakable. Like her progenitor, Mrs. Budd is a nautical Mrs. Malaprop, the victim of her deceased husband, a sea officer, who had exercised his wit by filling her mind with maritime misinformation which she now retails with unflinching conviction.

The nature of the metamorphosis which these materials undergo in *Jack Tier* unfolds in the first chapter, where Cooper with great swiftness and precision firmly sets the tone of the novel. The opening scene returns to the setting of *The Water-Witch*, the waterfront of New York, but in the earlier work the harbor is seen through the shimmer of a century's perspective, as quaint and clean as an anti-

quarian's reconstruction; here the time is the present and
the setting is sordidly commonplace, dominated by a Dutch
beer house and an old wooden wharf. At the wharf lies a
brigantine, a vessel that, in spite of her beauty, bears everywhere about her the marks of age and decay; she is a survi-
vor of the War of 1812 and is now too old to be insured.
Although Cooper had called her predecessors the *Ariel*, the
Dolphin, or the *Water-Witch*, he gives her the homely
name of *Molly Swash*. Unlike the Byronic Rover or the
god-like Tom Tiller, the master of the *Swash*, Stephen
Spike, is a brutish seaman who speaks in a "grum top-chain
voice," whose "coarse and vulgar features" are stained
with an "ambiguous red, in which liquor and the seasons
would seem to be blended in very equal quantities," and
whose characteristic gait is a waddle. He, too, is a victim
of age, a man of fifty-six who fears he is growing too old
for the sea. Again and again Cooper insists on the mood
of shabby senescence. Spike's crew have "lost the elasticity
of youth"; even the cabin boy is "an old, wrinkled, gray-
headed negro, of near sixty." The romantic Rose Budd
makes her entrance in a clumsy, overloaded cab drawn
by an ancient and sorrowful gray horse. She is accompanied
by her aunt Mrs. Budd, an overripe widow whose "very
countenance expressed imbecility and mental dependence,
credulity and a love of gossip," and the Irish maidservant
Biddy Noon, "pock-marked, red-faced, and red-armed."
Jack Tier, the female in disguise, bears little resemblance
to the willowy Roderick or the glamorous "Master Seadrift," for Jack is a gray-haired, "little dumpling-look-
ing person" who speaks in "a cracked, dwarfish sort of
voice" and chews tobacco incessantly. Even the hero and
heroine of the love story, slight and conventional though
they are, do not escape the withering touch of Cooper's
harsh tone. So ignorant of the affairs of the sea that she
"would have admired a horse-jockey bound to the West

Indies," Rose repeatedly makes "herself ridiculous" and gives Mulford pain by her abuse of nautical terminology. Mulford himself is something less than admirable in his passive submission to Spike; Mulford feels, "as it might be against his own will, bound to [Spike's] service."[4]

The only figure in this strange gallery of characters who rivals Spike in competing for the reader's interest is the blundering Mrs. Budd, "one of those inane, uncultivated beings who seem to be protected by a benevolent Providence in their pilgrimage on earth, for they do not seem to possess the power to protect themselves." It is difficult to escape the feeling that in the person of Mrs. Budd Cooper is satirizing the ignorant and credulous popular interest in maritime life, an interest capable of contenting itself with the productions of Ingraham and Judson. "All her prejudices being in favor of the sea, and sailors," Mrs. Budd comes aboard the *Swash* "ready to be delighted with any thing that was maritime"; to her, indeed, " 'a most remarkable region is the sea!' " But at last, after her vessel has foundered and she is cast adrift on the sea in a small boat, Mrs. Budd comes in contact with nautical fact: "the wreck and her present situation were so completely at variance with all her former notions of the sea and its incidents, that she was almost dumb-founded." This ordeal, however, is only the beginning of her initiation into the savage reality of maritime life, for once again she must experience shipwreck and the hardships of navigation in an open boat when the *Swash* is destroyed and Spike, his crew, and his passengers set out for land in a yawl. This time Mrs. Budd's providential protection deserts her. The yawl is pursued by a cutter from an American man-of-war, and Spike must lighten the craft if he is to make good his escape. With a savagery unequalled in any of his other novels, Cooper has Spike and his men murder all those characters who are particularly comic and particularly

AMERICAN SEALERS AT WORK

From Edmund Fanning's *Voyages round the World* (1833).

THE VOYAGE OF LIFE

Youth, the second painting in Thomas Cole's series (1842); courtesy
of the Munson-Williams-Proctor Institute, Utica, New York.

helpless. One by one, the Negro steward Josh, the cook Simon, and Biddy Noon are pitched into the turbulent waters of the Florida reef. But the ultimate act of brutality is reserved for Mrs. Budd. As she sinks into the sea, she clutches at the hand of the boatswain and screams for Spike to save her. At a command from Spike, "the boatswain drew his knife across the wrist of the hand that grasped his own, one shriek was heard, and the boat plunged into the trough of a sea, leaving the form of poor Mrs. Budd struggling with the wave on its summit, and amid the foam of its crest."[5]

Beneath the antiromanticism which seems to supply the primary impetus of the novel lie more lasting elements in Cooper's artistic and intellectual development. It is true that Spike, like Bird's Captain Brown, is designed to give the lie to the Byronic idealization of the nautical outlaw, but he also serves as an object lesson in the insufficiency of human ability unsupported by divine grace. As we have seen, the early romances may be read as a celebration of the noble self-reliance that is gained by the cultivation of a particular area of human skill, seamanship. Cooper had taken delight in drawing the contrast between the mariners of Latin countries who, in moments of crisis, let their prayers to God interfere with the exercise of their skill and the Anglo-Saxon sailor who depends for his safety on his own brain and muscle.[6] And in all the novels before *Jack Tier,* seamanship is dignified by the fact that it automatically entails moral excellence. If the Rover is not exactly the embodiment of the Christian virtues, neither is the moral frame of reference of the novel Christian; the values it does exalt, independence, daring, and honor, are possessed by the Rover in abundance. Conversely, in *Wing-and-Wing* Cooper takes pains to emphasize that the morally ambiguous Ithuel Bolt is a newcomer to the sea, unskilled in its ways. But in *Jack*

Tier seamanship is inadequate to cope with the power of the ocean and may, in fact, conceal from man his true dependence on divine mercy: even Mulford's "pride of profession and of manhood" offer themselves "as stumbling-blocks to prevent" him from asking "that succor from God which was so much needed." And, for once, the possession of superlative nautical skill is, in the person of Spike, clearly associated with evil.

The conjunction sets up tensions in Cooper's attitude toward the character; he seems to share Mulford's "profound respect for Spike's seamanship," and yet he must concede that the "only character in which [Spike] could be said to be respectable [was] that of a seaman." He tells us that, in performing the demanding task of threading Hell Gate, the master of the *Swash* "now manifested the sort of stuff of which he was really made," but "Spike was only great in a crisis, and then merely as a seaman." By the time Cooper comes to Spike's death scene, however, all suggestions of ambivalence have vanished:

We shall not enter into the details of the revolting scene, but simply add that curses, blasphemy, tremulous cries for mercy, agonized entreaties to be advised, and sullen defiance, were all strangely and fearfully blended. In the midst of one of these revolting paroxysms, Spike breathed his last. A few hours later, his body was interred in the sands of the shore. It may be well to say in this place, that the hurricane of 1846, which is known to have occurred only a few months later, swept off the frail covering, and that the body was washed away to leave its bones among the wrecks and relics of the Florida Reef.[7]

The scene offers a startling contrast to the triumphant death of the Rover; but, more than that, in the fate of Spike's body, the sea functions not as a merely natural force but as the agent of God's just power. In *Afloat and Ashore* Cooper had moved tentatively and incongruously toward the conception of the sea as the mirror of the divine mood. In *Jack Tier* he creates a moral environment that permits him to tighten the relation of nature to God: nature is not only in sympathy with God's purpose; it is the instrument and the expression of His will.

2

In Cooper's last sea novel, *The Sea Lions* (1849), the two great tendencies of his literary and philosophical development, the progress from romance to realism and the shift from a conception of the universe as the arena in which individual man wins fulfillment to a conception of the universe as the material expression of God's purpose, meet to produce what is, without doubt, his most complex and yet fully integrated fiction. The plot itself is simple enough. The novel opens in the summer of 1819, when a dying seaman tells the miserly Deacon Pratt, the leading citizen of Oyster Pond, a small agricultural and maritime community near Sag Harbor on the eastern tip of Long Island, of the existence of rich sealing grounds on an uncharted island near the Antarctic Circle and of a pirate's treasure buried in the sands of a small West Indian key. The Deacon commissions Roswell Gardiner, a young sealing officer, to command the schooner *Sea Lion* in an attempt to reap the harvest of seals and recover the buried gold. But business is not Gardiner's only connection with the Deacon, for he loves the old man's niece and ward, Mary. Although Mary returns Gardiner's love, she refuses to marry him because he, in the pride of his reason, is unable to believe in the divinity of Jesus.

Cheered by Mary's pledge that she will marry no one else in his absence, Gardiner quickly and efficiently prepares the schooner for her voyage and sets sail for the regions of the South Pole. Before he is out of sight of land, he discovers that he has acquired a consort, a schooner identical to his own in every respect, even in the name *Sea Lion*. It turns out that the Deacon's informant had relatives on Martha's Vineyard who have gained an inkling of the secret, have fitted out the vessel that now dogs Gardiner's, and are determined at least to share in the profits of the voyage. Reluctant though he is to admit another party to the venture, Gardiner finds that he is unable to outsail Daggett, the master of the Vineyard vessel, and the two schooners make their way southward in company. Although Daggett aids Gardiner in replacing a spar he has lost in a storm off Cape Hatteras, the relationship between the two men constantly threatens to disintegrate into a fierce competition, as when they nearly resort to violence in their struggle for the possession of a whale they have killed on the Brazil banks. At last, as the two *Sea Lions* approach Cape Horn, Gardiner manages to shake off his consort in the darkness of a misty night.

Forcing her way through the barrier of ice that rings the South Pole, the Oyster Pond *Sea Lion* finally reaches the secret sealing station and begins to take on her cargo. Before she can be filled, however, the schooner from the Vineyard arrives, and Gardiner feels obliged to remain at Sealer's Land until Daggett completes his cargo. Delayed by Daggett's late arrival and by the necessity of repairing an injury which his vessel has suffered, the *Sea Lions* find themselves trapped by the oncoming Antarctic winter. Daggett's schooner is crushed by the ice and driven on shore, a hopeless wreck, but Gardiner is able to moor his vessel in a cove sheltered from the drifting fields of ice. Gardiner is willing to make the best of the grim situation and invites Daggett's party to share the shed in which the men from Oyster Pond intend to spend the winter; Daggett, however, refuses to desert his vessel and requires his crew to winter in the wreck.

With these arrangements settled upon, the two crews

begin their long ordeal. At first intercourse between the wreck and the shed is frequent and friendly, but as the winter increases in severity, communication between the two camps becomes more difficult and eventually ceases altogether. As Gardiner reads the Bible Mary has given him, listens to the words of the devout old seaman Stephen Stimson, and contemplates the display of natural power that is ever before him, he slowly relinquishes his proud confidence in the supremacy of his own reason and becomes willing to admit the claims of faith. At the very moment when his spiritual regeneration reaches its climax, Gardiner hears a piercing scream from Daggett's camp. Hurrying to his rival's aid, he discovers that the stove in the wreck has gone out and that most of Daggett's party have frozen to death. Daggett himself lingers on a while, but he dies before the return of spring releases the Oyster Pond *Sea Lion* from the grip of the ice.

Although the upper works of Gardiner's schooner have been consumed as fuel during the winter, he is able to piece together a makeshift replacement for them with materials taken from the wreck. The survivors of the winter at Sealer's Land embark in the vessel, stop at the West Indies for the treasure, and at last, long overdue, return to Oyster Pond. Ironically, Deacon Pratt, whose health was failing even at the start of Gardiner's voyage, dies just as he learns that his venture has made a profit. Since Gardiner's religious views are now acceptable to Mary, the two are married, and, abandoning the sea, Gardiner settles with his family in an inland county of New York.

From one point of view, this plot seems nothing more than a realistic reworking of *Wing-and-Wing*. The conflict between French Deism and Italian Catholicism is reduced to a quarrel between Yankee Unitarianism and Yankee Congregationalism. The homely, comfortable scenery of Long Island and the forbidding wastes of Antarctica replace the magically beautiful Mediterranean setting of the earlier novel. The gallant Raoul Yvard, engaged in honorable warfare against the foes of his country, is transformed into Roswell Gardiner, engaged in the "skinning business," an occupation one degree lower on the nautical social scale than that pursued by Dana's despised "spouters." Although *The Sea Lions,* unlike *Jack Tier,* is far more than a grim revision of the nautical romances, such a reading of the novel serves to stress one of its most important aspects, its solid grounding in literal fact, its almost complete refusal to distort in the direction of idealization. Indeed, so convincing is the air of actuality of the novel, so closely do its incidents tally with the facts reported by Antarctic explorers, that many of its readers never penetrate beneath the surface of its narrative. To them, as to James Grossman, *The Sea Lion* remains "a competent story of thrilling adventure in the Antarctic and of the life of some nineteenth-century descendants of the Puritans," marred only by the "minor but bulky excrescence" of Cooper's concern for certain narrowly doctrinal religious issues.[8] An investigation of the origins of *The Sea Lions* provides one route to a fuller understanding of Cooper's intentions and achievements in the novel, for it reveals not only the sources of the rich factual matrix in which his narrative is embedded, but the influences which prompted him to expand the significance of that narrative to the point that it borders on allegorical statement.

3

The materials of *The Sea Lions,* like those of *Afloat and Ashore,* are the combined product of Cooper's personal experience and of his extensive reading in the literatures of maritime exploration and commercial enterprise. A pleasant memory of over thirty years' standing,

his daughter informs us, dictated his choice of eastern
Long Island as a setting for the novel:

In his early married life, Mr. Cooper had paid repeated visits,
during the summer months, to a relative of Mrs. Cooper,
living on one of the islands off the eastern shore of Long
Island. This gentleman [Charles T. Dering] led a sort of
semi-aquatic life, which had great attractions for a young
man still a seaman at heart. His estate covered an island of
some size, inhabited by his own family and dependents only,
and bearing the pleasing name of Shelter Island; and all
communications with the main land were carried on by
boats of different kinds. Here, cruising, fishing, shooting . . .
Mr. Cooper had passed many a pleasant hour, remembered
with pleasure through life. Familiarity with that part of the
country now induced him to send abroad his two sealers from
those waters.

An echo of this experience sounds in the concluding chapter of *The Sea Lions* and suggests that in Roswell
Gardiner, as in Miles Wallingford, Cooper saw something
of himself; like the young Mrs. Cooper, perhaps, Mary de-
tected "certain longings after the ocean" in her new husband "and did not consider him safe so long as he could
scent the odors of a salt marsh. There is a delight in this
fragrance that none can appreciate so thoroughly as those
who have enjoyed it in youth: it remains as long as human
senses retain their faculties."⁹

Still another association with the proprietor of Shelter
Island supplied Cooper with additional material for *The
Sea Lions,* for, in 1819, he and Dering became partners in
the ownership and management of the whaler *Union.*
Since it was Cooper's duty to supervise the fitting-out of
the *Union* at her home port of Sag Harbor, he must have
acquired an extensive acquaintance with the inhabitants
and activities of the maritime villages scattered along the
Long Island shore and the adjacent coast of Connecticut

during his three-year partnership with Dering.[10] Undoubtedly, Cooper's experience with the *Union* is reflected in his description of Gardiner's efforts to recruit a crew and prepare his vessel for sea, in the informed precision of his account of the financial transactions involving the whale oil taken by Deacon Pratt's schooner, and in the fact that the action of *The Sea Lions* takes place in the very years during which Cooper was engaged in his whaling venture.

But there was a still better reason for setting the novel in the period between 1819 and 1820. By a happy coincidence, Cooper's experience with the *Union* had occurred at the height of the American seal fishery, the years immediately following the discovery in 1819 of the rich sealing grounds on the South Shetland Islands, and it had made him familiar with the center of the sealing industry, Stonington, Connecticut. In an earlier work, *The Monikins* (1835), he had made incidental use of his acquaintance with the sealers, and in the character of Noah Poke, the Stonington sealer who conducts Sir John Goldencalf to the Monikin antiutopia at the South Pole, he drew a comic preliminary sketch of Daggett in *The Sea Lions.* Both men are fearless, greedy, and secretive, and both scorn the methods of formal navigation. Poke, who has "passed half his life in poking about among the sterile and uninhabited islands of the frozen ocean," takes "little account of charts" and relies upon his "scent" and his good luck to guide him to his destination. In his opinion, his instinctive method of navigation is " 'the very best way in the world to discover islands; and everybody knows that we sealers are always on the lookout for su'thin' of that sort.' " Daggett, who seems to navigate "by a positive nautical instinct," endorses a similar practice:

"I tell you . . . a man with a good judgment, can just as well jog about the 'arth, without any acquaintance with lunars, as he can with. Then, your sealer hasn't half as much need of your academy-sort of navigation as another man. More than half of our calling is luck; and all the best sealing stations I ever heard of, have been blundered on by some chap who has lost his way. I despise lunars, if the truth must be said."

In *The Monikins,* too, Cooper had first experimented with the glittering, frozen world of Antarctica as a setting and had provided himself with at least one illustration of the hazards of sailing in its ice-jammed seas that was to re-appear in *The Sea Lions.* When Poke's vessel, the *Walrus,* is nipped by the ice, she is wedged upwards as if in a "dry-dock" fitted with "ice-screws"; similarly, Daggett's *Sea Lion* is lifted by the wedge-like action of the ice on her bottom, a process which is likened to that of a screw-dock.[11]

Cooper's own knowledge of the sealers seems to have been sufficient to supply the needs of *The Monikins.* The memory of his days in Stonington was fifteen years old, but the sealing materials of the book were strictly inci-dental to the main action, and its satirical, blatantly al-legorical character demanded no scrupulous fidelity to fact. When he came to write *The Sea Lions,* he was separated from his experience with the sealers of Long Island Sound by the passage of thirty years. In the new novel, moreover, he was to move his sealing materials to the center of the stage, and, if he was not to reverse the whole tendency of his literary development over the past decade, he must treat them with a historian's concern for completeness and accuracy. In order to broaden and deepen his own first-hand knowledge of sealers and their lore and to acquaint himself with the remote seas on which they sailed, Cooper turned to an extensive body of writings relating to sealing and polar voyaging, the outgrowth of the energetic, daring, and intensely competitive exploitation of the newly dis-covered southern sealing grounds and the resumption of the great voyages of exploration after the close of the Napoleonic wars.

Like *Afloat and Ashore, The Sea Lions* so successfully captures the fact and spirit of the era in which it is set, so fully assimilates its source-materials into the fictional whole, that it is difficult to trace its origins with anything like absolute certainty. For example, Gardiner attempts to put off Daggett by implying that the *Sea Lion* is designed for a whaling voyage or for fishing off Newfoundland, when, of course, her real destination is Sealer's Land, a secret, untouched island where " 'the seals lie about on the beach like pigs in a pen, sunning themselves' "; and, although Gardiner's vessel sails before the first recorded American visits to the South Shetlands and Palmer's Land, several of his experienced hands, all recruited at Stonington, have "often visted [*sic*] the South Shetlands, New Georgia, Palmer's Land, and other known places in those seas."[12] These details may form a portion of the sealing lore that Cooper had acquired along the Connecticut waterfront in the days of his association with Dering, or they may come from research into the files of newspapers published in the era in which *The Sea Lions* is set. In 1820 both the New York *Mercantile Advertiser* and *Niles' Register* printed an article which, if it was not Cooper's source, at least testifies to the authenticity of his materials:

It is a singular fact that the newly discovered land in the Pacific Ocean, south of Cape Horn, has been known to *brother Jonathan,* at least so long that a voyage to and from the island [one of the South Shetlands] has actually been completed out of the port of Stonington, Connecticut. But less ambitious about the honor than the profit, he was content, from the experience of the first voyage, to move on quietly in the purchase of ships, which he has done to the extent of seven or eight within a few months—all of which have ostensibly *gone a whaling*, but they have been [*sic*] more probably gone a *sealing*. About two years ago, a ship was fitted out of this port, (New York,) on shares, for "an island unknown to any one except the captain, where the seals which have never been disturbed by man, were as tame as kittens, and more plenty than at any other place upon earth."[13]

There can be little doubt, however, that Cooper supplemented his knowledge of sealing with information drawn from two firsthand accounts of the southern fur trade, Benjamin Morrell's *A Narrative of Four Voyages* (1832) and Edmund Fanning's *Voyages Round the World* (1833). In addition to a mass of useful background material relating to the financing, equipment, and conduct of a sealing expedition, Morrell's book gave Cooper the authority for certain specific details that were to appear in *The Sea Lions*. Thus, the "good accounts" which the old seaman Stimson gives Gardiner of the passage through the Straits of Le Maire seem to be an echo of Morrell's recommendation of the route. Morrell, too, is the apparent source for Cooper's vivid account of the near destruction of the two *Sea Lions* by an overturning iceberg. And it seems likely that Cooper learned from Morrell the effectiveness of the device by which the writer suppresses information as if he were a party to the secrets of his characters. At one point, for example, Morrell interrupts his account with the warning that "we are now approaching a period of this eventful voyage, in the narrative of which I shall, *for reasons that must be obvious to every reader,* suppress dates, distances, bearings, and locations." The author of *The Sea Lions* must observe similar restrictions: "We are under obligations not to give the figures that stand on the chart, for the discovery is deemed to be important, by those who possess the secret, even to the present hour. We are at liberty to tell the whole story, with this one exception; and we shall proceed to do so, with a proper regard to the pledges made in the premises."[14]

Fanning's *Voyages* provided a still richer storehouse of materials. The prime source of information concerning the sealers of Stonington since the day of its publication, the book consists of accounts of nearly all the voyages conducted under the auspices of the Fanning family, the leading shipowners of Stonington in the first quarter of the nineteenth century. The history of one of these voyages probably gave Cooper the main outlines of the expedition of Gardiner's *Sea Lion*. According to Fanning, the brig *Hersilia* was dispatched from Connecticut in the summer of 1819 with instructions to sail south to latitude 63 degrees in the longitude of Cape Horn and then to turn east in the hope of discovering certain new sealing grounds that were supposed to exist in that region. In February of 1820 the *Hersilia* sighted the group of islands now known as the South Shetlands and stopped there to harvest the skins of the vast and apparently untouched herd of seals that lay along the shores.[15] Although the *Sea Lion* is instructed to sail to the west, rather than to the east, of the longitude of Cape Horn, the similarity between the two voyages, particularly in chronology and mission, is striking.

Still more convincing evidence of Cooper's indebtedness to Fanning is offered by his account of an excursion by Gardiner, Daggett, and Stimson to the top of the peak that overlooks the anchorage at Sealer's Land. When they reached the summit, "an extraordinary, and . . . a most brilliant view, rewarded the adventurers." On all sides "icebergs were visible," a "vast frozen fleet"; to the northward "the ocean was glittering under the brightness of an unclouded sun." The whole formed a spectacle in which "grandeur, sublimity, and even beauty were found." "After passing an hour on the bald cap of the mountain," the three men "undertook the descent." But "it is always much less dangerous to mount an acclivity than to go down it"; "the snow rendering the footing slippery," Gardiner proceeded "with due caution," but Daggett neglected to take the proper care, fell, and broke his leg. With great difficulty Gardiner and Stimson managed to bring him back to camp: "glad enough was the sufferer to find himself beneath a roof, and in a room that had its comforts; or what were deemed comforts on a sealing voyage." In his *Voyages* Fanning gives one account that must have especially interested Cooper, for it describes what was to be the central incident of *The Sea Lions,* a winter spent in a high southern latitude. In the course of that winter at South Georgia, Fanning, then in command of the sealer *Aspasia,* had tried to relieve the tedium by taking walks on the island:

On one of these excursions from the ship, the surgeon and myself had strolled, or rather climbed, to an elevated precipice of the mountain; from this position a wide and extensive view of the ocean was had, covered with fleets of immense iceislands. The brightness of a clear sun shining on these islands, and on the sea as it broke against their base, formed a view, which for grandeur and beauty, is seldom if ever surpassed. The position we occupied was an acre or upwards of table level, and from this to descend to our starting point, was a performance by no means easy, in consequence of the steepness and slipperiness of the descent, for we had found, in this instance at least, that it was easier to go up than to come down hill; however, by exercising all due caution, we at last safely attained more comfortable quarters.[16]

It is worth noticing that Cooper's one important departure from Fanning, Daggett's accident, not only plays an important role in the succeeding action of the novel, but is a natural outgrowth of Fanning's emphasis on the difficulty of the descent. The other changes are minor: the pompous revision of Fanning's little observation that "it was easier to go up than to come down hill" is unfortunate, but no one can regret Cooper's awareness of the irony in Fanning's mention of comfort in the context of a sealing voyage.

4

Cooper could not find many scenes like the prospect from the height of land on South Georgia in the narratives of either Morrell or Fanning, for both writers were far more concerned with recording the exploits of the sealers than with sketching the face of Antarctica. But to the novelist whose intention was "to portray man on a novel field of action," setting was all important. And if Cooper had some acquaintance with the sealers and their trade, the sea and land in the region of the South Pole lay, of course, far beyond the compass of his experience. Throughout his life, however, he had been an avid reader of the narratives of polar exploration, a man who loved to follow "the hardy mariners in their dangerous voyage," for "the heart of the scholar warms in proportion as the bodies of the adventurers freeze."[17] To the narratives of Wilkes, Parry, and Scoresby, then, Cooper turned for the icy setting of *The Sea Lions*.

In a review which appeared in the *Literary World* for April 28, 1849, Herman Melville remarked that the Antarctic descriptions in *The Sea Lions* remind the reader "of the appalling adventures of the United States Exploring Ship in the same part of the world, and of Scoresby's Greenland narrative."[18] As W. B. Gates has abundantly demonstrated, the resemblance between the novel and Wilkes's *Narrative of the United States Exploring Expedition* is more than accidental, for Cooper drew most of his descriptions of the topography in the vicinity of Cape Horn and the terrors of Antarctic navigation from the pages of the *Narrative*.[19] On four separate occasions the text of *The Sea Lions* refers to "the persevering and laborious Wilkes" by name; and once Cooper mentions Wilkes's graphic comparison of an iceberg to a ruined city fashioned of alabaster and then proceeds to describe a group of bergs in precisely the same figurative terms.[20] But the novelist's debt to Wilkes, Professor Gates shows, is vastly greater than these acknowledgements would indicate. The roster of the crew of Gardiner's *Sea Lion,* the description of the approach to Cape Horn, the account of the passage from the Cape to Sealer's Land and of the sealers' desperate efforts to escape to the north before the onset of winter, all have parallels in the *Narrative.* Time and again, incidental material from the *Narrative* finds its way into the novel in the speeches of Stimson, for the old seaman is made the mouthpiece for Wilkes, as he is for Morrell. Of the major constituents of the Antarctic portions of *The Sea Lions,* Professor Gates suggests, only the description of the winter at Sealer's Land comes not from Wilkes but from "Cooper's creative imagination."[21]

But inventive as that imagination was, Cooper did not, in this period of his literary career, rely on its productions alone. More than twenty-five years before he came to write *The Sea Lions* Cooper had published an enthusiastic review of William Parry's *Journal of a Voyage for the Discovery of a North-West Passage* (1821). Now, searching for the substance he needed for his description of the polar winter, he must have recalled Parry's detailed account of his enforced encampment at Melville Island in the winter of 1819–1820 and reread the *Journal* in the hope of finding the materials he lacked. A comparison of *The Sea Lions* with Parry's volume shows that the hope was not in vain. Late in the season of 1819, one of Parry's two vessels, the *Griper,* became caught in an ice field which collided with the shore, "piling up the enormous fragments of ice in the most awful and terrific manner"; the *Griper* was lifted bodily by the pressure of the ice and deposited intact on the shore. During the final attempt to escape from Sealer's Land before the advent of winter, Daggett's *Sea Lion* also is trapped in an ice field that is being driven with "vast pressure" against the shore; Gardiner's crew anxiously await the destruction of their consort:

They saw that the schooner, then less than a cable's length from them, was close to the rocks; and the next shock, if any thing like the last, must overwhelm her. To their astonishment, instead of being nipped, the schooner rose by a stately movement that was not without grandeur, upheld by broken cakes that had got beneath her bottom, and fairly reached the shelf of rocks almost unharmed. Not a man had left her; but there she was, placed on the shore, some twenty feet above the surface of the sea, on rocks worn smooth by the action of the waves!

Although Parry's vessel, unlike Daggett's, is salvaged, "the advanced period of the season, the unpromising appearance of the ice to the westward, and the risk to the ships with which the navigation had been attended for some days past, naturally led" him to the conclusion that "the time had arrived, when it became absolutely necessary to look out for winter-quarters." Gardiner, too, surveys his situation, "desolate, indeed, and nearly devoid of hope"; as he gazes "to the southward," where "stood clustering around the passage a line of gigantic bergs, placed like sentinels, as if purposely to stop all egress in that direction," "serious doubts darkened his mind as to his escaping from this frozen chain until the return of another summer," and he decides to make his preparations for the winter that "was already setting in."[22]

The first step taken by both Parry and Gardiner is the opening of a passage through the ice to a safe berth for their vessels. Parry's men hacked out a canal "four thousand and eighty-two yards, or nearly two miles and one-third" in length through ice having an "average thickness of . . . seven inches"; when his ships were finally moored in safety, the men "hailed the event with three loud cheers." As Gardiner's crew cut a passage for the *Sea Lion,* Cooper informs his readers that "new ice, an inch or two thick, or even six or eight inches thick, might have been cut even for a league, should it be necessary," for "such things were sometimes done"; and as the schooner enters her frozen dock, "three cheers broke spontaneously out of the throats of the men." Elaborate preparations for safeguarding the health of the crews constitute the next measure: both Parry and Gardiner go to great lengths to protect their shelters against what they consider their greatest threat, the incursion of moisture, and both commanders establish rigorous programs for hardening the men by requiring them to exercise in the frigid air. With these preparations completed, both parties begin their long hibernation. Although the routine followed by the large and well-equipped crews of the British men-of-war with their elegant theatricals, their weekly gazette, and their painstaking scientific observations was of little help to Cooper, he gleaned what material he could from the pages of the *Journal.* Parry had reported, for example, that "the distance at which sounds were heard in the open air, during the continuance of intense cold, was so great as constantly to afford matter of surprise to us, notwithstanding the frequency with which we had occasion to remark it. We have, for instance, often heard people distinctly conversing, in a common tone of voice, at the distance of a mile." Although Cooper, accustomed to the frosty winters of the Otsego valley, is less surprised than the Englishman was by the phenomenon, he does not hesitate to give his readers the benefit of Parry's observation: "the great distance to which sounds are conveyed in intensely cold and clear weather, is a fact known to most persons. Conversations in the ordinary tone had been heard by the sealers when the speakers were nearly a mile off." And in both the *Journal* and *The Sea Lions* the return of spring is signaled by a thaw which inundates the island in raging torrents and immense cataracts.[23]

To supplement Parry's information, Cooper may well have turned, as Melville suggests, to William Scoresby's descriptions of the Greenland whale fishery. He had reviewed Scoresby's *Account of the Arctic Regions* (1820) soon after its publication, and it seems likely that the recollection of Scoresby's careful study of the effects of intense cold contributed to the rich authenticity of the winter episodes in *The Sea Lions*. The only borrowings from Scoresby that may be identified with any certainty, however, appear not in the description of the winter at Sealer's Land but in the brief whaling episode. There can be little doubt that the accident by which Daggett's line becomes entangled in the mouth of the whale which Gardiner's men have harpooned was prompted by a passage describing a similar incident in Scoresby's *Account*, a passage quoted by Cooper in his review. Again, Daggett's peculiar defense of his claim to the whale seems to be derived from Scoresby: the Vineyarder contends that " 'there is a law above all whalers' law, and that is the law of Divine Providence. Providence has fastened us to this crittur', as if on purpose to give us a right in it; and I'm by no means so sure States' law won't uphold that doctrine.' " Scoresby offers a convenient precedent for the materialistic Daggett's ironical concern for the workings of Providence in his discussion of the rights of the Greenland whalers *Experiment* and *Neptune* to a whale first struck by the *Neptune*. The master of the *Experiment* had claimed the whale, " 'your harpoon, line, and boat, too; and by God's providence, I will have them.' This phrase was not without its meaning; for the people of Greenland, not the most cultivated and polished place in the world, had a notion that every thing they found afloat, God's providence sent, and so they kept it."[24]

From the narratives of sealers and polar explorers, then, Cooper assembled the extensive and detailed body of information required by the Antarctic setting of *The Sea Lions*. But it seems to have been a peculiarity of his creative method that such information, no matter how complete, could not become viable until he had found a means of translating the unfamiliar setting into terms which touched his own experience. By this process the solid ground of *The Prairie*, a terrain which Cooper knew only at second hand, is equated with the rolling, limitless sea. In *The Monikins* he had hit upon an analogous method for dealing with the icy world of Antarctica; as the *Walrus* approaches the great barrier of icebergs, Cooper's narrator searches for a way to describe the spectacle:

I can only compare the scene which now met my eyes, to a sudden view of the range of the Oberland Alps, when the spectator is unexpectedly placed on the verge of the precipice of the Weissenstein. There he would see before him a boundless barrier of glittering ice, broken into the glorious and fantastic forms of pinnacles, walls and valleys; while here, we saw all that was sublime in such a view heightened by the fearful action of the boisterous ocean, which beat upon the impassable boundary in ceaseless violence.

That Goldencalf's simile is founded on his creator's experience is revealed by a passage in Cooper's *Sketches of Switzerland* (1836), a description of an unexpected view of the Oberland from the Weissenstein:

Before this sublime sight, all that we had yet seen, even to the glittering peak of Mont Blanc, sunk into insignificance. It is not easy to convey a sufficiently vivid picture of a view so glorious with the pen, and I hardly know how to set about it; for I am fully aware that however kindly you may be disposed to be satisfied with an imperfect description, it is not easy for one who has actually looked upon it to please himself. You must imagine, therefore, as well as you can, what would be the appearance of frozen snow piled in the heavens to the height of a mile, and stretching twenty leagues across the boundary of an otherwise beautiful view, having its sides shaded by innumerable ravines, or rather valleys, with, here and there, a patch of hoary naked rock, and the upper line of all tossed into peaks, mountain tops, and swelling ridges, like the waves of a colossal ocean. The very *beau idéal* of whiteness is not purer than the congealed element, or chiselled marble better defined.[25]

Thus the memory of the Alps, a memory which Cooper had recorded with poetic intensity in the travel books, became the medium between his reading and his imagination; and in this description of the Oberland, with its reference to "a colossal ocean," one may see the completion of a triad of associations: the sea, the Alps, and the glittering polar ice, all linked in sublimity.

Throughout the Antarctic portions of *The Sea Lions*, Cooper reiterates again and again the equation he had discovered in *The Monikins*. Recalling the spectacle of the catastrophe at the Alpine village of Weggis, he observes that a floe of ice might drive Gardiner's vessel before it "as an avalanche of mud in the Alps is known to force cottages and hamlets in its front." The ceaseless grinding of field ice produces a rushing sound "like that of an incessant avalanche, attended by cracking noises that resembled the rending of a glacier," a medley Cooper had heard during his visit to the Jungfrau. The memory of his tour to the site of the landslide at Goldau finds its way into his description of the capsizing of an iceberg, an event producing "some such effect as would have been wrought by the falling of a portion of a Swiss mountain into a lake; a sort of accident of which there have been many and remarkable instances." The equation serves to

emphasize the difficulties that beset Gardiner: "to think
of sawing through ice as thick as that of the floe, for
any material distance, would be like a project to tunnel
the Alps"; Gardiner "might as well have expected to melt
the glaciers of Grinde[l]wald by lighting a fire on the
meadows at their base" as have hoped to keep the yard of
his winter camp free from ice and snow. Remembering
his Alpine excursions, Cooper is able to contrast a winter
at the southern tip of South America and a winter at
Gardiner's camp near the Antarctic Circle: "the difference
between Orange Harbor and Sealer's Land, in this respect, must be something like that which all the travelling
world knows to exist between a winter's residence at the
Hospital of the Great St. Bernard, and a winter's residence
at one of the villages a few leagues lower down the mountain." But if Antarctica resembles the Alps in kind, it
often exceeds them in degree. Indeed, "the glorious Alps
themselves, those wonders of the earth, could scarcely
compete in scenery with the views that nature lavished,
in that remote sea, on a seeming void." The "chiselled
marble" of the Alpine glaciers, marvelous though it is, is
not so impressive as the wonders of Antarctica:

Even the Alps, with all their peculiar grandeur, and certainly
on a scale so vastly more enlarged, possess no one aspect that is
so remarkable for its resemblance to the labors of man, composed of a material of the most beautiful transparency, and,
considered as the results of human ingenuity, on a scale so
gigantic. The glaciers have often been likened, and not un-
justly, to a frozen sea; but here were congealed mountains
seemingly hewed into all the forms of art, not by the chisel
it is true, but by the action of the unerring laws which produced them.[26]

Under the pressure of his continual comparison of Antarctica to the Swiss Alps, then, Cooper transfers the values
of the Alps, their power, their vastness, their beauty, and

their wonder, to his polar setting. But to Cooper the Alps were more than the supreme embodiment of earthly sublimity; they were a religious symbol, "the sublime altar that God has reared in his own honour." The contemplation of the Alpine terrain, "a world that bears about it, in every lineament, the very impression of its divine Creator," produced in him a state bordering on religious ecstasy: "it was impossible to look at [the Alps] without religious awe; and irreverent though it may seem, I could hardly persuade myself I was not gazing at some of the sublime mysteries that lie beyond the grave." At the same time, one could not confront the wild desolation of the upper reaches of the Alps without experiencing the complementary emotion, "an humbling sense of the dependence of man upon the grand and ceaseless Providence of God."[27] In the light of this attitude, it seems likely that Cooper's experience in Switzerland not only provided him with the means by which he could assimilate the raw material of his reading but helped to bring about the transformation of what might have been merely a realistic tale of a sealing expedition into a symbolic narrative, a narrative in which the action of the voyage and the detail of the setting function as an allegorical restatement of Roswell Gardiner's progress from impious pride in the human reason to a proper recognition of the feebleness of man and the majesty of God.

5

The peculiar meaning of his Alpine experience was only one of several inducements that Cooper had to expand the significance of his Antarctic narrative. No American writer of Cooper's day could have approached such a narrative without being aware of the existence of a literary convention which fixed the South Pole as the destination of the allegorical voyage. The journey to a

remote region where man can come in contact with a
reality more meaningful, more nearly absolute, than that
of ordinary life is, of course, as old as literature itself; but
influenced by Coleridge's *Ancient Mariner* and limited
by the fact that the South Pole was one of the few remaining unknown areas of the earth, American writers in the
first half of the nineteenth century came to regard Antarctica as the special province of symbolic fantasy. Thus,
in the course of a satire on Symmes's theory of concentric
spheres, the author of *Symzonia* (1820) sent his narrator,
an American sealing captain with a bent for exploration,
to the South Pole where he discovered a utopia whose
ruler, like Swift's King of Brobdingnag, was of the opinion
that men are "the most detestable reptiles" on the face
of the earth. In 1835 Cooper himself had chosen Antarctica as the antiutopian setting for an allegorical critique
of England and America, but "Peter Prospero," the pseudonymous author of "The Atlantis" (1838–1839), imagined the South Pole as a balmy paradise populated by the
spirits of the world's great thinkers. And as we have seen,
it was in the remote and mysterious world of Antarctica
that Poe set *The Narrative of Arthur Gordon Pym*, his attempt to fuse the allegorical structure of the traditional
imaginary voyage with the techniques and matter of the
modern sea novel. Different as these four works are, they
share a conception of the Antarctic as a place where events
have more than their common significance, a place which,
by its remoteness from everyday experience, sets man's
existence in a new and truer perspective.

If the fiction of the period depicted Antarctica as the
abode of fantasy and symbolic significance, the literature
of science and exploration conceived of the polar regions
in very different terms. It is ironic that J. N. Reynolds
should have been a source for Poe's dark and enigmatic
tales of Antarctic voyaging, for the buoyant scientific op-

timism of the early nineteenth century had no more articulate spokesman than Reynolds. He was confident that
the mysteries of Antarctica were about to enter the prosaic, daylight world of science, nationalism, and mercan-
tilism. "Who," he asked, "[is] so presumptuous as to set
limits to knowledge, which, by a wise law of Providence,
can never cease? As long as there is mind to act upon
matter, the realms of science must be enlarged." Reynolds
could easily envisage the day when an American flotilla
would "cast anchor on that point where all the meridians
terminate, where our eagle and star-spangled banner may
be unfurled and planted, and left to wave on the axis of
the earth itself!" His zeal for polar exploration was linked
with the irreverent commercialism that Cooper had always detested:

> A sober, business spirit is abroad, and neither Fauns nor
> Dryads can protect the grove when it is wanted for the saw or
> axe. It must fall if utility require the sacrifice. If any there be
> who mourn over these changes, we are not among them . . .
> It has not for years been difficult to discern the signs of
> the times. The watchword has been "onward!" and wonders
> exceeding the prodigies of ancient times have been the result.
> For the seven of olden time we can show an hundred, and
> these are but the earnest of our future achievements.[28]

But not even Reynolds could surpass Benjamin Morrell
in a jaunty confidence in the capabilities of the modern
mind. In his *Narrative of Four Voyages*, Morrell viewed
Antarctica as the arena in which science would win its
crowning triumph:

> Many enterprising navigators of the last and present cen-
> turies have made highly laudable, and some of them par-
> tially successful, attempts to penetrate the cloud of mystery
> which still hangs over the Antarctic seas. But every one has
> stopped at a certain point, timidly shrinking from the farther
> prosecution of what they deemed an impracticable project.
> Some, it is said, have even been deterred by a superstitious no-

tion that an attempt to reach the South Pole was a presumptuous intrusion on the awful confines of nature,—an unlawful
and sacrilegious prying into the secrets of the great Creator;
who, they contend, has guarded the "ends of the earth" with
an impassable bulwark of indissoluble ice; on which is written,
"Thus far shalt thou come, but no farther; and here thy
proud course be stayed." Such an idea would have become the
inquisitors of Spain in the days of Columbus.

Admitting for a moment, however, that such is the fact, and
that nothing less than a miracle could open the passage
through this formidable barrier, I contend that genius,
science, and energy combined can work miracles, and even
remove mountains; for what is a miracle but the power of
spirit over *matter*—the triumph of mind over physical im-
pediments. The march of intellect is irresistible; and were
the earth itself one globe of ice, the fire of genius, directed by
the wand of science, could melt a passage to its centre. The
day is not far distant when a visit to the South Pole will not
be thought more of a miracle than to cause an egg to stand
on its point.[29]

As a young man, Cooper had contemplated future polar
exploration with a similar faith in the power of the human
mind. He felt sure that "the time is approaching when we
are to prevail over the frozen barriers which have so
long hidden ten degrees of latitude from our investigation," for nature cannot halt "the march of knowledge";
the veil that conceals the "mysteries" of nature from "the
eye of theory" must fall at "the hands of enterprise and
perseverance."[30] By the time he wrote *The Sea Lions*,
however, his conception of man's place in the universe
had vastly changed. To Cooper in 1849, the "pride of
reason is one of the most insinuating of our foibles, and
is to be watched as a most potent enemy." In his preface
to *The Sea Lions*, he castigates "the want of a due sense
of humility," the exaggeration of the power and worth
of human reason, in words that seem to be a direct reply
to Morrell's cocky celebration of man's capabilities:

Very few men attain enough of human knowledge to be fully aware how much remains to be learned, and of that which they can never hope to acquire. We hear a great deal of god-like minds, and of the far-reaching faculties we possess; and it may all be worthy of our eulogiums, until we compare ourselves in these, as in other particulars, with Him who produced them. Then, indeed, the utter insignificance of our means becomes too apparent to admit of a cavil . . . Something that we cannot comprehend lies at the root of every distinct division of natural phenomena. Thus far shalt thou go and no farther, seems to be imprinted on every great fact of creation. There is a point attained in each and all of our acquisitions, where a mystery that no human mind can scan takes the place of demonstration and conjecture. This point may lie more remote with some intellects than with others; but it exists for all, arrests the inductions of all, conceals all.

In Cooper's mind, then, the icy barriers of Antarctica become the analogues of the mysteries which ultimately confront all rational inquiry and mark its farthest limits. In the narratives of the two most recent Antarctic expeditions, he found striking confirmation of his doctrine that "the most successful leaders of their fellow-men have had the clearest views of their own insufficiency to attain their own objects."[31] Wilkes's experience had revealed that nothing could guide the commander of men "in safety through, or shield from destruction those who have been entrusted to his charge, but the hand of an all-wise Providence."[32] Captain Ross had found that in moments of danger "comfort and peace of mind could only be obtained by casting our cares upon that Almighty Power which had already so often interposed to save us when human skill was wholly unavailing."[33] The lesson of man's explorations, whether physical or metaphysical, is the inadequacy of his means to achieve his ends.

In his Antarctic setting Cooper had the perfect field for the description of man's futile efforts to surpass his physical limitations; an equally specific instance of the attempt to push the human intellect beyond its capacities lay close at hand. The entry in Cooper's journal for March 5, 1848 (five days after the completion of the manuscript of *The Oak Openings* and a time when the novelist's mind must have been turning over the materials of his next work, *The Sea Lions*) records his reflections on reading the three epistles of St. John and the epistle of St. Jude: "The celebrated passage touching the divinity of Christ is so embedded in similar doctrine that it strikes me the whole chapter must go if these two verses go. But is not the entire new testament full of this doctrine? The pride of man makes him cavil at that which he cannot comprehend, while everything he sees has a mystery in it!"[34] It is thus, by objecting to a belief in the divinity of Christ, that Roswell Gardiner was to manifest his false estimate of the power and value of the human intellect. Mary Pratt sums up his error: " 'you worship your reason, instead of the only true and living God.' "[35] And in St. Jude's metaphorical description of those who deny the divinity of Christ, Cooper could find another link between the theme of his projected novel and its setting: they are "trees whose fruit withereth, without fruit, twice dead, plucked up by the roots;/Raging waves of the sea, foaming out their own shame; wandering stars, to whom is reserved the blackness of darkness for ever."[36] The pride of reason is equated with sterility, storm, and darkness: all primary properties of the appalling Antarctic winter.

6

As the most discerning of Cooper's critics have pointed out, all of his novels are informed by an interplay between the surface of the action and setting and an underlying moral vision; in the words of Marius Bewley, the incidents of Cooper's narratives, "exciting as they are considered simply as adventure tales, are merely the outward sign of a moral movement or pattern that makes up the real form of the novel."[37] But in the great bulk of Cooper's novels, that interplay is latent and general, while in *The Sea Lions,* as we shall see, it approaches the explicitness and particularity of allegory. No discussion of the origins of the novel would be complete without some attempt to account for the presence of that form, the means by which Cooper unites his realistic materials and his moral theme. Although the conventional literary treatment of Antarctica authorized some kind of symbolic narrative, it seems likely that the immediate suggestion for Cooper's choice of form came not from literature but from the work of the painter Thomas Cole.

Several recent studies have explored the relation of Cooper to the Hudson River school of painting in general and to Cole in particular. James F. Beard has traced Cooper's associations with his artistic contemporaries and indicated the resemblance of the novelist's scenic techniques to those of Cole.[38] Howard Mumford Jones has stressed the concern of Cooper and the members of the Hudson River group with common themes, one of which, "the grandeur of God working in the universe," occupies a central position in *The Sea Lions.*[39] Donald A. Ringe has found parallels in the work of Cole and Cooper which suggest that the painter may have exerted at least "an indirect or subconscious influence" on the writer.[40] Significantly, both of these parallels to the techniques of Cole occur in novels of the 1840's. In *Satanstoe* (1845) Cooper employs a series of contrasting landscapes to depict the English flotilla in attack and in retreat on Lake George, a device used by Cole in canvases like *Departure* and *Return* (1837). And in *The Crater* (1847), the immediate predecessor of *The Sea Lions,* Cooper not only states a theme closely related to the cyclical theory of history expressed in Cole's great series *The Course of Empire*

(1836), but also adopts Cole's use of a topographical reference point as a means of giving continuity to the description of drastic change. In this instance Cooper himself calls attention to the similarity between his technique and Cole's: the peak which alone marks the site of Woolston's colony "might be said to resemble . . . that sublime rock, which is recognized as a part of the 'everlasting hills,' in Cole's series of noble landscapes that is called 'The March of Empire;' ever the same amid the changes of time, and civilization, and decay."[41]

Both of these technical devices are used, though in a less striking manner, in *The Sea Lions*. The mountain and the volcano at Sealer's Land function as points of reference that identify the locale through the changes of the seasons. Contrasting views of the same scenes appear several times in the novel: the propitious departure of Gardiner's vessel from Oyster Pond and the arrival of "that tempest-tossed, crippled, ice-bound, and half-burned little craft" offer an obvious parallel to Cole's *Departure* and *Return;* the descriptions of the sealing camp at the beginning and at the end of winter serve to emphasize the "many marks of change, not to say of deterioration"; and the contrast between Gardiner's dismay at the sterile and forbidding aspect of Cape Horn during the outward passage and the relief he experiences on his way home at the sight of the landmark, which he now regards "as a sort of place of refuge," points up the terrors of the intervening months.[42] But the clearest indication of Cole's influence on *The Sea Lions* is not in these minor descriptive devices but in the design of the novel as a whole.

On January 6, 1849, at the very moment he was engaged in the composition of *The Sea Lions*,[43] Cooper took the time to write a brief appreciation of Cole at the request of Louis Noble, the painter's pastor and biographer. The novelist was glad to pay tribute to the man whom he considered "one of the very first geniuses of the age." In Cooper's judgment, *The Course of Empire* was "one of the noblest works of art that has ever been wrought"; indeed, "the day will come when . . . the series will command fifty thousand dollars." But he could not give the same degree of praise to all of Cole's works: "I do not place the more laboured allegorical landscapes of Cole as high as the Course of Empire. They are very fine pictures, and there is something noble in his constant efforts to unite the moral and the intellectual in landscape painting; but the first conception, I fancy, was produced most *con amore*."[44] The timing and the nature of this remark are intriguing: one recalls Cooper's dissatisfaction with a new English novel of manners, his boast that he could "write a better book than that," and his subsequent composition of *Precaution;* or his disappointment with Scott's lubberliness in *The Pirate,* his resolution "to show what can be done in this way by a sailor," and his composition of *The Pilot*.[45]

If any of Cole's works acted as a catalyst in the composition of *The Sea Lions,* it must have been the allegorical series entitled *The Voyage of Life* (1840), for these four canvases attempt within the context of a voyage to give symbolic expression to the very meanings which Cooper wished to attach to the voyage of the *Sea Lion*. In the first painting of the series a boat steered by an angelic form and bearing a laughing infant glides along a stream that issues from a deep cavern in the side of a mountain. In the second, the voyager, now a youth, guides the craft past the verdant banks of the river and gazes at a magnificent castle that rises in the distant sky. The third picture shows the boat rushing rudderless through the rapids of a ravine on its way to the ocean while the voyager, a middle-aged man, looks imploringly upward. In the fourth painting the shattered boat, now bearing an old man, sails over a gloomy ocean illuminated only by an opening in the clouds from which a procession of angels is descending. The second and third paintings are particularly relevant to *The Sea Lions,* for they depict that period in human experience, the evolution from youth to manhood, in which Roswell Gardiner is seen. In a descriptive guide to his work, Cole makes his meaning explicit. The voyager in the second painting "is now alone in the Boat, and takes the helm himself, and, in an attitude of confidence and eager expectation, gazes on a cloudy pile of Architecture, an air-built castle"; in its "aspirations after glory and fame," Youth "is forgetful that it is embarked on the Stream of Life, and that its current sweeps along with resistless force, and increases in swiftness, as it descends toward the great ocean of Eternity." The middle-aged voyager of the third painting gazes upward "as if heaven's aid alone could save him from the the perils that surround him," an act that "shows his dependence on a Superior Power; and *that* faith saves him from the destruction that seems inevitable."[46]

Blatant and hackneyed though Cole's allegory is, its intention must have held a peculiar interest for Cooper in the winter of 1848–1849, when Noble's request directed the writer's attention to the work of his great artistic contemporary. And because of its very clumsiness, *The Voyage of Life* may have prompted Cooper to attempt to unite successfully "the moral and the intellectual," to fuse his experience, his reading, and his religious convictions, in the crucible of *The Sea Lions.*

7

From origins as diverse as the works of Edmund Fanning and Thomas Cole, then, sprang Cooper's last sea novel. Although the total fabric of *The Sea Lions* rivals its origins in complexity, the thematic outlines of the novel can be traced rather simply. At the beginning of his voyage, Gardiner, like the figure in Cole's second canvas, is "young, active, and full of buoyancy," animated by "pride of profession, ambition . . . and the hardihood produced by experience in dangers often encountered and often escaped." "In the pride of his youth, strength, and, as he fancied, of his reason also," he doubts the divinity of Christ and puts his trust in his own powers. As he tells Daggett, " 'every man for himself in this world is a good maxim; it being pretty certain if we do not take care of ourselves, no one will take care of us.' "[47] Proud, capable, intelligent, well-intentioned, Gardiner is the kind of character that Cooper's early romances would have exalted, but here he is representative of the unregenerate natural man, the man whose talents, admirable though they may be, are misdirected, the man who can escape ultimate corruption only if he is born again into a realization of his true dependence upon an omnipotent God.

The forces working for Gardiner's regeneration during his long Antarctic ordeal are threefold. First, there is the influence of revelation in the form of the pocket Bible which Mary Pratt gives Gardiner at his departure "with an earnest request that he would not forget to consult its pages." Although Gardiner occasionally reads in the Bible during the succeeding months, he does not complete the program of study which Mary has laid out for him until the last four weeks of the winter at Sealer's Land; he is moved by his reading, but it alone is not sufficient to bring about his conversion: "There is a simple earnestness in the narrative portions of the Gospel that commends its truth to every mind, and it had its effect on that of Roswell Gardiner; though it failed to remove doubts that had so long been cherished, and which had their existence in pride of reason, or what passes for such, with those who merely skim the surface of things, as they seem to exist around them."[48]

But another force works to bring Gardiner to a clearer perception of reality, the pious admonitions of his constant companion, Stephen Stimson, for the old seaman from Kennebunk is the spokesman for religious as well as nautical authority. In the scheme of *The Sea Lions* he represents the power of simple faith, a faith which, being independent of education and intellect, "equalizes capacities, conditions, means, and ends, holding out the same encouragement and hope to the least, as to the most gifted of the race." Gardiner asks the old sealer whether his religious convictions stem from the teachings of his mother or from the influence of a parson: " 'My mother died afore I could listen to her talk, sir; and very little have I had to do with parsons, for the want of being where they are to be found. *Faith* tells me to believe this; and Faith comes from God.' "[49] Stimson's instinctive faith, of course, serves as the perfect foil for Gardiner's sophisticated doubts, but Stimson is more than a voice in the debate between belief and skepticism: he is the purest embodiment of Cooper's protean image of the seaman, that image which in some form enters into the composition of every portrait in the novelist's gallery of sailors, from Long Tom Coffin to Moses Marble. But, unlike his predecessors, Stimson is unalloyed by human failings: he never becomes angry, stubborn, or vengeful; he never blunders, never swears, never drinks, never even chews tobacco. He is as experienced in the intricacies of Antarctic navigation as Charles Wilkes, as zealous in religious matters as the apostles to whom he compares himself. The inevitable result is that Stimson becomes insufferable as, in Melville's words, he "discourses most unctuously upon various dogmas."[50]

It seems likely that the inordinate idealization of Stimson, the most annoying flaw in *The Sea Lions,* results from Cooper's inability to convey to the reader the full weight of the significance which the character held for him. During his youthful voyage in the *Sterling,* he had sailed with "a gigantic fellow from Kennebunk," a seaman named Steven Stimpson.[51] Thirty-eight years later the name turns up again in *Afloat and Ashore* in the roster of the brig *Sea Otter.*[52] The way the name seems to have haunted Cooper's imagination suggests that perhaps for him Stimpson was the archetypal seaman, a figure of immense strength and stature, but the unfortunate fact remains that none of these private associations, if indeed they did exist, find public expression in the Stimson of *The Sea Lions.*

But if Stimson merely annoys the reader, he has a powerful effect upon Roswell Gardiner: although "Stephen was no great logician," Newton himself "possessed no clearer demonstration of any of his problems than this simple, nay ignorant, man enjoyed in his religious faith, through the divine illumination it had received in the visit of the Holy Spirit." As the winter at Sealer's Land draws to a close and Gardiner completes his study of the Bible, Stimson holds an earnest conversation with his captain in which he points out that " 'we know too little of a thousand things to set up our weak judgments in the very face of revelation.' " Gardiner is struck by Stimson's arguments, and faith, "the great law of regeneration," begins to rout his proud skepticism.[53]

By far the most important cause of Gardiner's conversion, however, is the steady and overwhelming influence of his Antarctic environment. From one point of view, *The Sea Lions* may be regarded primarily as a fictional expansion of the proposition which Cooper sets forth in his preface, that the contemplation of the sublime phenomena of nature should fill our minds "with a proper sense of the power of the dread Being that created all" by leading us to a "due estimate of our own insignificance, as compared with the majesty of God."[54] In Cooper's early romances and in the work of writers like Peterson and Clark, natural sublimity is valued chiefly for its emotional effects, its capacity to produce awe and delight; ultimately, too, it serves to ennoble man, who gains stature by his association with his titanic environment and by his combat with his elemental antagonists. But in *The Sea Lions* natural sublimity as an end in itself is of secondary importance; Cooper's primary concern is with the implications of nature: its function as a demonstration of the power of the God who controls it, as a token of the qualities of the God who created it, and as man's means of access to that God.

The terrific world of Antarctica offers the sealers a continual demonstration of the divine power working through nature and of the corollary feebleness of man, a demonstration that Cooper does not hesitate to render thoroughly explicit. When, for example, Daggett's schooner is crushed by the ice floe, "then it was that the vast superiority of nature over the resources of man made itself apparent. The people of the two vessels stood aghast with this sad picture of their own insignificance before their eyes." But nature is not only the agent of God; it can be interpreted as a kind of moral allegory, for the individual natural phenomenon is a microcosmic emblem of the order and operation of the universe. Thus the sea instructs mariners in the fundamental facts of reality: "Its vastness reminds them of the time that has neither beginning nor end; its ceaseless movement, of the never-tiring impulses of human passions; and its accidents and dangers, of the Providence which protects all alike, and

which alone prevents our being abandoned to the dominion of chance."⁵⁵

The third function of nature, its service as an inter-
mediary between man and God, is given its fullest statement in the account of Gardiner's conversion. Impressive
as his readings in the Bible and his talks with Stimson
have been, Gardiner's great change of heart is accomplished by the "influence of those whisperings of the
Divine Spirit" which come to him as he walks in the
star-filled Antarctic night: "The night was coming in cold
and still. It was one of those last efforts of winter in which
all the terrible force of the season was concentrated . . .
The moon was young, but the stars gave forth a brightness
that is rarely seen, except in the clear cold nights of a high
latitude. Each and all of these sublime emblems of the
power of God were twinkling like bright torches glowing
in space." But the stars are more than the symbols of the
divine illumination that pierces the dark night of Gardiner's soul; the contemplation of them produces an experience that is nearly mystical in its sudden revelation
of the true relationship of God and man. The mind has
only to endow each star "with its probable or known
dimensions, its conjectural and reasonable uses, to form
a picture of the truest sublimity in which man is made
to occupy his real position"; Gardiner has never before
"been made so conscious of his own insignificance" as he
becomes "while looking on the firmament that night, glowing with its bright worlds and suns, doubtless the centres
of other systems in which distance swallowed up the lesser
orbs." Coming as it does "after so much reading, so many
conversations with Stephen, and addressing itself to one
whose heart was softened by the fearful circumstances that
had so long environed the sealers," the appearance of the
emblematic Southern Cross overhead produces a deep

impression on Gardiner's mind and marks the beginning of his epiphanal hour:

The hour that succeeded was probably the most important in Roswell Gardiner's life. So intense were his feelings, so active the workings of his mind, that he was quite insensible to the intensity of the cold; and his body keeping equal motion with his thoughts, if one may so express it, his frame actually set at defiance a temperature that might otherwise have chilled it, warmly and carefully as it was clad.

Truly there were many causes existing at that time and place, to bring any man to a just sense of his real position in the scale of created beings. The vault above Roswell was sparkling with orbs floating in space, most of them far more vast than this earth, and each of them doubtless having its present or destined use. What was that light, so brilliant and pervading throughout space, that converted each of those masses of dark matter into globes clothed with glorious brightness? Roswell had seen chemical experiments that produced wonderful illuminations; but faint, indeed, were the most glowing of those artificial torches, to the floods of light that came streaming out of the void, on missions of millions and millions of miles. Who, and what was the Dread Being —dread in his Majesty and Justice, but inexhaustible in Love and Mercy—who used these exceeding means as mere instruments of his pleasure?

The clearest evidence of Gardiner's "new-born faith," and one of its most significant consequences, is that he is now able to comprehend the full import of natural phenomena. On the passage homeward, his vessel must brush by the base of an active volcano:

A dozen times the Sea Lion had very narrow escapes when nearest to the danger, stones of a weight to pass through her decks and bottom falling even on the ice outside of her; but that Hand which had so benevolently stayed various other evils, was stretched forth to save, and nothing touched the schooner of a size to do any injury. These escapes made a deep impression on Roswell. Until the past winter he had been accustomed to look upon things and events as matters of course. This vacant indifference, so common to men in prosperity, was extended even to the sublimest exhibition of the Almighty power; our hero seeing nothing in the firmament of heaven, of a clear night, but the twinkling lights that seemed to him to be placed there merely to garnish and illumine the darkness of this globe. Now, how differently did he look upon natural objects, and their origin! If it were only an insect, his mind presented its wonderful mechanism, its beauty, its uses. No star seemed less than what science has taught us that it is; and the power of the Dread Being who had created all, who governed all, and who was judge of all, became an inseparable subject of contemplation, as he looked upon the least of his works.[56]

The process of Gardiner's conversion, the role played by natural sublimity in it, and the new vision of nature it effects, then, form the core of *The Sea Lions*. If the novel as a whole is approached from this center, the reader may be able to perceive a greater depth and unity in it than is indicated by Grossman's judgment that the religious content of the book is an insignificant but annoying excrescence on an otherwise skillful and stirring adventure story or by Alexander Cowie's converse opinion that in *The Sea Lions* a dull and inferior narrative "is harnessed to some interesting disquisitions on the theme of Unitarianism as opposed to Trinitarianism."[57] Whatever the reader's evaluation of the religious content or the narrative of the novel may be, he will see that neither is one a superfluous appendage to the other nor are they yoked arbitrarily together; on the contrary, he will see that the primary function of nearly every element of the narrative is to reinforce or to restate Cooper's great theme of regeneration.

8

Among those elements which help to deepen and expand Cooper's expression of his theme is the setting of the novel. The narrative opens in Oyster Pond, a village occupying "a long, low, fertile, and pleasant reach of land" at the eastern end of Long Island; the season is "the delightful month of September, when the earlier promises of the year are fast maturing into performance." Everything about Oyster Pond is on a small and comfortable scale, homely, fertile, and abundant:

Although Suffolk, as a whole, can scarcely be deemed a productive county, being generally of a thin, light soil, and still covered with a growth of small wood, it possesses, nevertheless, spots of exceeding fertility. A considerable portion of the northern prong of the fork has this latter character, and Oyster Pond is a sort of garden compared with much of the sterility that prevails around it. Plain but respectable dwellings, with numerous out-buildings, orchards, and fruit-trees, fences carefully preserved, a pains-taking tillage, good roads, and here and there a "meeting-house," gave the fork an air of rural and moral beauty . . . In a word, both the season and the place were charming, though most of the flowers had already faded; and the apple, and the pear, and the peach, were taking the places of the inviting cherry. Fruit abounded, notwithstanding the close vicinity of the district to salt water, the airs from the sea being broken, or somewhat tempered, by the land that lay to the southward.

Deacon Pratt's house, the locale of most of the action in the early portions of the novel, is in keeping with the verdant comfort of the general scene: "it stood on the edge of a fine apple-orchard, having a door-yard of nearly two acres in its front. This door-yard, which had been twice mown that summer, was prettily embellished with flowers, and was shaded by four rows of noble cherry trees"; altogether, an "unusually inviting" residence, set in "a smiling and fertile" landscape. Everywhere in his descriptions of Oyster Pond Cooper stresses its productivity, its abundance of food: its inhabitants send their surplus of "pigs and poultry, butter and eggs," to market in New York City; from its harbors are drawn eight- or ten-pound sheepsheads like the one that provides a "feast" at the Deacon's table.[58]

Oyster Pond is indeed "a spot as much favored by Divine Providence, in the way of abundance, as any other in highly-favored America," but like the Clawbonny of Miles Wallingford's youth, it presents a distorted image of reality. Just as Oyster Pond is sheltered from the blighting sea wind, so is it insulated from the sterner truths of existence, truths that Roswell Gardiner can encounter only when his vessel has "cast off the last ligaments which [connect] her with the land."[59] For the life of the village offers that kind of security which permits man merely to "skim the surface of things," that kind of prosperity which promotes a "vacant indifference" to the sublime manifestations of God's power.

The world to which Gardiner's voyage takes him presents a stark contrast to the tidy life of Oyster Pond. "Sterility, and a chill grandeur," Cooper tells us, "were the characteristics of all that region": a sterility that echoes the poverty and barrenness of Gardiner's skepticism; a grandeur that emanates from "the might and honor of God." Over and over Cooper's descriptive phrases reiterate these two characteristics and stress the contrast between Antarctica and Oyster Pond. If the topography of Oyster Pond is verdant, gentle, and inviting, that of the polar regions is "barren, rugged, inhospitable." If Oyster Pond offers society and abundance, Antarctica is a land of "solitude, desolation, want." If the aspect of Oyster Pond is smiling and secure, that of the Antarctic is "gloomy and menacing." But as Gardiner pursues his "pathless journey," he discovers sublimity as well as sterility. Standing on the "stern and imposing" peak of Cape Horn, he gazes on the "grand spectacle" formed by the meeting of the Atlantic, Pacific, and Antarctic oceans. Within "the mysterious depths of the antarctic circle," still more magnificent scenes meet his eye: "the striking and majestic" peak of Sealer's Land; the stately progress of an ice field, a motion that is slow but "absolutely grand, by its steadiness and power"; and the strange appearance of a group of icebergs, a "mysterious-looking, fantastical, yet sublime city of the ocean."[60]

This desolate and awesome environment plays its part, as we have seen, in working Gardiner's regeneration. On the morning after his epiphanal experience, the young sealing master discovers that a thaw has set in, bringing with it torrents of rain; every symptom is that of "settled spring." The balmy weather that follows the downpour has a "highly cheering and enlivening" effect on the men and gradually frees Sealer's Land from the grip of the ice and snow. Another severe rainstorm drenches the island, the thermometer rises to seventy, and summer appears "to have come in reality." As Gardiner prepares to sail for home, he notices that the rain has washed away all traces of Daggett's body and the carcasses of the seals; "in a word, the rocks were as naked and as clean as if man's foot had never passed over them."[61] Thus the end of Gardiner's long physical ordeal coincides with the moment of his spiritual rebirth, and the site of that rebirth is cleansed of all remnants of the greed which had inspired his voyage.

The extreme care with which *The Sea Lions* is constructed can be illustrated by tracing Cooper's handling of a single feature of his setting, the vast herds of seals that form the principal object of Gardiner's voyage. Before the arrival of the schooners, the seals are plentiful and tame; although they are of many different species, they live in perfect harmony. But to the Deacon, these symbols of the vitality, abundance, and order of nature exist only to be destroyed: "A man might walk in their midst without giving the smallest alarm. In a word, all that a gang of good hands would have to do, would be to kill, and skin, and secure the oil. It would be like picking up dollars on a sea-beach." To Gardiner and Daggett, too, the seals are merely potential sources of wealth, and they begin a systematic slaughter of the unresisting animals as soon as they reach Sealer's Land. With the start of the long Antarctic winter, however, the seals suddenly vanish; to the seamen, this is the first portent of the suffering they are about to undergo: " 'The seals are off, and that is a sign that *we* should be off, too. There's my explanation, and you may make what you please of it. Natur' gives sich hints, and no prudent seaman ought to overlook 'em. I say, that when the seal go, the sealers should go likewise.' " After the departure of the seals, no vestige of natural life remains on the island. The terrifying sterility of the place is pointed up by the ironic appearance of an ice field as it grinds against the shore:

It was an extraordinary sight to see the coast along which our party was hastening, just at that moment. As the cakes of ice were broken from the field, they were driven upward by the vast pressure from without, and the whole line of the shore seemed as if alive with creatures that were issuing from the ocean to clamber on the rocks. Roswell had often seen that very coast peopled with seals, as it now appeared to be in activity with fragments of ice, that were writhing, and turning, and rising, one upon another, as if possessed of the vital principle.

Within a week after Gardiner's conversion, however, the seals return to the island, an event which the sealers interpret as "a favorable augury," and which produces "a deep impression on Roswell Gardiner." The voyagers have learned their lesson: "These animals no longer awakened cupidity in the breasts of the sealers. The last no longer thought of gain, but simply of saving their lives,

and of restoring themselves to the humble places they had
held in the world, previously to having come on this ill-
fated voyage."[62] In this one detail, Cooper thus restates
in symbolic terms the main elements of his theme: man's
sinful pride and greed, the consequent sterility and desolation of his spirit, and the revivifying humility that comes
with a proper understanding of his place in the universe.[63]

9

In their relation to the theme of the novel, the characters of *The Sea Lions* are as carefully contrived as the setting. For once, Cooper resists the impulse to glorify the
professional attainments of his seamen. If Moses Marble
was not suited by temperament to the command of a vessel,
he was still a superb seaman, but Gardiner and Daggett
fall far short of a complete mastery of their profession.
Gardiner is deficient "in many attainments that mark the
thorough sea-dog"; he knows "little of the finesse of his
calling" and is "wanting in that in-and-in breeding which
converts habit into an instinct." Similarly, Daggett belongs
to that class of men who are "sailors without being seamen, in the severe signification of the term." And even
Stimson owes his authority to his moral superiority and
to his long experience in Antarctic navigation rather than
to a strictly professional excellence. For all his shortcom-
ings, Gardiner is "the best man in his little craft in nearly
every respect"; Stimson is "probably the next best seaman, after the master."[64] There is good reason for Cooper's refusal to characterize the technical skill of the sailors
of *The Sea Lions* in his customary unqualified superla-
tives. The realistic surface of the narrative demands, of
course, a relatively subdued tone, but, more than that,
the whole intention of the novel is to magnify the power
of God and minimize the abilities of man. This is no oc-

casion for the celebration of seamanship, the mastery of which can even lend dignity for a time to a figure as villainous as Stephen Spike.

But characterization in *The Sea Lions* not only harmonizes with Cooper's theme; in the person of Jason Daggett, the master of the schooner from Martha's Vineyard, it forms an integral part of the expression of that theme. If Daggett's function in the novel is overlooked, Gardiner's ordeal and the drama of his regeneration seem inordinately drastic consequences of failings as mild as his; he is, after all, a good fellow who, in Lounsbury's phrase, "merely denied the divinity of Christ, while he professed to hold him in reverence as the purest and most exalted of men."[65] Daggett, on the other hand, is clearly evil, a brutalized hypocrite whose only motive is greed. Appropriate though his name is to a native of the Vineyard, it seems to have been in Cooper's imagination a symbol of avarice, for the greedy usurper of Clawbonny in *Afloat and Ashore* is also called Daggett. But the Daggett of *The Sea Lions* does not serve as a villainous foil for an inoffensive Gardiner; rather, Cooper insists throughout the novel on the bonds that link the two characters together, on the resemblances between them. Indeed, so compelling is this steady process of equation that Gardiner and Daggett nearly merge into a single identity; their sins, Cooper seems to be saying, are equivalent, their guilt is the same.

From the start of the voyage, Gardiner finds himself forced into an association with Daggett. His duty to the Deacon demands that he shake off Daggett, and yet the very fact that he is pursuing the Deacon's mission of greed makes it impossible for him to escape the Vineyarder. Although their relationship oscillates between the poles of friendly cooperation and savage rivalry, a strengthening web of mutual obligations and shared experience steadily draws the two men closer together. When Gardiner loses a spar in the storm off Cape Hatteras and Daggett stands by to aid him, he is compelled to "express to Daggett a sense of the obligations he felt for the services the other had rendered." Daggett is quick to exploit Gardiner's feelings: " 'I like good-fellowship,' " he tells Gardiner; " 'when men have gone through such trials in company,' " they stick by each other. Gardiner has "not the smallest suspicion of the true motive of all this apparent good-fellowship:" " 'I really wish you would now quit me,' " he naïvely tells Daggett, but Daggett " 'couldn't think of it.' " Conscious of his debt to Daggett's "kindness," Gardiner agrees to continue southward in company with the vessel from Martha's Vineyard.[66]

In the whaling episode the equation of Gardiner and Daggett is made more explicit. In this brief bit of action, the movements of the two masters precisely parallel each other, as if they were performing some intricate and perfectly balanced dance. At the first sight of the whales, the boats of Gardiner and Daggett hit the water "about the same time." The two men see the whales reappear "at the same instant." When they fasten to the same whale, their crews perform precisely the same evolutions, letting out and hauling in the line in unison. At the moment of the kill, Gardiner and Daggett strike identical poses: "the two masters stood erect on their respective clumsy cleets, each poising his lance, waiting only to get near enough to strike." They hurl their lances "at the same instant," both weapons penetrating to the vitals of the whale, and "both crews [are] delighted to see the red of the blood mingling its deep hues with the white of the troubled water." Once again the two men match their movements as the ritual reaches a climax: "Gardiner and Daggett met, face to face, on the carcase of the whale. Each struck his lance into the blubber, steadying himself by its handle; and each eyed the other in a way that betokened feelings awakened by a keen desire to defend his rights."[67]

Although the controversy is resolved without violence, the pretense of friendship is shattered, and Gardiner is more determined than ever to elude his "pertinacious companion." The passage around Staten Land gives him his chance to escape, but as he prepares to sail alone into the Antarctic Ocean, he begins to question the wisdom of his action: "More than once, that morning, did our hero regret he had not entered into terms with the Vineyard men, that the effort might have been made in company. There was something so portentous in a lone vessel's venturing within the ice, in so remote a region, that, to say the truth, Roswell hesitated." By the time he reaches Sealer's Land, Gardiner is ready to admit that "it might be a good thing to have a consort in the event of any accident occurring to his own vessel." When Daggett's schooner does make its appearance, Gardiner's men, "so far from home, and in their imminently perilous condition," are greatly encouraged "to know that a countryman and a friend [is] so near them, to afford shelter and protection." In an overflow of good fellowship, the two masters forget "all feelings of competition and rivalry." When Daggett breaks his leg, Gardiner pledges that " 'the two vessels shall stick together,' " and resigns himself to the fact that "the necessities of the Vineyarders would seem to chain him to their fate."[68]

Like the whaling episode, the scene on the mountain top at Sealer's Land gives Cooper the opportunity to enforce the identity of Gardiner and his "brother-master." Of all the objects in the magnificent view, Daggett " 'likes its abundance of seal the most of all,' " and his imagination feeds "the lust of gold" that is "strong within him." While Daggett, "an intensely covetous man," dreams of profits, Gardiner's thoughts dwell on the "youthful beauty" of Mary Pratt. Different though the thoughts of Daggett and Gardiner seem, the substance of Stimson's contemplation reveals their common error:

And what was that rugged, uncultivated seaman, who stood near the two officers, thinking of, all this time? Did he, too, bend his thoughts on love, and profit, and the pleasures of this world? Of love, most truly, was his heart full to over-flowing; but it was the love of God, with that affection for all his creatures, that benevolence and faith, which glow as warmly in the hearts of the humblest and least educated, as in those of the great and learned. His mind was turned toward his Creator, and it converted the extraordinary view that lay before his sight into a vast, magnificent, gorgeous, though wild temple, for his worship and honor.[69]

Both Daggett and Gardiner are unregenerate; both are occupied with "the pleasures of this world"; and both are incapable of that deeply religious response to natural sublimity which, for Cooper, signifies the true perception of reality.

During the last weeks of the winter at Sealer's Land, Gardiner and Daggett gradually grow apart; as Daggett withdraws into the seclusion of the wreck and Gardiner devotes his time to the study of the Bible and to his talks with Stimson, "the connection [that] had been strangely continued" begins to weaken. At the epiphanal moment, just as Gardiner's heart is "warming with the new-born faith," he hears a shriek from Daggett's camp: "There was a strain of agony in the cry, as if he who made it uttered it in despair. Roswell's blood seemed to flow back to his heart; never had he before felt so appalling a sense of the dependence of man on a Divine Providence, as at that moment." Setting out for the wreck with the feeling that he is "now enlisted in the most important undertaking of his whole life," Gardiner discovers that the Vineyarders have let their fire go out. Stimson, appropriately, kindles a new blaze, but the warmth it generates does not come in time to save the dying Daggett. The sight of the dead gives Gardiner a new conception of "the majesty and judgment of God" and renders his estimate of himself "humbled and searching"; the burial of Daggett produces a particularly strong impression: "When Roswell Gardiner saw this man, who had so long adhered to him, like a leech, in the pursuit of gold, laid a senseless corpse among the frozen flakes of the antarctic seas, he felt that a lively admonition of the vanity of the world was administered to himself." The same night that brings new life to Gardiner brings death to Daggett, and the link between the two men is finally severed. The regenerate Gardiner is permitted to return home and to retire to an inland county, far from the ocean; Daggett's body, like that of Spike, is swept out to sea.[70]

10

By far the boldest instance of Cooper's expansion of the meaning of his narrative occurs in his treatment of the vessels in *The Sea Lions,* for the two schooners are the exact counterparts of their masters, Gardiner and Daggett. The plots of several of the earlier novels contain a double movement: in *The Red Rover* Wilder's quest for familial identity parallels the Rover's quest for national identity; in *The Bravo* Antonio's search for his grandson is elaborately balanced against the Duke's search for Violetta; and in *The Two Admirals* Tom Wycherly's pretensions to the Wychecombe estate are set against Prince Charlie's pretensions to the throne of England. But the use of ships as counterparts of characters had been only vaguely suggested before. As we have noticed, Ludlow's pursuit of Alida in *The Water-Witch* seems to be reflected in the pursuit of the brigantine by the man-of-war, and James Grossman has suggested that in *Homeward Bound* the corvette stands in the same relationship to the *Montauk* as Steadfast Dodge does to the Effinghams.[71] Yet these last two instances of parallelism are so little insisted upon that one would hesitate to ascribe them to any conscious design. In *The Sea Lions,* however, the correspondence between the two schooners and the two leading characters is rendered in such explicit detail that the novel seems a partial fulfillment of Cooper's earlier intention to write a tale "in which ships would be the only actors."[72]

The primary function of the two schooners in *The Sea Lions* is to reinforce the resemblance between Gardiner and Daggett before Gardiner's conversion. If this function is not recognized, Cooper's use of two vessels having precisely the same name and appearance seems only a source of gratuitous confusion.[73] In every other narrative centering on the synchronous movements of a pair of vessels, he takes pains to establish a distinct identity for each craft. Thus he employs a small schooner and a large, full-rigged frigate in *The Pilot;* a merchant brigantine and a full-rigged sloop of war in *The Water-Witch;* a packet ship and a sloop of war in *Homeward Bound;* a felucca and a frigate in *Wing-and-Wing;* and a brigantine and a full-rigged corvette in *Jack Tier.* In every case the vessels are differentiated by either size, rig, or function and, of course, always by name. But in *The Sea Lions* the two vessels are identical in every detail: they are fore-topsail sealing schooners of the same dimensions and tonnage; they are painted in the same way; and they have figureheads so nearly alike that, as Daggett remarks, " 'if they lay in a ship-yard, side by side, I don't think you could tell them apart.' " Even the performance of the two schooners is the same: "there was nothing remarkable in the fact that two vessels, built for the same trade, should have a close general resemblance to each other; but it was not common to find them so moulded, stowed, sparred, and handled, that their rate of sailing should be nearly identical."[74] Cooper obviously intends the identities of his twin *Sea Lions* to merge and, by so merging, to stress the equation of Gardiner and Daggett.

The symbolic relationship of the schooners to their masters becomes still more apparent as the moment of Gardiner's epiphany approaches. The wreck of the *Sea Lion* from Martha's Vineyard foreshadows Daggett's own destruction, but still the resemblance between the two vessels continues. Daggett's resistance to Gardiner's suggestion that the wreck be used as firewood forces the men from Oyster Pond to saw away the upper works of their vessel for fuel; "to render the obstinacy of the other crew more apparent, Daggett had been obliged to do the same!" But with Gardiner's conversion and the return of spring, the resemblance between the schooners ends, just as the connection between their masters is broken. Supplying himself with materials taken from the wreck, Gardiner begins to ready his vessel for sea. The job of reconstruction closely parallels his own spiritual experience, for he has "no idea of rebuilding his schooner strictly in her old form and proportions":

If the upper frame that was now got on the Sea Lion was not of a faultless mould, it was securely fastened, and rendered the craft even stronger than it had been originally. Some regard was had to resisting the pressure of ice, and experience had taught all the sealers where the principal defences against the effects of a "nip" ought to be placed. The lines were not perfect, it is true; but this was of less moment, as the bottom of the craft, which alone had any material influence on her sailing, was just as it had come from the hands of the artisan who had originally moulded her.

The correspondence between the physical reconstruction of the *Sea Lion* and the spiritual reconstruction of her master is ingeniously developed. At no point does the outermost layer of Cooper's meaning conflict with the realistic surface of his narrative, but the reader who has been alerted to the symbolic tendencies of the novel cannot miss the implied comparison of the rough and ready rebuilding of the upperworks to the extraordinary alteration of Gardiner's philosophy; of the experience which teaches the necessity and the means of strengthening the craft to Gardiner's "many lessons in humility, the most useful of all the lessons that man can receive in connection with the relation that really exists between the Deity and himself"; and of the excellent and undamaged underbody of the vessel to the unaltered moral impulses of Gardiner, impulses that had retained their original purity through all the errors into which his intellect had led him.[75]

When the *Sea Lion,* " 'a craft cut down and reduced,' " returns to Oyster Pond, Mary Pratt, who had vowed that she would never take Gardiner as her husband so long as he remained " 'unchanged,' " does not recognize the vessel: " 'that schooner does not look, to me, like the Sea Lion.' "[76] Fortunately, Gardiner is as much changed as his vessel, and at last Mary can accept him.

Before *The Sea Lions* Cooper had made two symbolic uses of his ships. In the early romances, particularly *The Water-Witch,* the vessel represents a way of life, a life in which freedom, wildness, and self-fulfillment are the paramount values. When the ship functions symbolically in the more realistic novels of Cooper's middle period, it becomes a microcosm of society, a miniature community of interest and effort whose members perform diversified and specialized roles within a hierarchical social structure. But in *The Sea Lions* the ship is a vehicle for neither the romantic celebration of wildness nor the realistic criticism of society. The two schooners are never the objects of ennobling metaphors or extensive descriptions that emphasize the qualities of speed, grace, and unreal lightness, nor do they ever offer any useful lessons in the discipline and government of large bodies of men. Rather, as we have seen, the ship exists to parallel and reiterate the experience of the human agents in the narrative. In a sense, Cooper's technique in *The Sea Lions* is an extension of the process of animation that had always informed his treatment of the ship, for now the vessel, once a sea bird on the wing or a fiery charger, has achieved the status of a character. The appearance, qualities, and actions of the ship no longer exist merely to satisfy the requirements of the plot; they play an integral and important part in the expression of the ultimate meaning of the novel.

It is difficult to exaggerate the significance of *The Sea Lions* in the evolution of nautical fiction. As the sea novel had taken shape in Cooper's hands during the 1820's, it depended for its primary interest upon the exotic environment and way of life it depicted; its value resided in its very remoteness from common experience. It was a literature of escape, a literature which, like Cooper's magical brigantine in *The Water-Witch*, offered the possibility of a flight from the pressures and restrictions of reality. Although the more realistic treatment accorded the sea in the fiction of the 1830's and early 1840's began to reveal that brutality, ugliness, and drudgery were as much a part of maritime life as freedom, beauty, and achievement, it still relied heavily on the exploitation of the singularity of the seaman's existence. If maritime life was no longer to be idealized, it nevertheless remained peculiar and unfamiliar, and it needed to be exposed, recorded, and preserved to its last strange detail. From this concern with the separateness of maritime life from common experience, the sea novel in England did not free itself until the appearance of Conrad. In America, however, the attempt to make the sea novel serve as a vehicle for meanings of universal relevance began much earlier. For all the diffuseness and uncertainty of Poe's *Arthur Gordon Pym,* its narrative continually verges on the borders of themes as universal as birth and death. And in Cooper's *Afloat and Ashore* the reader comes to understand with Miles Wallingford that maritime life offers no real escape from life on land, that the meaning of experience does not vary with man's environment. But *The Sea Lions* represents the first complete liberation of the sea novel from the notion that its principal function is the depiction of a special realm of experience. Although Cooper's narrative, unlike those of such pure allegories as Melville's *Mardi* (1849) or his own *The Monikins,* remains firmly embedded in a matrix of concrete plausibility, the reader's attention is never focused on the uniqueness of the sailor, the ship, and the ocean; rather, the seaman becomes the representative of all men, and his environment becomes an analogue of the condition of all human existence.

THE VOYAGE OF LIFE

Chapter VII

A Literary Leviathan

EPILOGUE

THE YEAR 1850 customarily serves marine historians as a bench mark in their record of the maritime experience of the American people, for the date is a convenient point at which to fix the start of the abrupt decline of American nautical activity and interest, a decline that reduced the United States from supremacy in many of the most important areas of commerce and shipping to near extinction as a maritime power in the years following the Civil War. In 1835 an observer as discerning as Tocqueville could prophesy with confidence that Americans would "one day become the foremost maritime power of the globe," because "they are born to rule the seas, as the Romans were to conquer the world";[1] by 1850 it was becoming apparent that the day would be long postponed.

For the most part, Americans now made their choice between two conceptions that had hitherto seemed equally attractive as routes to national greatness, the notion of a mercantile empire founded on command of the sea and the notion of an agrarian empire founded on the occupation and exploitation of the American continent.[2] A cluster of events occurring about mid-century caused the inland course of empire to become the dominant one in the American imagination. The war with Mexico, which both expressed and stimulated the imperialistic ambitions of the nation, had brought about an enormous and easy expansion of the national territory and, in marked contrast to the War of 1812, had exalted the army, rather than the navy, as the prime instrument of national power. The discovery of gold in California in 1848 made the continent seem as fertile ground for personal riches as it was for national wealth, a source of fortunes far larger and more sudden than the sea had ever offered. The increasing seriousness of the controversy over slavery turned the attention of Americans from commercial and naval competition with Great Britain to the tensions and rivalries within their own national boundaries. The effect of these events, when added to that of the accelerating shift of the center of population westward, away from the sea and its concerns, and to that of the increasing preoccupation of the older maritime states with the problems and profits of industrialization, was to produce, as the marine historian Carl Cutler has pointed out, a deepening national apathy to maritime affairs, even to the achievements of the marvelous clipper ships:

America, which had been sea-minded for two centuries, was nautically decadent in 1855. By 1860 the process could go little farther. There was an utter lack of anything resembling public interest in matters pertaining to shipbuilding or in the exploits of the ships themselves. New records escaped notice entirely or obtained a scant paragraph in almost unreadable marine columns instead of bold faced editorials on the news page.[3]

An inevitable result of this distraction of the American public from maritime life was a sharp decline in the market for sea fiction. As we have seen, nautical short stories began to deteriorate in quality in the late 1840's, when writers like Judson came to monopolize their production; but now they rapidly fell off in quantity as well, their place in the magazines usurped by the increasingly popular sentimental and domestic tales. Although the dime novels, unlike the magazines, sturdily resisted the trend toward the feminine, their contents offer striking evidence of the shift in interest from the sea to the continental frontier, for more and more in the years after 1850 the romantic young naval lieutenants, the Byronic pirates, and the homely old salts were shouldered from their pages by a swelling horde of fearless plainsmen, bloodthirsty Indians, and villainous Mexicans. Only in the field of the serious novel, and there only in the work of Herman Melville, did American sea fiction show continued energy and development. But Melville's work, like the great clipper ships which were its contemporaries, was something of a historical anomaly, the last, magnificent flowering of a plant that was dying at the roots.[4]

Only this sudden withering of American sea fiction and of the popular interest in maritime affairs can account for the extraordinary neglect which Cooper's nautical writings have encountered since his death. During his lifetime, his sea fiction was often considered his major literary achievement. His friend Charles Wilkes felt that in his early nautical romances Cooper had found his true vein; he assured the novelist that, like Britannia in Campbell's ballad, " 'your path is on the mountain wave' and your home is on the deep."[5] To the *Democratic Review,* Cooper was "our great naval novelist," a writer whose sea scenes had "made his reputation." The *Southern Literary Messenger* announced that "the open, the grand, and stirring sea" was Cooper's proper "element of fiction," his "forte." Even the usually hostile *North American Review* found words of praise for the sea novels: the ocean was Cooper's "favorite element," the quarter-deck was "his home"; all could agree that his "boldest and most triumphant march was on the mountain wave," and few could doubt that upon his sea novels his reputation would "ultimately depend." The *Knickerbocker,* too, added its voice to the chorus: "give our author 'the great and wide sea,' and he rides thereon like a literary leviathan."⁶

In the years since Cooper's death, however, his sea novels have been all but forgotten. The general reader, remembering a distant and brief encounter with *The Last of the Mohicans,* is content with the notion that Cooper is exclusively a delineator of the life of the forest frontier. In academic circles, although the work of Parrington and Spiller has expanded the image of Cooper to include his role as a social critic, that image remains for the most part the one created by Lounsbury, who wrote his biography of the novelist at a time when American interest in maritime affairs had reached its lowest point and when the westward movement was reaching its climax. Both the general reader and the serious student of literature are still largely unaware of the extent and excellence of Cooper's nautical writings, unaware that nearly half of his work is concerned with the sea, unaware that among his sea novels are to be found many of his most original and profound creations.

Although its intrinsic value alone is sufficient reason for a thorough knowledge of Cooper's sea fiction, the significant influence his nautical novels have exerted on the work of other writers provides further justification for a revival of interest in them. Conrad, who spoke of Cooper as "one of my masters" and "my constant companion," expressed his heavy indebtedness to the sublimity of Cooper's conception of maritime life.⁷ But perhaps the most important, and certainly the most neglected of Cooper's literary relations, is his influence on Melville. Too often Melville is treated as if he had no forerunners in the field of nautical writing except Smollett or the scribblers of nautical reminiscences who supplied materials for *White-Jacket* and *Moby-Dick.* To place Melville in a vacuum of this kind is to distort the nature of his contributions to the novel and to overlook the major role played by Cooper in the shaping of one of the finest achievements of American literature. For all the power and brilliance of Melville's creative genius, it seems unlikely that *Moby-Dick* could have attained its present form if Cooper had not performed three essential services for the fictional treatment of maritime subjects. In liberating the fictional treatment of the sea from the satirical tone of Smollett, he had demonstrated the successful use of two possible alternatives: a tone which, by evoking the mood of high romance, lent the narrative the aura of legend and a tone which created an atmosphere of sober realism, an atmosphere that gave the seaman the full dignity of a human being and made him, as a man, the center of the reader's concern. And in *The Sea Lions* Cooper had transformed the sea novel from a fiction in which the chief interest depends on the depiction of a special occupation and a special environment into a fiction in which that occupation and environment become the symbolic ground for the dramatic conflict of ideas and attitudes having universal significance.

In the middle of the nineteenth century, an era when even the clipper ships bore names like *Red Rover* and *Water Witch,* an American novelist who intended to deal with a serious maritime theme could scarcely escape the influence of Cooper, and Melville was no exception. Cooper's works, which were among the earliest Melville could remember, produced "a vivid and awakening power" upon his mind.[8] Shortly before the genesis of *Moby-Dick,* his acquaintance with Cooper's sea novels was renewed when he contributed reviews of *The Sea Lions* and of a new edition of *The Red Rover* to the *Literary World.* Leon Howard has indicated parallels between *The Red Rover* and *Moby-Dick* and suggested that Cooper's early romance contributed to the legendary flavor of Melville's novel.[9] A still closer and more significant relationship exists between *Moby-Dick* and *The Sea Lions*. Both novels open with striking portraits of small, closely knit maritime communities in which prowess in whaling is counted the chief civic virtue. Melville's Bildad is nearly a duplicate of Cooper's Deacon Pratt, whom Melville had described in his review as "a hard-handed, hard-hearted, psalm-singing old man, with a very stretchy conscience; intent upon getting to heaven, and getting money by the same course of conduct, in defiance of the scriptural maxim to the contrary." "There is," Melville had remarked, "a good deal of wisdom to be gathered from the story of the Deacon."[10] Both novels are richly larded with authentic detail drawn from factual sources, and yet in both the narrative continually transforms those details into analogies which open avenues to the exploration of a reality that lies beyond the physical. Both Cooper and Melville use vessels as emblems of human passions and attitudes. In both novels a sea hunt becomes a voyage into a strange world in which the absolute facts of existence seem to be less hidden, less masked than they are in ordinary life; and both Gardiner and Ahab, in their erroneous insistence on man's ability and right to know ultimate truth, arrogantly overestimate man's place in the cosmic order.

To indicate these resemblances, of course, is not to equate the two novels in value. Compared to *Moby-Dick*, *The Sea Lions* seems narrow in its conception, conventional in its characterization, and blatantly didactic in its meaning. Above all, *The Sea Lions* suffers from the relative poverty and monotony of Cooper's rhetoric. But in the dazzle of *Moby-Dick*, one must not lose sight of the magnitude of Cooper's achievement, for without *The Sea Lions* and its predecessors Melville's great novel could hardly have come into being. Indeed, in all likelihood, Melville's literary career itself owes its inception to

Cooper and his contemporaries, who, by establishing and sustaining the vogue for sea fiction in the first half of the nineteenth century, enabled Melville to turn his maritime experience into the materials of art.

Works Cited
Notes
Index

Works Cited

"An Affair of Honor," *Military and Naval Magazine*, 2:213–216 (1833).

Alaric [pseud.], "A Tale of the Sea," *Boston Spectator and Ladies Album*, 2:370, 385–386 (1827).

Albion, Robert Greenhalgh, and Jennie Barnes Pope, *Sea Lanes in Wartime: The American Experience, 1775–1942* (New York: Norton, 1942).

[Allen, Benjamin], *Columbia's Naval Triumphs* (New York: Inskeep and Bradford, 1813).

Almy, Robert F., "J. N. Reynolds: A Brief Biography with Particular Reference to Poe and Symmes," *Colophon*, new series, 2:227–245 (1937).

[Alsop, Richard], *Narrative of the Adventures and Sufferings of John R. Jewitt* (New York: no publ., 1815).

American Naval Songs and Ballads, ed. Robert W. Neeser (New Haven: Yale University Press, 1938).

[Ames, Nathaniel], *A Mariner's Sketches* (Providence: Cory, Marshall and Hammond, 1830).

——— *Nautical Reminiscences* (Providence: Marshall, 1832).

——— *An Old Sailor's Yarns* (New York: Dearborn, 1835).

Anderson, Charles R., "The Genesis of Billy Budd," *American Literature*, 12:329–346 (1940).

——— *Melville in the South Seas* (New York: Columbia University Press, 1939).

Ashley, Clifford W., *The Yankee Whaler* (Boston: Houghton Mifflin, 1938).

Bailey, J. O., "Sources for Poe's *Arthur Gordon Pym*, 'Hans Pfaal,' and Other Pieces," *PMLA*, 57:513–535 (1942).

Ballinger, R. H., "The Origins of James Fenimore Cooper's *The Two Admirals*," *American Literature*, 20:20–30 (1948).

Bancroft, Hubert H., *History of the Pacific States of North America* (San Francisco: History Co., 1884), vol. 22.

Beard, James F., "Cooper and His Artistic Contemporaries," *James*

Fenimore Cooper: A Re-Appraisal, ed. Mary E. Cunningham (Cooperstown: New York State Historical Association, 1954), pp. 112–127.

Beckett, S. B., "The Cruise of the Dart," *The Portland Sketch Book,* ed. Ann S. Stephens (Portland: Coleman and Chisholm, 1836), pp. 21–58.

Beechey, F[rederick] W., *Narrative of a Voyage to the Pacific and Bering's Strait,* 2 vols. (London: Colburn and Bentley, 1831).

Benton, Thomas H., *Thirty Years View; or, A History of the Workings of the American Government for Thirty Years, from 1820 to 1850,* 2 vols. (New York: Appleton, 1854).

Bewley, Marius, "Revaluations (XVI): James Fenimore Cooper," *Scrutiny,* 19:98–125 (Winter 1952–1953).

Bird, Mary Mayer, *Life of Robert Montgomery Bird,* ed. C. Seymour Thompson (Philadelphia: University of Pennsylvania Library, 1945).

[Bird, Robert Montgomery], *The Adventures of Robin Day,* 2 vols. (Philadelphia: Lea and Blanchard, 1839).

———— "The Ice-Island," *Philadelphia Monthly Magazine,* 1:109–114 (1827).

———— *Nick of the Woods, or The Jibbenainosay: A Tale of Kentucky,* rev. ed. (New York: Redfield, 1853).

Birss, John Howard, "A Book Review by Herman Melville," *New England Quarterly,* 5:346–348 (1932).

Blackbeard: A Page from the Colonial History of Philadelphia, 2 vols. (New York: Harper, 1835).

Block, Jack [pseud.], "The Cruise of the Mohawk," *American Monthly Magazine,* 5:417–425 (1835).

Bonaparte, Marie, *The Life and Works of Edgar Allan Poe: A Psycho-Analytic Interpretation,* trans. John Rodker (London: Imago, 1949).

[Bowen, Francis], rev. of Cooper's *Gleanings in Europe* in *North American Review,* 46:1–19 (1838).

Boynton, Henry W., *James Fenimore Cooper* (New York: Century, 1931).

Boynton, Percy H., *Literature and American Life* (Boston: Ginn, 1936).

"Breakers! A Scene at Sea," *Knickerbocker,* 6:495–500 (1835).

The Brigantine; or, Admiral Lowe (New York: Crowen and Decker, 1839).

[Briggs, Charles F.], *The Adventures of Harry Franco: A Tale of the Great Panic*, 2 vols. (New York: Saunder, 1839).

———— "A Veritable Sea Story," *Knickerbocker*, 23:151–152 (1844).

———— *Working a Passage: or, Life in a Liner* (New York: Allen, 1844).

Brown, T. Allston, *A History of the New York Stage* (New York: Dodd, Mead, 1903), vol. 1.

Browne, J. Ross, *Etchings of a Whaling Cruise* (New York: Harper, 1846).

"The Bucaneer," *Ladies' Companion*, 13:247–252 (1841).

Burton, William E., "A Cape Codder Among the Mermaids," *Burton's Gentleman's Magazine*, 5:287–292 (1839).

B[urts], R[obert], "The Escape," *Knickerbocker*, 8:270–275 (1836).

———— "The Flying Dutchman," *Knickerbocker*, 8:545–547 (1836).

———— "Jack Marlinspike's Yarn," *Knickerbocker*, 8:202–209 (1836).

———— "The Man Overboard," *Military and Naval Magazine*, 6:92–94 (1835).

———— "Naval Fragments," *Military and Naval Magazine*, 4:419–421 (1835).

———— "The Privateer," *Knickerbocker*, 8:650–655 (1836).

———— *The Scourge of the Ocean: A Story of the Atlantic*, 2 vols. (Philadelphia: Carey and Hart, 1837).

Byrne, Frank [pseud.?], "The Cruise of the Gentile," *Graham's Magazine*, 32:133–147, 205–217 (1848).

Byron, George Gordon, Lord, *The Poetical Works*, ed. Ernest Hartley Coleridge (London: Murray, 1905).

Calkins, Carlos Gilman, "Repression of Piracy in the West Indies, 1814–1825," *United States Naval Institute Proceedings*, 37:1197–1238 (1911).

[Channing, E. T.], rev. of Dana's *Two Years Before the Mast* in *North American Review*, 52:56–75 (1841).

Chapelle, Howard I., *The History of the American Sailing Navy: The Ships and Their Development* (New York: Norton, 1949).

"A Chapter of Sea Life," *New-England Magazine*, 4:47–51 (1833).

"A Chapter on Sharking," *Knickerbocker*, 7:841–858 (1836).

Charvat, William, "Cooper as Professional Author," *James Fenimore Cooper: A Re-Appraisal*, ed. Mary E. Cunningham (Cooperstown: New York State Historical Association, 1954), pp. 128–143.

Clagett, John Henry, "Cooper and the Sea: Naval Life and Naval

History in the Writings of James Fenimore Cooper," unpubl.
diss., 2 vols. (Yale, 1954).

Clark, Henry A., "The Cruise of the Raker," *Graham's Magazine*,
33:69–74, 129–136, 188–196, 257–266 (1848).

Clavel, Marcel, *Fenimore Cooper and His Critics: American, British, and French Criticisms of the Novelist's Early Works* (Aix-en-Provence: Imprimerie Universitaire de Provence, 1938).

———— *Fenimore Cooper, sa vie et son œuvre: La jeunesse (1789–1826)* (Aix-en-Provence: Imprimerie Universitaire de Provence, 1938).

"The Clerk's Yarn," *Knickerbocker*, 9:268–275 (1837).

Cleveland, Richard J., *A Narrative of Voyages and Commercial Enterprises*, 3rd ed. (Boston: Pierce, 1850).

C[linch], J. H., "The Pirate," *Ladies' Companion*, 7:244–248 (1837).

Clymer, W. B. Shubrick, *James Fenimore Cooper* (Boston: Small, Maynard, 1900).

[Coates, Reynell, ed.], *Friendship's Offering: A Christmas, New Year, and Birthday Present, for MDCCCL* (Boston: Phillips, Sampson, 1850).

[Codman, John], *Sailors' Life and Sailors' Yarns* (New York: Francis, 1847).

[Colton, Walter], *Ship and Shore: or Leaves from the Journal of a Cruise to the Levant* (New York: Leavitt, Lord, 1835).

Conrad, Joseph, *Notes on Life and Letters* (London: Dent, 1921).

Cook, James, *Voyages*, 2 vols. (London: Smith, 1842).

Cooper, James Fenimore, *The American Democrat or Hints on the Social and Civic Relations of the United States of America* (New York: Vintage, 1956).

———— *Correspondence of James Fenimore-Cooper*, ed. James Fenimore Cooper, 2 vols. (New Haven: Yale University Press, 1922).

———— *Early Critical Essays (1820–1822)*, ed. James F. Beard (Gainesville, Fla.: Scholars' Facsimiles and Reprints, 1955).

———— *Excursions in Italy* (Paris: Baudry, 1838).

———— *Excursions in Switzerland* (Paris: Baudry, 1836).

———— *Gleanings in Europe*, ed. Robert E. Spiller, 2 vols. (New York: Oxford University Press, 1928–1930).

———— *The History of the Navy of the United States of America*, 2 vols. (London: Bentley, 1839).

———— *A Letter to His Countrymen* (New York: Wiley, 1834).

———— *The Letters and Journals of James Fenimore Cooper*, ed.

James F. Beard, 2 vols. (Cambridge, Mass.: Harvard University Press, 1960).

—— *Ned Myers; or, A Life Before the Mast* (Philadelphia: Lea and Blanchard, 1843).

—— *Notions of the Americans: Picked up by a Travelling Bachelor,* 2 vols. (Philadelphia: Carey, Lea and Carey, 1828).

—— *Novels,* 32 vols. (New York: Townsend, 1859–1861).

—— *The Pilot,* 5th ed., 2 vols. (Philadelphia: Carey and Lea, 1832).

—— *The Red Rover,* new ed., 2 vols. (Philadelphia: Carey, Lea and Blanchard, 1836).

—— *A Residence in France; with an Excursion up the Rhine, and a Second Visit to Switzerland* (Paris: Baudry, 1836).

—— "Review of the Proceedings of the Naval Court Martial," *Proceedings of the Naval Court Martial in the Case of Alexander Slidell Mackenzie* (New York: Langley, 1844), pp. [263]–344.

—— *The Water-Witch,* new ed., 2 vols. (New York: Stringer and Townsend, 1852).

Cooper, Susan Fenimore, *The Cooper Gallery; or, Pages and Pictures from the Writings of James Fenimore Cooper* (New York: Miller, 1865).

Cowie, Alexander, *The Rise of the American Novel* (New York: American Book Co., 1948).

"The Cruise of the Enterprize," *United States Magazine and Democratic Review,* 6:33–42 (1839).

Cutler, Carl C., *Greyhounds of the Sea: The Story of the American Clipper Ship* (New York: Halcyon House, 1930).

Dana, Richard Henry, *Two Years Before the Mast* (New York: Macmillan, 1911).

Davidson, Edward H., *Poe: A Critical Study* (Cambridge, Mass.: Harvard University Press, 1957).

[Dawes, Rufus], *Nix's Mate: An Historical Romance of America,* 2 vols. (New York: Colman, 1839).

"The Dead Man's Sermon," *Knickerbocker,* 26:203–212 (1845).

Delano, Amasa, *A Narrative of Voyages and Travels, in the Northern and Southern Hemispheres* (Boston: House, 1817).

Delta [pseud.], "Extract from a Log," *Military and Naval Magazine,* 4:353–355 (1835).

—— "Life in a Steerage," *Military and Naval Magazine,* 4:356–358 (1835).

[Dow, J. E.], "Sketches from the Log of Old Ironsides," *Burton's Gentleman's Magazine*, 5:13–17, 101–104, 138–144, 179–181, 272–276, 300–303 (1839).

Drake, Samuel Adams, *Nooks and Corners of the New England Coast* (New York: Harper, 1875).

Duer, John K., *The Matricide* (New York: Graham, 1846).

Dunlap, W[illiam], *Yankee Chronology; or, Huzza for the Constitution!* (New York: Longworth, 1812).

Durand, James R., *Life and Adventures* (Rochester: Peck, 1820).

Duyckinck, Evert A. and George L., *Cyclopaedia of American Literature*, 2 vols. (New York: Scribner, 1856).

Dwight, Timothy, "Columbia," *American Museum*, 1:484–485 (1787).

Ellison, James, *The American Captive, or Siege of Tripoli* (Boston: Belcher, 1812).

"An Execution at Sea," *Knickerbocker*, 7:285–288 (1836).

Fanning, Edmund, *Voyages round the World; with Selected Sketches of Voyages to the South Seas, North and South Pacific Oceans, China, etc., Performed under the Command and Agency of the Author* (New York: Collins and Hannay, 1833).

"The Farewell at Sea," *Boston Pearl and Literary Gazette*, 4:373–375 (1835).

[Fitz-roy, Robert, *et al.*], *Narrative of the Surveying Voyages of His Majesty's Ships Adventure and Beagle*, 3 vols. (London: Colburn, 1839).

Fleurieu, C. P. Claret, *A Voyage round the World, Performed during the Years 1790, 1791, and 1792, by Étienne Marchand*, 2 vols. (London: Longman and Rees, 1801).

"The Freebooter," *Parlour Journal*, 2:113–115 (1834).

Freeman, F. Barron, *Melville's Billy Budd* (Cambridge, Mass.: Harvard University Press, 1948).

Freneau, Philip, *The Last Poems*, ed. Lewis Leary (New Brunswick, N. J.: Rutgers University Press, 1945).

———— *Poems*, ed. Fred Lewis Pattee, 3 vols. (Princeton: Princeton University Library, 1902).

Garnett, R. S., "Moby-Dick and Mocha Dick: A Literary Find," *Blackwood's*, 226:841–858 (1929).

Gates, W. B., "Cooper's Indebtedness to Shakespeare," *PMLA*, 67:716–731 (1952).

———— "Cooper's *The Sea Lions* and Wilkes' *Narrative*," *PMLA*, 65:1069–1075 (1950).

Gould, John W., *Forecastle Yarns*, ed. Edward S. Gould (Baltimore: Taylor, 1845).

―――― *Private Journal of a Voyage from New-York to Rio de Janeiro; Together with a Brief Sketch of His Life, and His Occasional Writings* (New York: no publ., 1839).

Greenough, Horatio, "American Architecture," *United States Magazine and Democratic Review*, 13:206–210 (1843).

Grossman, James, *James Fenimore Cooper* (New York: Sloane, 1949).

Hart, James D., "Richard Henry Dana, Jr.," unpubl. diss. (Harvard, 1936).

[Hart, Joseph C.], *Miriam Coffin; or, The Whale-Fishermen*, 2 vols. (New York: Carvill, 1834).

Harwood, A. A., "Mess-Table Chat," *The Gift: A Christmas and New Year's Present for 1840* (Philadelphia: Carey and Hart, [1839], pp. 17–53.

Hazzard, Samuel, "Extracts from a Sea Book," *The Legendary*, ed. Nathaniel P. Willis (Boston: Goodrich, 1828), II, 146–181.

―――― "A Mystery of the Sea," *American Monthly Magazine*, 1:303–312 (1829).

Herbert, Henry William, *Ringwood the Rover: A Tale of Florida* (Philadelphia: Graham, 1843).

The History of Lorenzo and Virginia; or, Virtue Rewarded (Concord, N. H.: Eastman and Chadwick, 1834).

Holland, Edwin, "The Pillar of Glory," *Port Folio*, 3rd ser., 2:552 (1813).

[Hope, Thomas], *Anastasius, or, Memoirs of a Greek*, 2nd ed., 3 vols. (London: Murray, 1820).

Howard, Leon, *Herman Melville: A Biography* (Berkeley: University of California Press, 1951).

―――― "A Predecessor of Moby-Dick," *Modern Language Notes*, 49:310–311 (1934).

Howay, F. W., "Early Days of the Maritime Fur Trade on the Northwest Coast," *Canadian Historical Review*, 4:26–44 (1923).

Humphreys, [David], "Poem on the Happiness of America," *American Museum*, 1:240–263 (1787).

"Hunting a Devil Fish," *Military and Naval Magazine*, 6:364–366 (1836).

Huntress, Keith, "Another Source for Poe's *Narrative of Arthur Gordon Pym*," *American Literature*, 16:19–25 (1944).

———— "Melville's Use of a Source for *White-Jacket*," *American Literature*, 17:66–74 (1945).

Ichabod [pseud.], "The Ice Ship," *Bower of Taste*, 1:257–260 (1828).

Ireland, Joseph N., *Records of the New York Stage, from 1750 to 1860* (New York: Morrell, 1866), vol. 1.

Irving, Washington, *Astoria or, Anecdotes of an Enterprise beyond the Rocky Mountains*, rev. ed. (New York: Putnam, 1849).

———— *The Sketch Book of Geoffrey Crayon, Gent. No. 1* (New York: Van Winkle, 1819).

———— *Tales of a Traveler* (Philadelphia: Carey and Lea, 1824).

Isaacs, Nicholas Peter, *Twenty Years Before the Mast* (New York: Beckwith, 1845).

James, Reese D., *Old Drury of Philadelphia* (Philadelphia: University of Pennsylvania Press, 1932).

Jean-Aubry, G., *Joseph Conrad: Life and Letters*, 2 vols. (New York: Doubleday, 1927).

[Johnson, Charles], *The History of the Pirates* (Haverhill, Mass.: Carey, 1825).

Johnson, Samuel, *Lives of the English Poets*, ed. George Birkbeck Hill, 3 vols. (Oxford: Clarendon Press, 1905).

Jones, Alexander, *The Privateer; or, The Black Boatswain of the Atlantic* (Boston: Redding, 1846).

[Jones, George], *Sketches of Naval Life*, 2 vols. (New Haven: Howe, 1829).

Jones, Howard Mumford, "Prose and Pictures: James Fenimore Cooper," *Tulane Studies in English*, 3:133–154 (1952).

[Judah, Samuel B.], *The Buccaneers: A Romance of Our Own Country, in Its Ancient Day*, 2 vols. (Boston: Munroe and Francis, 1827).

[Judson, Edward Z. C.], "A Chronicle of Our Navy," *Knickerbocker*, 28:527–531 (1846).

———— *Cruisings, Afloat and Ashore, from the Private Log of Ned Buntline* (New York: Craighead, 1848).

———— "A Dream That Was Not All Dream," *Knickerbocker*, 28:244–247 (1846).

———— "Running a Blockade in the Last War," *Knickerbocker*, 29:306–309 (1847).

———— "A Visit to Lafitte," *Knickerbocker*, 29:254–261 (1847).

Kaplan, Sidney, ed., *The Narrative of Arthur Gordon Pym* (New York: Hill and Wang, [1960]).

Kelpie [pseud.], "The Pirates: A Sea Tale," *Illinois Monthly Magazine*, 1:481–491 (1831).

[Kenrick, William], rev. of Falconer's *The Shipwreck* in *Monthly Review*, 27:197–201 (1762).

Lafitte or the Baratarian Chief (New York: no publ., 1828).

Lann, Wilder, "Pirate Law," *Burton's Gentleman's Magazine*, 2:305–308 (1838).

La Pérouse, J[ean] F. de G., *A Voyage round the World*, 2nd ed., 3 vols. (London: Johnson, 1799).

Leggett, William, *Naval Stories* (New York: Carvill, 1834).

—— *Tales and Sketches by a Country Schoolmaster* (New York: Harper, 1829).

Leech, Samuel, *Thirty Years from Home, or A Voice from the Main Deck* (Boston: Tappan and Dennet, 1843).

Levin, Harry, *The Power of Blackness: Hawthorne, Poe, Melville* (New York: Knopf, 1958).

Lewis, Charles Lee, *Books of the Sea: An Introduction to Nautical Literature* (Annapolis: United States Naval Institute, 1943).

—— "Edgar Allan Poe and the Sea," *Southern Literary Messenger*, new series, 3:5–10 (1941).

Lewis, Meriwether, *History of the Expedition of Captains Lewis and Clark*, ed. James K. Hosmer, 2 vols. (Chicago: McClurg, 1902).

Lewis, R. W. B., *The American Adam: Innocence, Tragedy, and Tradition in the Nineteenth Century* (Chicago: University of Chicago Press, 1955).

Lincoln, Barnabas, *Narrative of the Capture, Sufferings and Escape of Capt. Barnabas Lincoln and His Crew, Who Were Taken by a Piratical Schooner, December, 1821, off Key Largo* (Boston: Lincoln, 1822).

Lindsley, A. B., *Love and Friendship; or, Yankee Notions* (New York: Longworth, 1809).

"The Lost Fisherman," *Burton's Gentleman's Magazine*, 3:340–347 (1838).

"The Lost Sailor," *Military and Naval Magazine*, 6:366–367 (1836).

Lounsbury, Thomas R., *James Fenimore Cooper* (Boston: Houghton Mifflin, 1889).

McCloskey, John C., "The Campaign of Periodicals after the War of 1812 for National American Literature," *PMLA*, 50:262–273 (1935).

McKeithan, D. M., "Two Sources of Poe's 'Narrative of Arthur

Gordon Pym,' " *University of Texas Studies in English*, 13:116–137 (1933).

Mackenzie, Alexander, *Voyages from Montreal, on the River St. Laurence, through the Continent of North America, to the Frozen and Pacific Oceans; in the Years 1789 and 1793*, 2 vols. (London: Cadell and Davies, 1802).

Maclay, Edgar Stanton, *A History of American Privateers* (New York: Appleton, 1899).

McNally, William, *Evils and Abuses in the Naval and Merchant Service, Exposed; with Proposals for Their Remedy and Redress* (Boston: Cassady and March, 1839).

The Mariner's Library or Voyager's Companion (Boston: Gaylord, 1840).

Maritime Scraps, or Scenes in the Frigate United States during a Cruise in the Mediterranean (Boston: no publ., 1838).

M[ayo], W[illiam] S., "The Captain's Story," *United States Magazine and Democratic Review*, 18:305–311 (1846).

———— "The Escape of the Atalanta," *Ladies' Companion*, 19:24–26 (1843).

———— *Kaloolah; or, Journeyings to the Djebel Kumri* (New York: Putnam, 1849).

———— "A Real Pirate," *United States Magazine and Democratic Review*, 22:263–269 (1848).

[Mellen, Grenville], rev. of Cooper's *The Red Rover* in *North American Review*, 27:139–154 (1828).

Melville, Herman, *Novels*, 16 vols. (London: Constable, 1922–1924).

———— rev. of Browne's *Etchings of a Whaling Cruise* and Codman's *Sailors' Life and Sailors' Yarns* in *Literary World*, 1:105–106 (1847).

———— rev. of Cooper's *The Sea Lions* in *Literary World*, 4:370 (1849).

———— "A Thought on Book-Binding," *Literary World*, 6:276–277 (1850).

Memorial of James Fenimore Cooper (New York: Putnam, 1852).

[Mercier, Henry James, and William Gallop], *Life in a Man-of-War, or Scenes in "Old Ironsides" During Her Cruise in the Pacific* (Philadelphia: Bailey, 1841).

"A Midsummer Night Watch," *The Gift . . . for 1837* (Philadelphia: Carey and Hart, [1836]), pp. 17–53.

Miller, Perry, *The Raven and the Whale: The War of Words and*

Wits in the Era of Poe and Melville (New York: Harcourt Brace, 1956).

[Mitchell, Donald G.], "A Man Overboard," *Southern Literary Messenger*, 14:10–11 (1848).

Morrell, Benjamin, *A Narrative of Four Voyages to the South Sea, North and South Pacific Ocean, Chinese Sea, Ethiopic and Southern Atlantic Ocean, Indian and Antarctic Ocean* (New York: Harper, 1832).

Morris, George P., *Poems* (New York: Scribner, 1860).

Mott, Frank Luther, *A History of American Magazines: 1741–1850* (Cambridge, Mass.: Harvard University Press, 1939).

Munro, Wilfred Harold, *Tales of an Old Sea Port* (Princeton: Princeton University Press, 1917).

Mutiny and Murder: Confession of Charles Gibbs, a Native of Rhode Island (Providence: Smith, 1831).

"Naval Life," *Military and Naval Magazine*, 3:364–368, 4:5–14 (1834).

"Naval Reminiscence," *American Monthly Magazine*, 5:349–353 (1835).

Nevens, William, *Forty Years at Sea* (Portland: Thurston, Fenley, 1846).

"A Night at Sea," *Philadelphia Monthly Magazine*, 2:338–343 (1828).

Noble, Louis L., *The Course of Empire, Voyage of Life and Other Pictures of Thomas Cole* (New York: Cornish, Lamport, 1853).

"The Nobleman and the Fisherman," *New-England Magazine*, 6:280–289 (1834).

Noel, Mary, *Villains Galore: The Heyday of the Popular Story Weekly* (New York: Macmillan, 1954).

"The Old Seaman, a Sketch from Nature," *Portfolio*, 15:456–459 (1823).

Olmstead, Francis Allyn, *Incidents of a Whaling Voyage* (New York: Appleton, 1841).

"Opportunity for the Escape of Napoleon from St. Helena," *Military and Naval Magazine*, 5:11–14 (1835).

Orians, G. Harrison, "Lafitte: A Bibliographical Note," *American Literature*, 9:351–353 (1937).

Orson [pseud.], "Life at Sea," *Knickerbocker*, 8:66–70 (1836).

[Palfrey, J. G.], rev. of Bird's *The Adventures of Robin Day* in *North American Review*, 49:220–237 (1839).

Parry, William Edward, *Journal of a Voyage for the Discovery of a*

WORKS CITED

North-West Passage from the Atlantic to the Pacific; Performed in the Years 1819-20 (Philadelphia: Small, 1821).

Pattee, Fred Lewis, The Development of the American Short Story (New York: Harper, 1923).

Paulding, J[ames] K[irke], "The Ghost," The Atlantic Souvenir for MDCCCXXX (Philadelphia: Carey, Lea and Carey, 1830) pp. 296-323.

Paullin, Charles Oscar, "Naval Administration Under Naval Commissioners: 1815-1842," United States Naval Institute Proceedings, 33:597-641 (1907).

[Peabody, O. W. B.], rev. of Cooper's The Water-Witch in North American Review, 32:508-523 (1831).

Peterson, Charles J., The American Navy (Philadephia: Peterson, 1857).

——— "The Black Rover," Sartain's Magazine, 4:37-44, 119-126, 202-210 (1849).

——— Cruising in the Last War (Philadelphia: Peterson, 1850).

——— "Getting to Sea," Graham's Magazine, 26:105-109 (1844).

——— "Off Calais," Graham's Magazine, 28:214-218 (1845).

——— "The Union Jack," Graham's Magazine, 23:105-109 (1843).

"The Phantom Ship," New-England Magazine, 3:122-127 (1832).

Philadelphia Songster; or a Complete Vocal Pocket Companion (Philadelphia: Graves, 1805).

"A Piratical Sketch," Ladies' Companion, 9:9-11 (1838).

Poe, Edgar Allan, Complete Works, ed. James A. Harrison, 17 vols. (New York: Society of English and French Literature, 1902).

Pollock, Thomas Clark, The Philadelphia Theatre in the Eighteenth Century (Philadelphia: University of Pennsylvania Press, 1933).

Pond, Fred E., Life and Adventures of "Ned Buntline" (New York: Cadmus, 1919).

[Prescott, William H.], rev. of English Literature of the Nineteenth Century in North American Review, 35:165-195 (1832).

Proctor, Page S., "A Source for the Flogging Incident in White-Jacket," American Literature, 22:176-182 (1950).

——— "William Leggett (1801-1839): Journalist and Literator," Papers of the Bibliographical Society of America, 44:239-253 (1950).

Prospero, Peter [pseud.], "The Atlantis," American Museum of Science, Literature and the Arts, 1:42-65, 222-255, 321-341, 419-437 (1838); 2:37-41, 231-240 (1839).

Quinn, Arthur Hobson, *American Fiction: An Historical and Critical Survey* (New York: Appleton-Century, 1936).

—— *Edgar Allan Poe: A Critical Biography* (New York: Appleton-Century, 1941).

—— *A History of the American Drama: From the Beginning to the Civil War* (New York: Harper, 1923).

Quinn, Patrick F., *The French Face of Edgar Poe* (Carbondale: University of Illinois Press, 1957).

Ramon, the Rover of Cuba, and Other Tales (New York: Nafis and Cornish, 1843).

"Recollections of a Sailor," *Military and Naval Magazine*, 5:340–[345]; 6:43–49 (1835).

"The Reefer's First Cruise," *American Monthly Magazine*, 3:105–112, 185–192 (1834).

A Report of the Trial of Pedro Gibert, Bernardo de Soto, Francisco Ruiz, Nicola Costa, Antonio Ferrer, Manuel Boyga, Domingo de Guzman, Juan Antonio Portana, Manuel Castillo, Angel Garcia, Jose Velazquez, and Juan Montegro . . . on an Indictment . . . of Piracy, on Board of the Brig Mexican, of Salem (Boston: Russell, Odiorne and Metcalf, 1834).

Review of Bird's *The Adventures of Robin Day* in *Burton's Gentleman's Magazine*, 4:358 (1839).

Review of *Blackbeard* in *New-England Magazine*, 9:77–79 (1835).

Review of Burts's *The Scourge of the Ocean* in *Burton's Gentleman's Magazine*, 1:287–289 (1837).

Review of Channing's *Sermons and Tracts* in *Edinburgh Review*, 50: 125–144 (1829).

Review of Cooper's *Afloat and Ashore* in *Spectator*, 17:567–568 (1844).

Review of Cooper's *The Crater* in *United States Magazine and Democratic Review*, 21:438–447 (1847).

Review of Cooper's *Homeward Bound* in *Knickerbocker*, 12:263–267 (1838).

Review of Cooper's *Homeward Bound* in *Southern Literary Messenger*, 4:724–728 (1838).

Review of Cooper's *The Monikins* in *American Monthly Magazine*, 5:487 (1835).

Review of Cooper's *The Monikins* in *Knickerbocker*, 6:152–153 (1835).

Review of Cooper's *The Two Admirals* in *Southern Literary Messenger*, 8:361–362 (1842).

Review of Cooper's *The Wing-and-Wing* in *United States Magazine and Democratic Review*, 11:665–666 (1842).

Review of Cooper's *Works* in *United States Magazine and Democratic Review*, 25:51–55 (1849).

Review of Dana's *Two Years Before the Mast* in *Knickerbocker*, 16:348–352 (1840).

Review of Dana's *Two Years Before the Mast* in *New York Review*, 7:535–537 (1840).

Review of Dana's *Two Years Before the Mast* in *Southern Literary Messenger*, 6:781 (1840).

Review of Dana's *Two Years Before the Mast* in *United States Magazine and Democratic Review*, 8:318–332 (1840).

Review of Hart's *Miriam Coffin* in *Knickerbocker*, 4:67–72 (1834).

Reynolds, J[eremiah] N., *Address, on the Subject of a Surveying and Exploring Expedition to the Pacific Ocean and South Seas* (New York: Harper, 1836).

——— "Mocha Dick; or the White Whale of the Pacific," *Knickerbocker*, 13:377–392 (1839).

——— "Report . . . in Relation to Islands, Reefs, and Shoals in the Pacific Ocean, &c.," House Exec. Doc. No. 105, 23rd Cong., 2nd Sess., 1835.

——— *Voyage of the United States Frigate Potomac* (New York: Harper, 1835).

Rhea, Robert Lee, "Some Observations on Poe's Origins," *University of Texas Studies in English*, 10:135–146 (1930).

Ringe, Donald A., "James Fenimore Cooper and Thomas Cole: An Analogous Technique," *American Literature*, 30:26–36 (1958).

Robinson, Charles Napier, and John Leyland, *The British Tar in Fact and Fiction: The Poetry, Pathos, and Humour of the Sailor's Life* (New York: Harper, 1909).

Ross, Ernest C., *The Development of the English Sea Novel from Defoe to Conrad* (Ann Arbor, Mich.: Edward, n. d.).

Ross, James Clark, *A Voyage of Discovery and Research in the Southern and Antarctic Regions, during the Years 1839–43*, 2 vols. (London: Murray, 1847).

Rourke, Constance, *American Humor: A Study of the National Character* (New York: Doubleday, 1955).

Ruschenberger, W[illiam] S. W., *Three Years in the Pacific* (Philadelphia: Carey, Lea and Blanchard, 1834).

The Saga of the Bounty, ed. Irvin Anthony (New York: Putnam, 1935).

[Sargent, Charles Lenox], *The Life of Alexander Smith, Captain of the Island of Pitcairn, One of the Mutineers on Board His Majesty's Ship Bounty, Commanded by Lieut Wm. Bligh* (Boston: Goss, 1819).

Sargent, Emma W., and Charles S. Sargent, *Epes Sargent of Gloucester and His Descendants* (Boston: Houghton Mifflin, 1923).

"Scene on the Bahama Banks," *Hartford Pearl and Literary Gazette,* 4:33–34 (1834).

"Scenes in a Life," *Southern and Western Magazine,* 2:43–50 (1845).

Scoresby, W[illiam], *An Account of the Arctic Regions,* 2 vols. (Edinburgh: Constable, 1820).

Scott, Sir Walter, *The Pirate* (London: Dent, 1907).

Scudder, H. H., "Cooper and the Barbary Coast," *PMLA,* 62:784–792 (1947).

Seaborn, Adam [pseud.], *Symzonia: A Voyage of Discovery* (New York: Seymour, 1820).

Seadrift [pseud.], "The Deserters," *Military and Naval Magazine,* 2:216–219 (1833).

[Sedgwick, Catharine M.], "Modern Chivalry," *The Atlantic Souvenir . . . 1827* (Philadelphia: Carey and Lea, [1826]), pp. 5–47.

"The Shipwrecked Coaster," *Boston Pearl and Literary Gazette,* 4:149–151 (1835).

Simms, William Gilmore, "A Sea-Piece," *The Atlantic Club-Book* (New York: Harper, 1834), I, 264–279.

[Sleeper, John Sherburne], *Tales of the Ocean, and Essays for the Forecastle* (Boston: Dickinson, 1841).

Smallfull, Jerry [pseud.], "Adventures of a Reefer," *Military and Naval Magazine,* 5:222–226 (1835).

Smith, Elizabeth Oakes, "Jack Spanker and the Mermaid," *Graham's Magazine,* 23:68–71 (1843).

Smith, Henry Nash, *Virgin Land: The American West as Symbol and Myth* (Cambridge, Mass.: Harvard University Press, 1950).

Smith, Thomas W., *A Narrative of the Life, Travels and Sufferings of Thomas W. Smith* (Boston: Hill, 1844).

Spiller, Robert E., *Fenimore Cooper: Critic of His Times* (New York: Minton, Balch, 1931).

———— *James Fenimore Cooper: Representative Selections* (New York: American Book Co., 1936).

Spiller, Robert E., and Philip C. Blackburn, *A Descriptive Bibliography of the Writings of James Fenimore Cooper* (New York: Bowker, 1934).

Stackpole, Edouard A., *The Voyage of the Huron and the Huntress: The American Sealers and the Discovery of the Continent of Antarctica* (Mystic, Conn.: Marine Historical Association, 1955).

Stanton, Dick [pseud.], "Off the Cape," *Burton's Gentleman's Magazine*, 4:233–236 (1839).

Starke, Aubrey, "Poe's Friend Reynolds," *American Literature*, 11:152–159 (1939).

Starr, Nathan Comfort, "The Sea in the English Novel from Defoe to Melville," unpubl. diss. (Harvard, 1928).

Stedman, Edmund Clarence, and George Edward Woodberry, eds., *The Works of Edgar Allan Poe* (New York: Scribner, 1914), vol. 5.

Stewart, C. S., *A Visit to the South Seas*, 2 vols. (New York: Haven, 1831).

Stone, William Leete, "The Dead of the Wreck," *The Atlantic Souvenir for MDCCCXXXI* (Philadelphia: Carey, Lea and Carey, 1830), pp. 164–193.

———— "The Spectre Fire-Ship," *Knickerbocker*, 3:361–370 (1834).

Swifter, Jack [pseud.], "Ashore and Afloat," *New World*, 3:141 (1841).

Thomas, R., *An Authentic Account of the Most Remarkable Events: Containing the Lives of the Most Noted Pirates and Piracies. Also, the Most Remarkable Shipwrecks, Fires, Famines, Calamities, Providential Deliveries, and Lamentable Disasters on the Seas, in Most Parts of the World*, 2 vols. in 1 (New York: Strong, 1837).

Tocqueville, Alexis de, *Democracy in America*, ed. Phillips Bradley, 2 vols. (New York: Knopf, 1945).

Triton [pseud.], "The Character of a Sailor," *Military and Naval Magazine*, 4:115–117 (1834).

Tuckerman, Henry T., "Captain Millar," *Ladies' Companion*, 19:95–97 (1843).

[Tyler, Royall], *The Algerine Captive; or, The Life and Adventures of Doctor Updike Underhill*, 2 vols. (Walpole, N. H.: Carlisle, 1797).

Vail, James E., "The Sea Voyage," *Ladies' Companion*, 7:285–287 (1837).

Vancouver, George, *A Voyage of Discovery to the North Pacific Ocean*, 6 vols. (London: Stockdale, 1801).

Vandiver, Edward P., "James Fenimore Cooper and Shakspere," *Shakespeare Association Bulletin*, 15:110–117 (1940).

Vincent, Howard P., *The Trying-Out of Moby-Dick* (Boston: Houghton Mifflin, 1949).

"Voyaging," *New-England Magazine*, 7:447–448 (1834).

Wade, Robert L., "The Doomed Ship," *Knickerbocker*, 22:403–411 (1843).

Walker, Warren, "Ames vs. Cooper: The Case Re-Opened," *Modern Language Notes*, 70:27–32 (1955).

Wallace, Godfrey, "The Esmeralda," *The Atlantic Souvenir . . . 1829* (Philadelphia: Carey, Lea and Carey, [1828]), pp. 306–327.

——— "Giles Heatherby, the Free Trader," *The Atlantic Souvenir for MDCCCXXXI* (Philadelphia: Carey and Lea, 1831), pp. 220–262.

[Warren, Mercy], *The Motley Assembly* (Boston: Coverley, 1779).

Waterhouse, Benjamin, "A Journal of a Young Man of Massachusetts," *Magazine of History with Notes and Queries*, 5:199–470 (1911–1912).

Watson, Harold Francis, *The Sailor in English Fiction and Drama: 1500–1800* (New York: Columbia University Press, 1931).

[Weld, Horatio Hastings], "A Chapter on Whaling," *New-England Magazine*, 8:445–449 (1835).

——— *Ribs and Trucks, from Davy's Locker* (Boston: Strong, 1842).

W[estcott], A[llan], "William Leggett," *Dictionary of American Biography*, ed. Dumas Malone (New York: Scribner, 1933), XI, 147–148.

Whittier, John Greenleaf, *Whittier on Writers and Writing: The Uncollected Critical Writings of John Greenleaf Whittier*, ed. Edwin Harrison Cady and Harry Hayden Clark (Syracuse: Syracuse University Press, 1950).

Wilkes, Charles, *Narrative of the United States Exploring Expedition during the Years 1838, 1839, 1840, 1841, 1842*, 5 vols. and atlas (Philadelphia: Lea and Blanchard, 1845).

Wilkinson, Cuthbert S., *The Wake of the Bounty* (London: Cassell, 1953).

Williams, Stanley T., "James Fenimore Cooper," *Literary History of the United States*, ed. Robert E. Spiller, *et al.* (New York: Macmillan, 1953), pp. 253–269.

[Willis, Nathaniel P.], "The Archipelago in a Levanter," *New Mirror*, 1:241–245 (1843).

————— *Pencillings by the Way*, new ed. (London: Virtue, 1842).

Winters, Yvor, *Maule's Curse: Seven Studies in the History of American Obscurantism* (Norfolk, Conn.: New Directions, 1938).

Woodberry, George E., *The Life of Edgar Allan Poe*, 2 vols. (Boston: Houghton Mifflin, 1909).

Woodworth, Samuel, *The Champions of Freedom; or, The Mysterious Chief* (New York: Graham, 1847).

————— *The Poems, Odes, Songs, and Other Metrical Effusions, of Samuel Woodworth* (New York: Asten and Lopez, 1818).

Wright, Lyle H., *American Fiction, 1774–1850: A Contribution toward a Bibliography*, rev. ed. (San Marino: Huntington Library Publications, 1948).

"The Yacht," *New Mirror*, 2:392–396 (1844).

"A Yankee's Adventures with the Flying Dutchman," *Burton's Gentleman's Magazine*, 1:331–333 (1837).

Notes

I

Dread Neptune's Wild Unsocial Sea

1. *Port Folio*, 3rd ser., 2:115 (1813).
2. *The Red Rover*, p. vii. This and all subsequent quotations of the final prefaces and texts of the novels are from the Townsend edition of *Cooper's Novels*, 32 vols, (New York, 1859–1861).
3. Samuel Johnson, *Lives of the English Poets*, ed. G. B. Hill (Oxford, 1905), I, 433.
4. [William Kenrick], rev. of *The Shipwreck* in *Monthly Review*, 27:198 (1762).
5. *Gleanings in Europe*, ed. Robert E. Spiller (New York, 1928–1930), II, 8.
6. *Childe Harold*, Canto IV, stanzas 178, 180, 183. All quotations of Byron's poetry are from *The Poetical Works of Lord Byron*, ed. Ernest H. Coleridge (London, 1905).
7. *Poems of Philip Freneau*, ed. Fred Lewis Pattee (Princeton, 1902), II, 24.
8. *Ibid.*, II, 342–345.
9. "On the Crew of a Certain Vessel," *Poems of Philip Freneau*, II, 317.
10. "The Nautical Rendezvous," *Poems of Philip Freneau*, III, 243.
11. "The British Prison Ship," *Poems of Philip Freneau*, II, 20–21.
12. "The Argonaut," *Poems of Philip Freneau*, II, 128.
13. "Lines Written at Sea," *Poems of Philip Freneau*, III, 232.
14. "To a Lady Remarkably Fond of Sleep," *The Last Poems of Philip Freneau*, ed. Lewis Leary (New Brunswick, N. J., 1945), p. 88.
15. "Captain Jones's Invitation," *Poems of Philip Freneau*, I, 291.
16. *Poems of Philip Freneau*, II, 129.

17. "A Midnight Storm in the Gulph Stream," *Last Poems,* p. 86.

18. "Captain Jones's Invitation," *Poems of Philip Freneau,* I, 292.

19. "Commerce," *Poems of Philip Freneau,* III, 220. Contrast, for example, Timothy Dwight's prophecy of America's future naval and commercial supremacy in his song "Columbia," first published in the *American Museum,* 1:484-485 (1787):

> Thy fleets to all regions thy pow'r shall display,
> The nations admire, and the ocean obey;
> Each shore to thy glory its tribute unfold,
> And the east and the south yield their spices and gold.

In David Humphreys' eyes, too, the future of America lay on the sea. In his "Poem on the Happiness of America," *American Museum,* 1:252 (1787), Humphreys pointed to the inevitable greatness of his country as a sea power:

> Where lives the nation fraught with such resource,
> Such vast materials for a naval force?
> Where grow so rife, the iron, masts, and spars,
> The hemp, the timber and the daring tars?
> Where gallant youths, inur'd to heat and cold,
> Thro' ev'ry zone, more hardy, strong, and bold?

20. "On the Launching of the . . . Independence," *Poems of Philip Freneau,* III, 374-375.

21. From a broadside in the Isaiah Thomas Collection of Ballads, reprinted in *American Naval Songs and Ballads,* ed. Robert W. Neeser (New Haven, 1938), pp. 48-50.

22. "The Freedom of the Seas," a song added to William Dunlap's *Yankee Chronology* (New York, 1812), pp. 13-14.

23. "The Pillar of Glory," first printed in *Port Folio,* 3rd ser., 2:552 (1813).

24. Samuel Woodworth, *Poems, Odes, Songs, and Other Metrical Effusions* (New York, 1818), p. 135. The lines are from "Victory No. 5. Hornet and Peacock," one of seven ballads which Woodworth wrote to commemorate the naval victories of the War of 1812.

25. For example, the *Philadelphia Songster* (Philadelphia, 1805), a typical song book of its period, contains thirty-five sea songs, only one of which, Susanna Rowson's "America, Commerce and Freedom," utilizes American materials; the place names and allusions of three others have been Americanized.

26. Benjamin Waterhouse, "A Journal of a Young Man of Massa-

chusetts," *Magazine of History with Notes and Queries*, 5:292–293 (1911–1912).

27. The Isaiah Thomas Collection of Ballads in the library of the American Antiquarian Society, Worcester, Mass., provides a convenient cross section of American taste in sea songs at the height of the War of 1812. Of the 349 songs in the collection approximately fifty are American naval ballads. A slightly smaller number, about forty, are English sea songs.

28. See Joseph N. Ireland, *Records of the New York Stage, from 1750 to 1860* (New York, 1866), I, 4; Thomas C. Pollock, *The Philadelphia Theatre in the Eighteenth Century* (Philadelphia, 1933), pp. 417, 420.

29. See T. Allston Brown, *A History of the New York Stage* (New York, 1903), I, 8. The sailor had made a still earlier appearance in the American drama when the author of *The Motley Assembly* (1779), probably Mercy Warren, introduced the character of Captain Careless, "an honest young sea-captain."

30. *The American Captive; or Siege of Tripoli* (Boston, 1812), pp. 3, 17, 19, 37, 47–48.

31. *Love and Friendship; or, Yankee Notions* (New York, 1809), p. 39. "Carter's mountain" apparently refers to some kind of block ship or floating battery.

32. *Ibid.*, pp. 40, 57. As his name indicates, Jonathan is a stage Yankee, just as much a stereotype as the stage sailor. Like Hardweather, however, Jonathan does not completely conform to the mold. Although he speaks in a comic New England dialect, he is not merely a hayseed, for his speech and the experience it suggests show the influence of salt water. Moreover, his greenness and awkwardness are less the result of provincialism than of youth.

33. See Arthur H. Quinn, *A History of the American Drama: From the Beginning to the Civil War* (New York, 1923), pp. 427, 462; Reese D. James, *Old Drury of Philadelphia* (Philadelphia, 1932), p. 116.

34. Quoted in James, *Old Drury of Philadelphia*, pp. 137–138.

35. *Yankee Chronology; or, Huzza for the Constitution!* (New York, 1812), pp. 7–8.

36. See, for example, Arthur H. Quinn, *American Fiction: An Historical and Critical Survey* (New York, 1936), p. 23; Alexander Cowie, *The Rise of the American Novel* (New York, 1948), p. 30. In *Literature and American Life* (Boston, 1936), pp. 195–196, Percy H. Boynton suggests that *Constantius and Pulchera* may have been

intended as a parody of contemporary prose romances. Whatever the intention of the author may have been, the publishing history of the book seems to indicate that its readers regarded it as a serious narrative. It is hard to imagine that a book considered to be only a literary burlesque would have enjoyed at least eleven printings between 1794 and 1834 in such communities as Suffield, Conn., Leominster, Mass., and Concord, N.H.; see Lyle H. Wright, *American Fiction: 1774–1850*, rev. ed. (San Marino, 1948), pp. 128–129.

37. *History of Lorenzo and Virginia; or, Virtue Rewarded* (Concord, N.H., 1834), pp. 19–21. The names of the protagonists were altered in this latest edition of *Constantius and Pulchera;* see Wright, *American Fiction: 1774–1850*, p. 129. In *The Sailor in English Fiction and Drama: 1500–1800* (New York, 1931), p. 48, Harold F. Watson lists the ingredients of the formulaic storm of romance: "The chief elements are (1) good weather; (2) sudden wind and mountainous waves; (3) darkness and a figure of speech suggesting a struggle; (4) deafening noise; (5) fright of the sailors; (6) destruction of rigging, mast, or oars; (7) wreck of the ship. These do not always appear in the same order but are nearly always found together."

38. See Evert A. and George L. Duyckinck, *Cyclopaedia of American Literature* (New York, 1856), I, 416.

39. *The Algerine Captive; or, The Life and Adventures of Doctor Updike Underhill* (Walpole, N.H., 1797), I, 209, 206.

40. *Ibid.*, I, 196–199.

41. *Ibid.*, II, 101, 116, 241.

42. In their preface to Woodworth's *Poems, Odes, Songs*, p. x, Abraham Asten and Matthias Lopez describe the pressures to which Woodworth was subjected: "In writing the Champions of Freedom, the author was confined, by the conditions of his engagement with the publisher, within a compass circumscribed by the latter. By these conditions he was compelled to connect *fiction* with *truth;* and, at all events, to give a complete and accurate account of the late war, however much the history of his hero and heroine might suffer in consequence."

43. Samuel Woodworth, *The Champions of Freedom; or, The Mysterious Chief* (New York, 1847), p. 82.

44. The little evidence that exists suggests that Smith was a native of London; at least both Captain Mayhew Folger and Sir Thomas Staines, commanders of the first two vessels to visit Pitcairn after the arrival of the mutineers, believed him to be English. See

the record of Folger's visit in Amasa Delano, *A Narrative of Voyages and Travels* (Boston, 1817), pp. 141–142, and Staines's report to the Admiralty of his stay at Pitcairn, reprinted in *The Saga of the Bounty*, ed. Irvin Anthony (New York, 1935), pp. 354–356.

45. Attempts to devise a more satisfying ending to the *Bounty* incident than the accepted version provides continue to be made; according to Cuthbert Wilkinson in *The Wake of the Bounty* (London, 1953), Christian left Pitcairn about 1795 and with the aid of William Wordsworth took up secret residence in England where he served as the model for Coleridge's ancient mariner and lived out his remaining days in happiness.

46. See Hubert H. Bancroft, *History of the Pacific States of North America* (San Francisco, 1884), XXII, 358; F. W. Howay, "Early Days of the Maritime Fur Trade on the Northwest Coast," *Canadian Historical Review*, 4:27 (1923).

47. Sargent may have drawn on literary sources for some of this detail: *Robinson Crusoe* is an obvious parallel; Delano's *Voyages*, published two years before *Alexander Smith*, includes a detailed description of St. Felix Island (pp. 354–355), an account of the marooning of Alexander Selkirk on Juan Fernandez (pp. 308–309), and a lengthy discussion of the *Bounty* affair (chaps. 5–6); and Richard Alsop's very popular *Narrative of the Adventures and Sufferings of John R. Jewitt* (1815) is a rich source of information about life among the Northwest Indians. Due allowance must be made for the possibility of Sargent's personal familiarity with his material; according to Emma W. and Charles S. Sargent, *Epes Sargent of Gloucester* (Boston, 1923), p. 23, he "was a sea captain in the East India mercantile service," and his book may be in part "an account of his own career."

48. *The Life of Alexander Smith* (Boston, 1819), pp. 9, 94.

49. [Washington Irving], *The Sketch Book of Geoffrey Crayon, Gent. No. 1* (New York, 1819), pp. 14, 20. Contrast Irving's description with that of a very similar storm encountered by the narrator on a voyage to Tunis on board a Moslem vessel in Tyler's *Algerine Captive* (II, 235): "A tremendous storm arose, and the gale struck us with such violence, that our sails were instantly flittered into rags. We could not shew a yard of canvass, and were obliged to scud under bare poles. The night was excessively dark; and to increase our distress, our ballast shifted and we were obliged to cut away our masts by the board, to save us from foundering. The vessel righted, but being strong and light, and the hatchways well

secured, our captain was only fearful of being driven on some Christian coast." One suspects that, together with the creation of verisimilitude, a primary purpose of Tyler's account is to permit the inclusion of his ironical inversion of the conventional fear of shipwreck on a heathen coast. At any rate, the narrator's view of the sea is clearly detached and objectified.

II

The Tempestuous Ocean for a World

1. Throughout this discussion the terms *sea novel* and *sea story* will be reserved for those works of fiction in which nautical elements are predominant rather than incidental. In *Fenimore Cooper: La jeunesse (1789–1826)* (Aix-en-Provence, 1938), p. 428, Marcel Clavel describes the sea novel as including the ocean as the principal scene of action, seamen as principal characters, and a style which satisfies the technical interest of sailors without repelling the lay reader. Thus a peculiar concern of sea fiction in this sense becomes the relationship between the ocean and man. The sea is not merely a setting that permits extravagant action, as it is, for example, in Defoe's *Captain Singleton;* nor is the sailor of interest only for his grotesque eccentricity, as he is in Smollett's *Peregrine Pickle.* Rather, as in Cooper, Melville, and Conrad, a central theme of the sea novel is the significance of the ocean to man in its roles as a shaper of human character and as an index of the nature of the universe.

2. See his letters written to his brother Richard and dated November 7, 1808, December 19, 1808, and May 18, 1810, published in *The Letters and Journals of James Fenimore Cooper,* ed. James F. Beard (Cambridge, Mass., 1960), I, 11–12, 17–18. There is considerable evidence of Cooper's longing for military glory and nautical authority during the years just prior to the composition of *The Pilot.* See, for example, Susan Fenimore Cooper's description in "Small Family Memories," *Correspondence of James Fenimore-Cooper,* ed. James F. Cooper (New Haven, 1922), I, 37, of her father's grand appearance in the magnificent uniform of a colonel

in the New York militia and of his playing master of the *Union*, the whaler in which he had a part interest.

3. *Correspondence*, I, 35.

4. For a comprehensive discussion of such appeals see John C. McCloskey, "The Campaign of Periodicals After the War of 1812 for National American Literature," *PMLA*, 50:262–273 (1935).

5. For an account of the history of the *Repository* and of Cooper's connection with it see James F. Beard's introduction to his facsimile edition of Cooper's *Early Critical Essays (1820–1822)* (Gainesville, Fla., 1955), pp. [vii–xiv]. Coleman's prospectus is quoted on p. [ix].

6. *Ibid.*, p. 140.

7. *Ibid.*, pp. 97–98.

8. *Ibid.*, pp. 4, 19–20.

9. *Ibid.*, p. 29.

10. *Notions of the Americans: Picked up by a Travelling Bachelor* (Philadelphia, 1828), II, 73–74.

11. *Ibid.*, II, 79.

12. *Ibid.*, I, 7, 19–21, 42.

13. *Ibid.*, I, 9; II, 87, 72. Cooper's grandiose vision of the future maritime supremacy of the United States was satirized in Fitz-Greene Halleck's "Red Jacket" (1828), which predicted that in fifty years "our brave fleet, eight frigates and a schooner,/Will sweep the seas from Zembla to the Line."

14. *Notions of the Americans*, I, 12–16.

15. *Ibid.*, II, 83–84, 86; I, 337, note B.

16. *The Pilot*, 5th ed. (Philadelphia, 1832), I, 6.

17. From the final preface to *The Pilot*, p. viii. For a full account of Cooper's objections to *The Pirate* and of his contention that a work "with the scene laid on the ocean, whose machinery would be the ships and the waves, whose principal characters should be seamen, acting and talking as such, might be written with perfect professional accuracy, and yet possess equal interest with a similar book connected with the land," see Susan Fenimore Cooper's reminiscences in *The Cooper Gallery; or, Pages and Pictures from the Writings of James Fenimore Cooper* (New York, 1865), pp. 72–73, and in "Small Family Memories," *Correspondence*, I, 52–53.

18. *The Red Rover*, pp. vii–viii.

19. See, for example, the highly expository whaling episode in chap. 17 of *The Pilot* in which Cooper, leaning heavily on his earlier account of the American whale fishery in a review of Scoresby's

Account of the Arctic Regions (*Early Critical Essays*, pp. 59–63), seems to revise from the point of view of the deep-water sailor Scott's description (*The Pirate*, chap. 17) of the Zetlanders' lubberly attack on a stranded whale.

20. *The Red Rover*, new ed. (Philadelphia, 1836), I, 4; *The Pilot*, 5th ed., I, 5–6. In later years Cooper regarded the attempt in his early novels to achieve a compromise between romantic invention and historical fidelity as a failure. In *The Cooper Gallery*, p. 77, Susan Fenimore Cooper recalls her father's later dissatisfaction with *The Pilot*. He viewed the characterization of Jones as more idealized than the facts of Jones's life would justify. He would gladly have severed the link between the pilot and Jones and "left the pilot as vaguely connected with the annals of the country, as the ship he steered." As early as 1833, the date of the second and final preface to *The Water-Witch*, Cooper ascribed the unpopularity of that book to its attempt to blend "too much of the real with the purely ideal. Halfway measures will not do in matters of this sort; and it is always safer to preserve the identity of a book by a fixed and determinate character, than to make the effort to steer between the true and the false" (*The Water-Witch*, p. vi).

21. *Early Critical Essays*, pp. 100–101.

22. *The Cooper Gallery*, p. 18.

23. See Edward P. Vandiver, "James Fenimore Cooper and Shakspere," *Shakespeare Association Bulletin*, 15:110–117 (1940).

24. The ratio of chapters of action on land to those of action on shipboard in *The Pilot* is approximately 4:3. In *The Red Rover* the ratio is 1:3 and in *The Water-Witch* 3:4.

25. See Vandiver, *Shakespeare Association Bulletin*, 15:116, and Yvor Winters' discussion of the rhetoric of *The Water-Witch* in *Maule's Curse* (Norfolk, Conn., 1938), pp. 47–49.

26. See *The Cooper Gallery*, p. 178, and Cooper's letter to Moore, October 20, 1827, in *Letters and Journals*, I, 228.

27. In certain details Cooper's account of this race in *Gleanings in Europe*, I, 12–13, suggests the description of the pursuit of the *Royal Caroline* by the *Dolphin* in *The Red Rover*, chaps. 14–16. The climax of both chases occurs when the pursuing vessel sheers off to leeward before the gale and is lost in the mist.

28. *Notions of the Americans*, II, 62–63.

29. *The Red Rover*, pp. 15–17.

30. *Ibid.*, pp. 167, 410, 494–495.

31. *Ibid.*, pp. 354–355.

32. *Ibid.*, p. 522.

33. See the unpubl. diss. (Yale, 1954) by John H. Clagett, "Cooper and the Sea: Naval Life and Naval History in the Writings of James Fenimore Cooper," I, 341–342.

34. First preface (1830); see *The Water-Witch*, new ed. (New York, 1852), I, v. The supposed commander of the brigantine, for example, likes " 'neither this manner of ruling a nation by deputy, nor the principle which says that one bit of earth is to make laws for another' " (*The Water-Witch*, p. 189).

35. *The Pilot*, p. 9.

36. *The Red Rover*, p. viii.

37. Stock romantic devices are equally prominent in *The Pilot* and *The Water-Witch*. In *The Pilot* Katherine Plowden masquerades as a man, and Mr. Gray and Alice Dunscombe enjoy a remarkable reunion. In *The Water-Witch* Alida is abducted aboard ship by the supposed Master Seadrift, actually the girl Eudora who, in an elaborate recognition scene, proves to be Alida's cousin. It should be noted that Cooper does not employ two of the most familiar conventions of romance, the formulaic storm and the miraculous rescue from shipwreck. Storms and rescues, of course, abound in his sea novels, but they never follow a set conventional pattern. Cooper never sacrifices authenticity in matters of seamanship for romantic effect. Thus, although the rescue of the survivors of the *Caroline* in *The Red Rover* is extraordinary, it is in no sense miraculous, for Cooper keeps the incident firmly within the bounds of nautical probability by surrounding it with convincing circumstantial detail.

38. Clavel, *Fenimore Cooper: La jeunesse*, pp. 431–432.

39. For a comprehensive discussion of the conventional devices of romance shared by Cooper and Shakespeare, see W. B. Gates, "Cooper's Indebtedness to Shakespeare," *PMLA*, 67:716–731 (1952).

40. *The Red Rover*, pp. 28–29, 233–235, 240.

41. *The Red Rover*, pp. 40, 111; *The Corsair*, Canto I, lines 193–211.

42. " 'None can look into the secret heart' " of the Rover (p. 363), but with his "penetrating . . . glances" he can "read the countenance of his associates" (p. 99); Conrad has "the skill, when Cunning's gaze would seek/To probe his heart and watch his changing cheek,/At once the observer's purpose to espy,/And on himself roll back his scrutiny" (Canto I, lines 217–220).

43. *The Red Rover,* pp. 338, 355–356; *The Corsair,* Canto I, lines 539–544, 253–264.

44. *The Red Rover,* pp. 102, 307, 91–92. Compare the Rover's weapons with Selim's accouterments in *The Bride of Abydos,* Canto II, lines 613–632. In a note appended to *The Giaour,* line 355, Byron describes the "ataghan" as "a long dagger worn with pistols in the belt." The description of the Rover's cabin parallels those of Lambro's house in *Don Juan,* Canto III, stanzas 61–69, and of the interior of the harem in Canto V, stanzas 93–94. Cooper's remark that in the furnishing of the Rover's cabin "splendour and elegance seemed to have been much more consulted than propriety or taste" (p. 92) echoes Byron's criticism of the decoration of the harem, where "wealth had done wonders—taste not much" (Canto V, stanza 94).

45. There is some evidence for the supposition that *The Red Rover* was influenced by Thomas Hope's oriental tale *Anastasius* (1819). For one thing, Cooper adopts Hope's, not Byron's, spelling of the word *yatagan,* and, according to the *New English Dictionary,* the first known instance of such a spelling is in *Anastasius.* More important, certain details of plot and characterization in *Anastasius* parallel *The Red Rover.* In both novels the equivocal conduct of the master of a merchant ship leads the passengers to suspect that he intends to deliver the ship into the hands of pirates; both refer to the tendency of Mediterranean sailors to substitute prayer for effort in moments of crisis; and in both a strange vessel seen during a storm is assumed to be the *Flying Dutchman.* The Rover and Anastasius resemble each other in that both are ruled by pride; they share a love of excitement and a delight in struggle (both refer to this characteristic in terms of the metaphor of storm); they affirm a common belief in the finality of death and the necessity of seizing pleasure while they may; and both heroes, after being frustrated in the expression of their patriotism, become enemies of all organized societies.

46. [William H. Prescott], rev. of *English Literature of the Nineteenth Century* in *North American Review,* 35:190 (1832).

47. "The sublime spectacle of the ocean in unbridled fury, the nobility of the seaman triumphant over the elements by the exercise of his wit and skill, the valor of the ship that struggles for survival like a living creature, the glory that illumines the carnage, of all these Smollett had seen hardly anything, had felt nothing": Clavel, *Fenimore Cooper: La jeunesse,* p. 437.

48. *The Corsair,* Canto I, lines 1–3, 13–16, 93–94.

49. *The Red Rover,* pp. 223, 230.

50. *Ibid.,* pp. 259–261, 263, 274. The metaphor of sleep is a favorite device of Cooper for describing the latent vitality of a calm sea; cf. *The Water-Witch,* pp. 82–83: "the surface of the immense waste was perfectly unruffled . . . but the body of the element was heaving and settling heavily, in a manner to resemble the sleeping respiration of some being of huge physical frame."

51. Stanley T. Williams, "James Fenimore Cooper," *Literary History of the United States,* ed. Robert E. Spiller *et al.* (New York, 1953), p. 261.

52. *The Prairie,* pp. 14–15.

53. *Ibid.,* p. 29.

54. *Satanstoe,* pp. 421–422.

55. *The Prairie,* p. 232.

56. *The Wept of Wish-Ton-Wish,* p. 424. It must be pointed out that Cooper's association of woods and water works only one way; that is, although he frequently compares the forest to the ocean, he rarely compares the ocean to the forest. For Cooper, and perhaps for the majority of his audience, the process consisted in part of the translation of the unfamiliar into the familiar. Thus *The Prairie,* the locale of which Cooper had not visited (see *The Cooper Gallery,* pp. 142–143), contains more nautical similes and analogies than any of his other novels of the wilderness.

57. Boynton, *Literature and American Life,* pp. 263–264; R. W. B. Lewis, *The American Adam: Innocence, Tragedy and Tradition in the Nineteenth Century* (Chicago, 1955), p. 99.

58. *The Pathfinder,* pp. 4, 115.

59. *The Water-Witch,* pp. 405, 445.

60. *The Red Rover,* p. 228.

61. *Ibid.,* pp. 291–292.

62. Joseph Conrad, *Notes on Life and Letters* (London, 1921), p. 76.

63. *The Red Rover,* p. 348.

64. *Ibid.,* pp. 225, 333.

65. *Ibid.,* p. 347.

66. *The Water-Witch,* pp. 125, 461.

67. *The Pilot,* pp. 99, 11.

68. *The Water-Witch,* p. 169.

69. *The Red Rover,* p. 300.

70. *Ibid.,* p. 255.

71. *The Water-Witch,* pp. 98, 257. For other examples of the metaphor of the bird, see *The Pilot,* pp. 103, 309; *The Red Rover,* pp. 197, 383, 426, 470, 483; *The Water-Witch,* pp. 252, 340.

72. *The Red Rover,* pp. 177, 220. For other examples of the metaphor of the horse, see *The Pilot,* p. 217; *The Red Rover,* pp. 237, 252, 425; *The Water-Witch,* p. 211. Susan Fenimore Cooper testifies to her father's fondness for fiery stallions; see her account of his Gilpin-like experience with "Bullhead" in "Small Family Memories," *Correspondence,* I, 36–37.

73. *The Pilot,* p. 301.

74. *The Water-Witch,* p. 77; see also pp. 125, 165, 197, 229, 340, 353.

75. *The Pilot,* p. 52.

76. *The Red Rover,* pp. 143–145, 207.

77. *The Water-Witch,* pp. 231, 396, 211, 384, 165.

78. *The Red Rover,* pp. 469–471.

79. Cooper's friend Horatio Greenough, the sculptor and aesthetician, held a remarkably similar conception of the ship. In "American Architecture," *United States Magazine and Democratic Review,* 13:208 (1843), Greenough celebrates the functional beauty of naval architecture in descriptive terms very like those of Cooper: he urges his fellow artists to "observe a ship at sea! Mark the majestic form of her hull as she rushes through the water, observe the graceful bend of her body, the gentle transition from round to flat, the grasp of her keel, the leap of her bows, the symmetry and rich tracery of her spars and rigging, and those grand wind muscles, her sails! Behold an organization second only to that of an animal, obedient as the horse, swift as the stag, and bearing the burthen of a thousand camels from pole to pole! What Academy of Design, what research of connoisseurship, what imitation of the Greeks produced this marvel of construction?" For a discussion of the interplay of opinions and attitudes between Greenough and Cooper, see James F. Beard, "Cooper and His Artistic Contemporaries," *James Fenimore Cooper: A Re-Appraisal,* ed. Mary E. Cunningham (Cooperstown, 1954), p. 114.

80. *The Pilot,* pp. 20, 325, 292.

81. *The Red Rover,* pp. 227, 462, 226, 473–474.

82. *The Water-Witch,* p. 93.

83. *The Red Rover,* pp. 311, 132, 224.

84. *The Water-Witch,* p. 257.

85. *The Red Rover,* p. 211.

86. *Ibid.*, p. 300.

87. *The Water-Witch*, p. 76.

88. *The Pilot*, p. 484. There seems to be more than a suggestion of Cooper's conception of himself in characters like Griffith and Ludlow. Griffith's withdrawal from the sea clearly parallels Cooper's; moreover, like Cooper, Griffith was born in New Jersey, attended a good college, and inherited property. In the early romances the further Cooper moves from the duplication of his own experience toward the imaginative fulfillment of his abortive naval career, the more successful he seems to be. The very different effect of autobiographical elements in *Afloat and Ashore* is discussed in a later chapter.

89. *The Red Rover*, pp. 319, 33–34; cf. the description of Boltrope, "a hard-featured, square-built, athletic man," having "small, hard eyes" (*The Pilot*, pp. 79, 470).

90. *The Pilot*, p. 19; *The Water-Witch*, p. 38.

91. Samuel Adams Drake, *Nooks and Corners of the New England Coast* (New York, 1875), p. 334, identifies Reuben Chase, the Nantucket-born midshipman of the *Bon Homme Richard*, as the model for Coffin; W. B. Shubrick Clymer, *James Fenimore Cooper* (Boston, 1900), pp. 35–36, suggests Mr. Irish, first mate of the *Sterling*, as a prototype; Clavel, *Fenimore Cooper: La jeunesse*, p. 495, note 209, thinks Philadelphia Bill of the *Sterling* a more likely candidate; and Clagett, "Cooper and the Sea," I, 17, offers Stephen Stimpson, another member of the crew of the *Sterling*, as a source for Coffin, Moses Marble in *Afloat and Ashore*, and Stephen Stimson in *The Sea Lions*.

92. *The Water-Witch*, pp. 39, 350, 428–429.

III

The Dangers of the Deep

1. *The Pilot*, pp. viii, xi. The first part of the final preface, from which these passages are quoted, is identical to the preface in the Bentley edition.

2. A long succession of sketches of life in the Royal Navy offered additional models for American authors. Ranging from the purely

reportorial to the purely fictional, these sketches include Moor's *Original Anecdotes of a Naval Officer* (1795), Thelwall's *Trident of Albion* (1805), Urquhart's *Naval Sketches* (1814), Warneford's *The Jolly Boat* (1815), Glascock's *The Naval Sketch Book* (1826), Bower's *Naval Adventures* (1833), and James Scott's *Recollections of Naval Life* (1834). Emphasizing naval manners rather than the sea and its influence on man, such sketches are in the tradition of Smollett's naval episodes and the service novels of Marryat, Chamier, and Howard. The influence of Cooper's more general interest in the sea, the ship, and the sailor distinguishes the work of the better American chroniclers of naval life from that of their British counterparts. For a survey of British naval sketches see Charles N. Robinson and John Leyland, *The British Tar in Fact and Fiction* (New York, 1909), pp. 298–308.

3. See Charles Oscar Paullin, "Naval Administration Under Naval Commissioners: 1815–1842," *United States Naval Institute Proceedings*, 33:598, 613–614, 629–631 (1907); Howard I. Chapelle, *The History of the American Sailing Navy* (New York, 1949), p. 338.

4. *Thirty Years View* (New York, 1854), II, 144.

5. [Nathaniel Ames], *Nautical Reminiscences* (Providence, 1832), p. [3].

6. *Pencillings by the Way*, new ed. (London, 1842), pp. 170–171. Other examples of the mixture of travelogue and naval sketching include *Sketches of Naval Life* (1829) by George Jones, a schoolmaster; *A Visit to the South Seas* (1831) by C. S. Stewart, a chaplain; *Three Years in the Pacific* (1834) by William S. W. Ruschenberger, a surgeon; *Ship and Shore: or Leaves from the Journal of a Cruise to the Levant* (1835) by Walter Colton, a chaplain; and *Voyage of the United States Frigate Potomac* (1835) by J. N. Reynolds, private secretary to Commodore Downes.

7. *Niles' Weekly Register*, June 22, 1822, p. 264.

8. See *Niles' Weekly Register*, May 24, 1823, p. 177; Robert Greenhalgh Albion and Jennie Barnes Pope, *Sea Lanes in Wartime: The American Experience, 1775–1942* (New York, 1942), p. 142.

9. *Niles' Weekly Register*, October 20, 1821, p. 118.

10. Quoted in Carlos Gilman Calkins, "Repression of Piracy in the West Indies, 1814–1825," *United States Naval Institute Proceedings*, 37:1207 (1911). Unless otherwise noted, the factual material in this paragraph is drawn from Calkins' article, pp. 1197–1238.

11. *Niles' Weekly Register,* January 8, 1820, p. 309.

12. Examples include *Narrative of the Capture, Sufferings and Escape of Capt. Barnabas Lincoln and His Crew, Who Were Taken by a Piratical Schooner, December, 1821, off Key Largo* (1822); *Mutiny and Murder: Confession of Charles Gibbs, a Native of Rhode Island* (1831); and *A Report of the Trial of [Twelve Spanish Seamen for] . . . Piracy, on Board of the Brig Mexican, of Salem* (1834).

13. Irving, too, had shown that piracy could be glamourized if it were cloaked in the supernatural and located in the past (pt. iv, "The Money-Diggers," of *Tales of a Traveler* [1824]). But though their style and tone were vastly influential on the shorter fiction of the period, Irving's sketches, like Scott's *The Pirate,* gave no precedent for the treatment of piracy as a maritime subject: his quaint and rambling legends make no attempt to utilize the sea, seamen, and ships as fictional materials.

14. Kidd's face is marked by "passion uncontrolled and unrestrained" and by "stern and darksome thought," but his manner betokens "an acquaintance with the courteous rules of the world, somewhat above the sphere in which he was acting"; see *The Buccaneers: A Romance of Our Country, in Its Ancient Day* (Boston, 1827), I, 214–215. Judah's novel also offers several striking parallels to *The Water-Witch:* the setting of the two novels is nearly identical in time and place; Vanderspeigl, a receiver of stolen goods, and his negro servant Yonne are very like Van Beverout and Bonnie; and Judah's experiments with portraiture by dialect and characteristic metaphor strongly resemble Cooper's manipulation of dialogue.

15. Like Cooper, the anonymous author of *The Memoirs* seems to have used *The Corsair* as a model: Lafitte's form is slight but active, his fair complexion has been tanned by exposure except where it is shaded by his curling hair, his features are "femininely regular, his forehead high and proudly arched," and his eyes appear "to flash lightning, and at a glance penetrate the secret recesses of the heart"; see *Lafitte or the Baratarian Chief* (New York, 1828), pp. 8–9.

16. Anon. rev. of *Blackbeard* in *New-England Magazine,* 9:77 (1835).

17. *Ramon, the Rover of Cuba, and Other Tales* (New York, 1843), pp. 32, 110.

18. *Ibid.,* p. 39.

19. Although *The Memoirs of Lafitte* purports to record the history of the famous pirate of the Gulf, the narrative pays little heed to the facts of Lafitte's career and makes no attempt to represent the maritime life of the era.

20. *Ramon, the Rover*, pp. 103, 124, 50, 59–60.

21. *Ibid.*, pp. 129, 78, 84.

22. *Ibid.*, pp. 98–99, 100.

23. [Joseph C. Hart], *Miriam Coffin; or, The Whale-Fishermen* (New York, 1834), II, 205–206.

24. *Ibid.*, I, 190; II, 107; I, 189, 30. In his effort to root American maritime activity in the past, Hart predates the American exploitation of the Pacific whaling grounds by nearly twenty years. The first whaler to enter the Pacific was not, as Hart says, an American vessel in the early 1770's but the British ship *Amelia* in 1788. The first American whaler to round the Horn was the *Beaver* of Nantucket in 1791; see Clifford W. Ashley, *The Yankee Whaler* (Boston, 1938), p. 38.

25. *Miriam Coffin*, I, 197–198.

26. *Ibid.*, I, 32; II, 81, 25–26, 108, 83. Leon Howard, "A Predecessor of Moby-Dick," *Modern Language Notes*, 49:310–311 (1934), and Charles R. Anderson, *Melville in the South Seas* (New York, 1939), pp. 55–56, 448, note 25, point out that several of the names and details of *Moby-Dick* parallel those of *Miriam Coffin*, from which Melville quotes in "Extracts." In both novels the action is intensified by being foreshadowed by a prophecy of doom, whalers are sunk by collision with enormous bull whales, men perish in the jaws of sperm whales, and characters are named Starbuck and Peleg. It seems worth noting that broader, but equally striking, similarities in characterization and tone also exist.

27. *Miriam Coffin*, I, 197; II, 37, 41–42.

28. *Ibid.*, II, 183.

29. *Ibid.*, II, 202–203.

30. An example is the anonymous sketch "The Old Seaman" (1823), a static caricature in the manner of Dibdin.

31. "Modern Chivalry," *The Atlantic Souvenir* (Philadelphia, [1826], p. 36. Another sentimental sea story that follows Cooper in the use of a historical setting is Godfrey Wallace's "Giles Heatherby, the Free Trader" (1830).

32. Stories of contemporary piracy include "A Tale of the Sea" (1827) by "Alaric"; Samuel Hazzard's "Extracts from a Sea Book" (1828); "The Pirates: A Sea Tale" (1831) by "Kelpie"; the anony-

mous "Naval Life" (1834), "The Freebooter" (1834), and "Scene on the Bahama Banks" (1834); John W. Gould's "Cruise of a Guinea-Man" (1835) and "The Pirate of the South Pacific" (1835); Ames's "The Pirate of Masafuero" (1835); and the anonymous "The Fare-well at Sea" (1835).

33. Stories of contemporary naval life include Godfrey Wallace's "The Esmeralda" (1829); the anonymous "An Affair of Honor" (1833); "The Deserters" (1833) by "Seadrift"; the anonymous "The Reefer's First Cruise" (1834); Gould's "Off Cape Horn" (1834), "A Portugue Breakfast" (1834) and "My First and Last Flogging" (1834); "Extract from a Log" (1835) and "Life in a Steerage" (1835) by "Delta"; Robert Burts's "Naval Fragments" (1835); the anony-mous "Recollections of a Sailor" (1835); "Adventures of a Reefer" (1835) by "Jerry Smallfull"; "The Cruise of the Mohawk" (1835) by "Jack Block"; Burts's "The Man Overboard" (1835); and the anonymous "Breakers! A Scene at Sea" (1835). Only four of the naval stories that I have examined are set in the past: the anony-mous "A Chapter of Sea Life" (1833); Gould's "The Capture of the Frigate President" (1834) and "Capture of the Cyane and Levant" (1834); and the anonymous "Naval Reminiscence" (1835).

34. Weld's story, which was first published in the *New-England Magazine* in 1835, reprinted a month later in the *Military and Naval Magazine,* and pressed into service as the first chapter of Weld's book *Ribs and Trucks* (1842), may have served as a source for Melville. In *The Trying-Out of Moby-Dick* (Boston, 1949), pp. 331–332, Howard P. Vincent points out the close resemblance of the description of the try-works in *Ribs and Trucks* to chap. 96 of *Moby-Dick,* but he does not mention that the description first appeared in 1835 or that it was written by Weld. John Gould's story "The Mutiny" (1834) is another early fictional treatment of the whale fishery.

35. Approximately two thirds of the short sea stories published in the period 1827–1835 are narrated in the first person; of the sea stories mentioned in this chapter, seventeen are yarns in the sense that they pretend to be narrated by a seaman in nautical dialect.

36. Ames's stories were collected in *An Old Sailor's Yarns* (1835), and Gould's were published posthumously together with his other literary remains in *Private Journal of a Voyage from New-York to Rio de Janeiro* (1839) and by themselves in *Forecastle Yarns* (1845).

37. *The Development of the American Short Story* (New York, 1923), p. 55.

38. By 1835 "The Main-Truck," for example, had made at least four separate appearances: in the *New York Mirror*, August 28, 1830, pp. 60–61; in *The Mariner's Library or Voyager's Companion* (Boston, 1832), pp. 356–364; in *Naval Stories* (New York, 1834), pp. 109–126; and in *The Atlantic Club-Book* (New York, 1834), I, 51–65. The success of the story prompted George P. Morris to write a metrical version of it; see his *Poems* (New York, 1860), pp. 54–55.

39. Biographical material in this paragraph is drawn from Allan Westcott in *Dictionary of American Biography, s.v.* "Leggett, William"; Page S. Proctor, "William Leggett (1801–1839): Journalist and Literator," *Papers of the Bibliographical Society of America*, 44:239–253 (1950).

40. *Tales and Sketches by a Country Schoolmaster* (New York, 1829), pp. 145, 141, 143.

41. *Ibid.*, pp. 208, 215.

42. Simms's story "A Sea-Piece," apparently derived from "A Watch in the Main-Top," is frankly cast in the form of a dream.

43. *Naval Stories*, pp. 83, 123.

44. *Ibid.*, pp. 23–26, 29–30.

45. *Tales and Sketches*, pp. 205, 210; *Naval Stories*, pp. 90–91.

46. *Naval Stories*, pp. 154–156.

47. *Ibid.*, pp. 164–165, 168–169, 173. Melville makes a very similar use of the ironic juxtaposition of the solemn words of worship and the curses of nautical commands: see *White-Jacket*, p. 195. In references to Melville's novels pagination and text are those of the Constable edition, 16 vols. (London, 1922–1924).

48. *Naval Stories*, pp. 174–175; cf. *White-Jacket*, p. 175. Page S. Proctor, "A Source for the Flogging Incident in *White-Jacket*," *American Literature*, 22:176–182 (1950), identifies this incident as the source for White Jacket's plan to leap into the sea with Captain Claret in his arms if he is to be flogged (*White-Jacket*, pp. 352–353). A curious historical parallel to the incident used by Leggett and Melville exists in Fletcher Christian's threat on the day before he led the mutiny aboard the *Bounty:* if Bligh were to flog him, " 'it would be the death of us both, for I am sure I should take him in my arms and jump overboard with him' " (quoted in Wilkinson, *The Wake of the Bounty*, p. 38, from a pamphlet by Edward Christian published in 1794).

49. Most of Ames's protests against injustice in the naval and

merchant services are contained in *A Mariner's Sketches* (1830), a book which is a major source for *White-Jacket* but which, as a work of nonfiction, lies beyond the scope of this study. Only a feeble undercurrent of protest is evident in Ames's fiction; in "The Rivals," for example, he refers in passing to "that tyranny that but too many of our navy officers think indispensable" (*An Old Sailor's Yarns*, pp. 90–91).

50. From Edward Gould's "Biographical Sketch," *Private Journal*, p. 5. Gould's humanitarian outrage is only rarely expressed in his fiction, chiefly in the story "My First and Last Flogging," which, after giving in its opening pages an effective portrait of a sadistic officer aboard the frigate *Java*, quickly degenerates into adolescent fantasy of the most blatant sort.

IV

The Light and Dark Together

1. *American Humor: A Study of the National Character* (New York, 1955), p. 110.

2. [Francis Bowen], rev. of Cooper's *Gleanings in Europe* in *North American Review*, 46:12–13 (1838).

3. *An Old Sailor's Yarns*, p. 372; *A Mariner's Sketches* (Providence, 1830), pp. 238–239. For a discussion of Ames's jealousy of Cooper see Warren Walker, "Ames vs. Cooper: The Case Reopened," *Modern Language Notes*, 70:27–32 (1955).

4. *Knickerbocker*, 23:151 (1844).

5. Anon. rev., *Gentleman's Magazine*, 1:288 (1837).

6. Anon. rev., *United States Magazine and Democratic Review*, 8:318–332 (1840); rev. [by E. T. Channing], *North American Review*, 52:56–75 (1841); anon. rev., *Knickerbocker*, 16:348–352 (1840); anon. rev., *New York Review*, 7:535–537 (1840). *The Southern Literary Messenger*, 6:781 (1840), ran counter to the general praise of Dana's book: an anonymous reviewer found that it "contains little that is new or striking" and suspected that it was written in the hope of enlarging the author's legal practice among seamen. It should be noted, however, that this magazine consistently opposed

any realistic treatment of the sea in the books that it reviewed.

7. *Two Years Before the Mast* (New York, 1911), p. 1. Ames, of course, had published two additional volumes describing maritime life, *An Old Sailor's Yarns* and *Nautical Reminiscences*. Moreover, other common seamen had previously published accounts of their nautical experiences, but most of these books, such as James R. Durand's *Life and Adventures* (1820), a somber history of hardship and injustice afloat, and William McNally's bitter *Evils and Abuses in the Naval and Merchant Service, Exposed* (1839), were so obscurely published and so nearly illiterate that they were virtually unknown. In sending a copy of *Two Years Before the Mast* to Cooper, R. H. Dana, Sr., apologized for his son's ignorance of Cooper's service in the merchant marine as a foremast hand; see *Correspondence*, II, 422–424.

8. *Two Years Before the Mast*, pp. 1, 40.

9. *Ibid.*, pp. 2, 396–397.

10. Rev. of Browne's *Etchings of a Whaling Cruise* and Codman's *Sailors' Life and Sailors' Yarns* in *Literary World*, 1:105 (1847).

11. From a review of *The Wept of Wish-Ton-Wish* in the *Essex Gazette* for January 2, 1830, reprinted in Edwin Harrison Cady and Harry Hayden Clark, eds., *Whittier on Writers and Writing: The Uncollected Critical Writings of John Greenleaf Whittier* (Syracuse, 1950), pp. 26–27. The editors point out that Whittier's "opinions are unusually significant testimony to the reception, vogue, and general reputation of other writers" (p. 1).

12. Anon. rev. of Channing's *Sermons and Tracts* in *Edinburgh Review*, 50:128 (1829).

13. See *Correspondence*, I, 295, 309.

14. *A Letter to His Countrymen* (New York, 1834), p. 98; *Correspondence*, I, 334.

15. *The Monikins* was notorious as the book no one read; see *United States Magazine and Democratic Review*, 21:444 (1847). The *American Monthly Magazine*, 5:487 (1835), refused to review the book, terming it "a monument of human delusion," while the *Knickerbocker*, 6:152–153 (1835), ascribed the failure of the book to its attempt to mingle politics and fiction: "one is the *reality*, the other the *ideality* of life." For an account of the reception of the critical nonfiction see Robert E. Spiller's introduction to *Gleanings*, I, xiv–xxx.

16. *Homeward Bound*, pp. [v], 154, 130, 126.

17. *The Red Rover*, pp. [vii], viii.

18. The work was conceived as early as 1825, according to *Niles' Weekly Register*, February 26, 1825, p. 416.

19. *The History of the Navy of the United States of America* (London, 1839), I, vi, viii.

20. See *Gleanings*, II, 313–314.

21. *History of the Navy*, I, [xi], 4.

22. *Mercedes of Castile*, p. 150.

23. *Gleanings*, II, 157. According to Spiller, the first draft of this passage was composed in 1828, although it was not published until 1837.

24. For a thorough demonstration of the close connections between the *History of the Navy* and *The Two Admirals*, see R. H. Ballinger, "The Origins of James Fenimore Cooper's *The Two Admirals*," *American Literature*, 20:20–24 (1948).

25. Robert E. Spiller, *James Fenimore Cooper: Representative Selections* (New York, [1936]), p. 347, describes the book as "an eddy rather than a part of the current of Cooper's literary development"; in *James Fenimore Cooper* (New York, 1949), pp. 173–174, James Grossman views *Wing-and-Wing* as an attempt to return to the mood of magical unreality in *The Water-Witch*.

26. *Wing-and-Wing*, pp. 283, 58, 323.

27. See Cooper's *Excursions in Italy* (Paris, 1838), pp. 89–103, 133–148.

28. *Correspondence*, II, 490–491, 495–496, 519.

29. *Ned Myers; or, A Life Before the Mast*, ed. J. Fenimore Cooper (Philadelphia, 1843), pp. iii, vi.

30. *Ibid.*, pp. 221, 23.

31. *Afloat and Ashore*, I, 58–59; cf. *Ned Myers*, p. 204: " 'You look as if you had been dragged through h—, and beaten with a soot-bag!' " In this study the title *Afloat and Ashore* refers to both volumes of the novel; thus the volume titled *Afloat and Ashore* in the Townsend edition is cited as *Afloat and Ashore*, I, and that titled *Miles Wallingford* is cited as *Afloat and Ashore*, II.

32. *Gleanings*, II, 9, 241, 244–248; *Ned Myers*, pp. 26, 33; *Afloat and Ashore*, I, 60, 163–171, 173–175.

33. *Afloat and Ashore*, II, 211, 202; *Ned Myers*, pp. 25, 36.

34. *Afloat and Ashore*, I, 11, 14, 50, 103–105, 300; II, 244. Cf. *History of the Navy*, I, 243–246, 318–319.

35. *History of the Navy*, I, 187.

36. *Afloat and Ashore*, II, 433.

37. In writing *Homeward Bound*, Cooper drew the details of the

episode that takes place on the west coast of Africa from Judah Paddock's *Narrative of the Shipwreck of the Ship Oswego* (1818); see H. H. Scudder, "Cooper and the Barbary Coast," *PMLA*, 62: 784–792 (1947).

38. On August 23, 1844, when he was working on the last one hundred pages of the second volume of *Afloat and Ashore*, Cooper wrote to his wife from a hotel in Philadelphia that "Charles Wilkes is in this house, superintending the publication of his work. It will be a very magnificent book, and I make no doubt will do him credit" (*Correspondence*, II, 525–526).

39. See *Afloat and Ashore*, I, 274: "I see that Captain Beechy [*sic*], in his voyage, speaks of a wreck that occurred in 1792, on a *reef*, where in 1826 he found an island near three leagues long, bearing tall trees."

40. Anon. rev., *Spectator*, 17:567–568 (1844).

41. Cooper makes specific reference to Cook's *Voyages* in at least two works which antedate *Afloat and Ashore*: see *Early Critical Essays*, p. 95, and *Excursions in Italy*, p. 196. Susan Fenimore Cooper lists Mackenzie and Lewis and Clark among the authorities whom her father consulted for information about Indians: see *The Cooper Gallery*, p. 129. Evidence of Cooper's familiarity with Cleveland's *Narrative* and Irving's *Astoria* is given in my text.

42. *Afloat and Ashore*, I, 218, 204–205, 213; Washington Irving, *Astoria or, Anecdotes of an Enterprise beyond the Rocky Mountains*, rev. ed., (New York, 1849), pp. 115, 109, 92.

43. James Cook, *Voyages* (London, 1842), II, 279–280, 263.

44. *Afloat and Ashore*, I, 202–203, 205.

45. *Ibid.*, I, pp. 217–219, 224, 228.

46. For an account of Mackenzie's unmerited attack on Cooper's *History of the Navy*, see Grossman, *James Fenimore Cooper*, pp. 188–189.

47. *Correspondence*, II, 510.

48. "Review of the Proceedings of the Naval Court Martial," *Proceedings of the Naval Court Martial in the Case of Alexander Slidell Mackenzie* (New York, 1844), p. 265.

49. *Afloat and Ashore*, I, 244–245.

50. See, for example, Anderson, *Melville in the South Seas*, and Vincent, *The Trying-Out of Moby-Dick*, two extended studies of the origins of Melville's fiction. A strikingly specific instance of the similarity of the techniques of Cooper in *Afloat and Ashore* and of Melville (whose cousin Guert Gansevoort was Mackenzie's first

lieutenant) is their common use of the *Somers* affair for fictional purposes; see Charles R. Anderson, "The Genesis of Billy Budd," *American Literature*, 12:329–346 (1940), and F. Barron Freeman, *Melville's Billy Budd* (Cambridge, Mass., 1948), pp. 57–65. Dana, too, was concerned with the issues raised by Mackenzie's action, but, unlike Cooper, he chose to defend the hangings; for an account of Dana's part in the controversy see James D. Hart, "Richard Henry Dana, Jr.," unpubl. diss. (Harvard, 1936), p. 158.

51. *Gleanings*, I, vii.

52. *Afloat and Ashore*, I, 51, 131, 138; II, 242. Compare the model at Clawbonny with the glass ship in Melville's *Redburn*, pp. 7–9.

53. *Afloat and Ashore*, I, 68, 159, 285, 450; II, 287.

54. *Ibid.*, I, 444, 448; II, 225, 315.

55. *Ibid.*, I, 306, 240; II, 363.

56. *Ibid.*, II, 32; I, 458–459, 96; II, 320; I, 184, 275.

57. *Ibid.*, I, 331, 456; II, 434.

58. *Ned Myers*, pp. v, 170, 201, 211.

59. *Afloat and Ashore*, I, 107, 109, 448; II, 317, 322, 329.

60. *Ibid.*, I, 61, 272, 137–138.

61. *Ibid.*, I, v–vi.

62. In *The Development of the English Sea Novel from Defoe to Conrad* (Ann Arbor, n.d.), p. 21, Ernest Carson Ross describes *Afloat and Ashore* as "a long tale of adventure, which has little unity other than what it gains from the central character"; were it not for the fact that its two volumes "derive some charm from being told in the first person, and reflect some of the author's early experiences afloat, they would hardly deserve a perusal by the lover of sea stories." In *James Fenimore Cooper*, p. 194, James Grossman, reading *Afloat and Ashore* as "an amusing compendium of all of Cooper's notions and a splendid collection of exciting adventures," praises the book as an anthology rather than as a novel. Stanley T. Williams, in his article on Cooper in *Literary History of the United States*, p. 268, finds that the scenes ashore blend "imperfectly with the romance of action" at sea.

63. *Ned Myers*, p. vi.

64. *Letters and Journals*, II, 369, 384; see also Grossman, *James Fenimore Cooper*, pp. 194–195.

65. *Afloat and Ashore*, II, 440; J. Fenimore Cooper, *A Residence in France; with an Excursion up the Rhine, and a Second Visit to Switzerland* (Paris, 1836), p. 293.

66. *Afloat and Ashore*, II, 382.

67. *Ibid.*, I, 48, 175, 421–422; II, 115–116, 81.

68. *Ibid.*, II, 415.

69. *Ibid.*, II, 435.

70. *Ibid.*, I, 457; II, 169, 129. Compare Miles's response to the frustrations of civilization with the emotions expressed in Cooper's letter from Paris to his nephew Richard in 1831: "now my longing is for a Wilderness—Cooperstown is far too populous and artificial for me and it is my intention to plunge somewhere into the forest, for six months in the year, at my return" (*Letters and Journals*, II, 89).

71. *Afloat and Ashore*, I, 378, 483, 404–405; II, 16.

72. *Ibid.*, II, 241, 288, 329.

73. *Ibid.*, II, 464; *The American Democrat or Hints on the Social and Civic Relations of the United States* (New York, 1956), p. 181; *The Heidenmauer*, p. 59.

74. In stressing the contrast between *Afloat and Ashore* and its predecessors, however, one must not overlook the fact that in *Afloat and Ashore* Cooper retains in large measure the serious tone that he had established in the early romances. Although he abandons characterizations as the embodiment of a few fixed traits, he does not abandon his notion of the essential dignity of the seaman. If *Afloat and Ashore* moves in the direction of realism, it does not constitute a return to the mood of Smollett's satirical exposé; rather, the novel attempts to elevate the problems and concerns of the seaman and his society to the stature of seriousness, an attempt that places *Afloat and Ashore* squarely in the mainstream of nineteenth-century fiction.

V

An Ocean Unapproachable and Unknown

1. For a study of Melville's indebtedness to *Life in a Man-of-War*, see Keith Huntress, "Melville's Use of a Source for *White-Jacket*," *American Literature*, 17:66–74 (1945). For an examination of the relation of both *Working a Passage* and Briggs's *Adventures of Harry Franco* (1839), a picaresque novel containing substantial nautical

elements, to *Redburn,* see Perry Miller, *The Raven and the Whale: The War of Words and Wits in the Era of Poe and Melville* (New York, 1956), pp. 55–56.

2. [Charles F. Briggs], *Working a Passage: or, Life in a Liner* (New York, 1844), pp. 18–19.

3. From an advertisement by the publisher in the story paper *The Flag of Our Union* for February 26, 1848; quoted in Mary Noel, *Villains Galore: The Heyday of the Popular Story Weekly* (New York, 1954), p. 33.

4. *The Complete Works of Edgar Allan Poe,* ed. James A. Harrison (New York, [1902]), III, 17.

5. *Ibid.,* III, 242.

6. *Ibid.,* III, 112–113.

7. Arthur Hobson Quinn, *Edgar Allan Poe: A Critical Biography* (New York, 1941), p. 264.

8. Poe, *Works,* III, 2–3, 101.

9. For an account of Poe's nautical background see Charles Lee Lewis, "Edgar Allan Poe and the Sea," *Southern Literary Messenger,* new series, 3:5–10 (1941). For studies of Poe's sources, see Edmund C. Stedman and George E. Woodberry, eds., *The Works of Edgar Allan Poe* (New York, 1914), V, 433–438; Woodberry, *The Life of Edgar Allan Poe* (Boston, 1909), I, 191; Robert Lee Rhea, "Some Observations on Poe's Origins," *University of Texas Studies in English,* 10:135–146 (1930); D. M. McKeithan, "Two Sources of Poe's 'Narrative of Arthur Gordon Pym,'" *University of Texas Studies in English,* 13:116–137 (1933); Keith Huntress, "Another Source for Poe's *Narrative of Arthur Gordon Pym,*" *American Literature,* 16:19–25 (1944). McKeithan identifies *The Mariner's Chronicle* (1806) as the nautical anthology that Poe ransacked. Huntress establishes the fact that Poe used some later anthology and suggests *Remarkable Events and Remarkable Shipwrecks* (1836) as the likeliest possibility. Certain identification of the anthologies used by Poe, however, is impossible in the absence of conclusive external evidence. The compilers of the dozen or more anthologies available to Poe freely borrowed material from each other; as a result, accounts of each of the individual incidents that Poe used appear in at least three different anthologies. In "Sources for Poe's *Arthur Gordon Pym,* 'Hans Pfaal,' and Other Pieces," *PMLA,* 57:513–535 (1942), J. O. Bailey contends that the general plan and some details of *Pym* were drawn from the little novel *Symzonia* (1820) by the pseudonymous "Adam Seaborn." But, unlike most of Poe's probable

sources, *Symzonia* bears no close verbal resemblance to *Pym*, and most of the information it offers would have been available to Poe in a nautical anthology like *Remarkable Events*. The argument for the resemblance in design of *Pym* and *Symzonia* is substantially undermined by its failure to recognize that *Symzonia,* far from being a serious imaginary voyage, is a satirical attack on Symmes's theory and a parody of the style of conventional narratives of travel and exploration.

10. See A. H. Quinn, *Edgar Allan Poe,* p. 264.

11. Patrick F. Quinn, *The French Face of Edgar Poe* (Carbondale, Ill., 1957), pp. 202–205.

12. Marie Bonaparte, *The Life and Works of Edgar Allan Poe: A Psycho-Analytic Interpretation,* trans. John Rodker (London, 1949), p. 312.

13. Quoted in P. F. Quinn, *The French Face of Edgar Poe,* p. 191.

14. Edward H. Davidson, *Poe: A Critical Study* (Cambridge, Mass., 1957), pp. 168–169.

15. For discussions of the pattern of deception and revolt and of the stress on black and white in *Pym,* see P. F. Quinn, *The French Face of Edgar Poe,* p. 176; Harry Levin, *The Power of Blackness* (New York, 1958), pp. 120–125. In his introduction to a new edition of *The Narrative of Arthur Gordon Pym* (New York, [1960]), pp. vii–xxv, Sidney Kaplan develops a cogent argument to the effect that the puzzling second half of the novel was intended as an allegorical defense of slavery, a defense based on a fundamentalist belief in the divinely ordained inferiority of the black race.

16. Mustering an impressive array of parallels between *Pym* and *Moby-Dick* in respect to both general symbolic strategy and the use of particular symbols, P. F. Quinn concludes that *Pym* is a forerunner and perhaps the prototype of Melville's novel; he concedes, however, that the symbolic intention of *Moby-Dick* is made manifest, while that of *Pym* remains latent and inferential: see *The French Face of Edgar Poe,* pp. 205–215. The problem of relating the symbols of *Pym* in a coherent and meaningful pattern is illuminated by Yvor Winter's interpretation of Poe's conception of poetry in *Maule's Curse,* p. 105: "the subject-matter of poetry . . . is by definition incomprehensible and unattainable; the poet, in dealing with something else, toward which he has no moral or intellectual responsibilities whatever . . . should merely endeavor to *suggest that a higher meaning exists*—in other words, should endeavor to suggest the presence of meaning when he is aware of none. The poet has

only to write a good description of something physically impressive, with an air of mystery, an air of meaning concealed."

17. For a study of Poe's relation to Reynolds, see Aubrey Starke, "Poe's Friend Reynolds," *American Literature*, 11: 152–159 (1939); for an explication of Reynolds' theories, see Robert F. Almy, "J. N. Reynolds: A Brief Biography with Particular Reference to Poe and Symmes," *Colophon*, new series, 2:227–245 (1937).

18. Poe, *Works*, III, 167, 178.

19. The resemblance and indebtedness of *Robin Day* to the work of Smollett and Marryat was noticed by at least two contemporary reviewers: see [John G. Palfrey], rev. of *Robin Day* in *North American Review*, 49:220–237 (1839); anon. rev. of *Robin Day* in *Burton's Gentleman's Magazine*, 4:358 (1839).

20. [Robert Montgomery Bird], *The Adventures of Robin Day* (Philadelphia, 1839), I, 43, 89, 164–165, 82.

21. *Ibid.*, I, 36, 223.

22. *Ibid.*, II, 73.

23. Palfrey, *North American Review*, 49:237.

24. *Robin Day*, II, 189.

25. Mary Mayer Bird, *Life of Robert Montgomery Bird*, ed. C. Seymour Thompson (Philadelphia, 1945), p. 14.

26. From Bird's letter, Liverpool, May 13, 1834, to Mary and Caroline Mayer; quoted in Mary Bird, *Life*, p. 77.

27. *Robin Day*, I, 212.

28. Robert Montgomery Bird, *Nick of the Woods, or The Jibbenainosay: A Tale of Kentucky*, rev. ed, (New York, 1853), p. iv. In the preface to this edition Bird goes on to say that his intention was to dispel "the poetical illusion" which "the genius of Chateaubriand and of our own Cooper had thrown . . . over the Indian character." The uncivilized Indian is, according to Bird, "ignorant, violent, debased, brutal" (pp. iv–v).

29. *Robin Day*, II, 191.

30. Although serial publication of a sea novel was a novelty in America in 1839, many English sea novels had been serialized by that time. *The Man-of-War's-Man* by "Bill Truck" had begun publication in the *Edinburgh Magazine* as early as 1821. Four of Marryat's novels had been published serially in his own *Metropolitan Magazine* between 1832 and 1836.

31. Charles J. Peterson, *Cruising in the Last War* (Philadelphia, 1850), p. 7.

32. In her three-year career as a privateer, the *Yankee* took forty

English vessels as prizes, seized or destroyed property valued at
five million dollars, and sent into Bristol alone one million dollars
worth of goods; see Edgar Stanton Maclay, *A History of American
Privateers* (New York, 1899), p. 274. The journal of the second cruise
of the *Yankee* is published in Wilfred Harold Munro, *Tales of an
Old Sea Port* (Princeton, 1917), pp. 225–288.

33. At times Peterson follows his source almost literally. *Cruising
in the Last War*, p. 32, offers an example:

"For more than a week, we had heavy gales, during which the
brig suffered much damage, having carried away three of her spars,
stove the arm-chests, injured the bulwarks, and strained her in
every part.

" 'I have crossed the old herring pond, at least twenty times,'
said Taffrail, . . . 'but I have always sailed *over* the Atlantic before,
not *under* it.' "

Cf. *Tales of an Old Sea Port*, p. 230: "It is something singular that
since we left port [nine days ago] we have had only one pleasant
day. There has been a continual succession of gales of wind from
all parts of the compass, attended with torrents of rain, squalls,
whirlwinds, thunder and lightning, and a tremendous sea frequently
breaking on board and occasioning considerable damage; carrying
away several spars and staving the arm-chests. Indeed it may be said
that our vessel has sailed thus far under but not over the Atlantic
Ocean."

34. Two other instances of specific borrowing from Cooper occur
in *Cruising in the Last War*. The interpolated account of the combat between the *Constitution* and the *Guerrière* (pp. 70–78) is drawn
from Cooper's *History of the Navy*, II, chap. 10. Peterson's description of the near collision of two scudding vessels (pp. 215–217) offers
verbal parallels to a similar description in *Homeward Bound*, chap.
13.

35. Charles J. Peterson, *The American Navy* (Philadelphia, 1857),
pp. 5–6; the first edition appeared in 1852.

36. *Cruising in the Last War*, pp. 12, 14, 139, 144, 78. Contrast
Peterson's characterization of the victory of the *Constitution* with
the tone and substance of Cooper's remarks in *History of the Navy*,
II, 197–198: "After making all proper allowance for the difference
in force, which certainly existed in favour of the Constitution, as
well as for the excuses the defeated party freely offered to the world,
men on both sides of the Atlantic, who were competent to form

intelligent opinions on such subjects, saw the promise of many future successes in [the victory of the American frigate]."

37. *Cruising in the Last War*, pp. 177, 42.

38. *Ibid.*, p. 166.

39. For example, within thirty pages (pp. 14–54) of *Cruising in the Last War* Peterson uses the two metaphors with virtually no variation on seven occasions.

40. *Cruising in the Last War*, pp. 33, 39, 101, 125.

41. *Ibid.*, p. 156.

42. The extraordinary stylistic and thematic uniformity of the cheap sea novels is in part a result of the fact that they were written by a relatively small number of men. Of the more than one hundred such works published between 1842 and 1850, two thirds were produced by just seven writers: E. Z. C. Judson had written five cheap sea novels by 1850, Justin Jones six, Charles E. Averill seven, "Harry Halyard" eight, Maturin Murray Ballou nine, Benjamin Barker nine, and Joseph Holt Ingraham no less than twenty-nine.

43. Fred E. Pond, *Life and Adventures of "Ned Buntline"* (New York, 1919), pp. 52–53.

44. Thus Alexander Jones's *The Privateer*, which first appeared serially in *Burton's Gentleman's Magazine* in 1839, was issued as a cheap novel in 1846, and Henry William Herbert's *Ringwood the Rover*, published serially in *Coleman's Monthly Miscellany* in 1839, appeared as a cheap novel in 1843. The 1850 edition of *Cruising in the Last War* itself appeared in paper covers bearing the imprint of "T. B. Peterson's Cheap Book, Magazine and Publishing Establishment," sellers of "books for everybody, printed for the 'million,' at greatly reduced rates."

45. [William S. Mayo], "A Real Pirate," *United States Magazine and Democratic Review*, 22:263–264 (1848). Of the sea tales that I have examined, only three published after 1835 are predominantly sentimental: the anonymous "The Lost Fisherman" (1838); Henry T. Tuckerman's "Captain Millar" (1843); and the anonymous "The Yacht" (1844). The vast majority of the piratical tales I have examined appeared before 1840: S. B. Beckett's "The Cruise of the Dart" (1836); Robert Burts's "The Escape" (1836); J. H. Clinch's "The Pirate" (1837); the anonymous "The Clerk's Yarn" (1837); James E. Vail's "The Sea Voyage" (1837); Wilder Lann's "Pirate Law" (1838); the anonymous "A Piratical Sketch" (1838); the

anonymous "The Cruise of the Enterprize" (1839); and John Sherburne Sleeper's "The Pirate off Cape St. Antonio" (c. 1838) and "Encounter with a Pirate" (c. 1838). Only five were published after 1840: the anonymous "The Bucaneer" (1841); Peterson's "The Union Jack" (1843) and "The Black Rover" (1849); Judson's "A Visit to Lafitte" (1847); and Mayo's "A Real Pirate" (1848).

46. Serious supernatural tales include Burts's "The Flying Dutchman" (1836); Sleeper's "The Haunted Ship" (c. 1838) and "The Spirit Bird" (c. 1838); Robert L. Wade's "The Doomed Ship" (1843); and the anonymous "The Dead Man's Sermon" (1845). Comic treatments of the supernatural include Burts's "Jack Marlinspike's Yarn" (1836); the anonymous "A Yankee's Adventure with the Flying Dutchman" (1837); William E. Burton's "A Cape Codder Among the Mermaids" (1839); and Elizabeth Oakes Smith's "Jack Spanker and the Mermaid" (1843).

47. Reynolds' story was first linked with *Moby-Dick* by Nathan Comfort Starr in his unpubl. diss. (Harvard, 1928), "The Sea in the English Novel from Defoe to Melville"; see also R. S. Garnett, "Moby-Dick and Mocha Dick: A Literary Find," *Blackwood's Magazine*, 226:841–858 (1929). For a discussion of the folk origins of stories concerning marine beasts, see Rourke, *American Humor*, p. 155.

48. [John Codman], *Sailors' Life and Sailors' Yarns* (New York, 1847), pp. 173–181, 246, 251, 20–21.

49. Rev. of Browne's *Etchings of a Whaling Cruise* and Codman's *Sailors' Life and Sailors' Yarns* in *Literary World*, 1:106 (1847).

50. *Sailors' Life*, pp. 117–118.

51. W. S. Mayo, "The Escape of the Atalanta," *Ladies' Companion*, 19:24 (1843). With slight alteration, this story later appeared in chap. 1 of Mayo's novel *Kaloolah* (1849).

52. Two examples are Judson's "A Dream that Was Not All Dream" (1846) and "The Cruise of the Gentile" (1848) by Frank Byrne.

53. W. S. M[ayo], "The Captain's Story," *United States Magazine and Democratic Review*, 18:306–307 (1846).

54. [Judson], *Cruisings, Afloat and Ashore, from the Private Log of Ned Buntline* (New York, 1848), p. [5]. The *Knickerbocker* pub-

lished five of Judson's stories of contemporary naval life: "Running the Blockade" (1844), "A Race on the Bahama Banks" (1845), "A Chapter on Middies" (1845), "A Chronicle of Our Navy" (1846), and "The Captured Banner" (1848). The fact that the *Knickerbocker*, which had begun its service as a vehicle for American sea fiction with the publication of William Leggett's "The Encounter" in 1834, should give over its pages in the middle and late 1840's to "Ned Buntline" substantiates the observation by Frank Luther Mott in *A History of American Magazines: 1741–1850* (Cambridge, Mass., 1939), p. 611, that by "1850 the *Knickerbocker* had plainly deteriorated."

55. Stories of privateering in the War of 1812 include Burts's "The Privateer" (1836); Gould's "The Cruise of the Sparkler" (1836); Sleeper's "A Stratagem of War" (c. 1838); "Off the Cape" (1839) by "Dick Stanton"; Peterson's "Getting to Sea" (1844); the anonymous "Scenes in a Life" (1845); Peterson's "Off Calais" (1845); Judson's "Running a Blockade in the Last War" (1847); and Henry A. Clark's "The Cruise of the Raker" (1848). Of the stories I have examined, only one first published after 1835, J. E. Dow's "Sketches from the Log of Old Ironsides" (1839), deals with the activities of the regular navy in the War of 1812.

56. "The Cruise of the Raker," *Graham's Magazine*, 33:69, 134 (1848).

57. *Ibid.*, pp. 69, 132. Abandoning a narrative thread even so rudimentary as Clark's, a number of short sketches published between 1835 and 1850 consist almost entirely of the delineation of a magnificently sublime storm scene: "Life at Sea" (1836) by "Orson"; the anonymous "The Lost Sailor" (1836); Gould's "Man Overboard" (1838); N. P. Willis' "The Archipelago in a Levanter" (1843); D. G. Mitchell's "A Man Overboard" (1848); and Peterson's "Overboard in the Gulf" (1848). For examples of the stress on maritime sublimity in the visual arts, see the gift book *Friendship's Offering* (Boston, 1850), pp. 92, 216, containing engravings by Sartain of two scenes from Turner: "The White Squall," full of lowering black clouds, streaks of lightning, and the flash of a signal gun; and "Fire at Sea," a night scene illuminated by pale moonlight and the glare of a burning ship.

VI

The Voyage of Life

1. The novel was issued in book form in 1848 as *Jack Tier; or The Florida Reefs* in America and as *Captain Spike; or The Islets of the Gulf* in England. It was published serially between November 1846 and March 1848 in both *Graham's Magazine* and *Bentley's Miscellany*.

2. One other effect of serial publication on *Jack Tier* is the slipshod finish of its narrative. Although Cooper's novels are never impeccable in their details, *Jack Tier* contains more than its share of inconsistent and tautological passages: Spike's boatswain, for example, is variously named Rove (p. 36), Clench (p. 72), and Strand (p. 463); the reader is first told that Spike knows the name of a certain naval officer (p. 127), but later in the narrative it appears that he does not (p. 178); a bag of gold has been stowed aboard a schooner first by Mulford (p. 321) and then by Jack (p. 439); Cooper's phobia against "Hurl Gate" as a bowdlerized version of "Hell Gate" manifests itself twice in the novel (pp. 35, 81–82); and two tedious, nearly identical, and entirely unnecessary explanations of the method of determining longitude are supplied (pp. 94–99, 223–227).

3. Grossman, *James Fenimore Cooper*, pp. 225–228.

4. *Jack Tier*, pp. 10–32, *passim*. Cooper uses the verb *waddle* again and again to reinforce the antiromantic tone of the novel: see pp. 17, 23, 49, 86, 88, 292, 484.

5. *Ibid.*, pp. 29, 209, 73, 253, 474. The only incident in Cooper's other novels that is comparable to the death of Mrs. Budd is the murder of Parson Amen by Scalping Peter in the nearly contemporaneous *Oak Openings* (1848). But the noble death of the gentle, comic Amen becomes the occasion of the conversion of his murderer. By contrast, in the harsher world of *Jack Tier* Mrs. Budd dies as she has lived, bumbling, pitiful, and ineffectual, and Spike remains untouched by her death. It seems likely that Cooper based the grisly scene in the open boat on an actual incident involving the survivors of the wreck of the immigrant ship *William Brown* in the winter of 1841; see Carl C. Cutler, *Greyhounds of the Sea: The Story of the American Clipper Ship* (New York, 1930), pp. 108–109.

6. See, for example, *The Red Rover,* p. 242; *The Water-Witch,* p. 212.

7. *Jack Tier,* pp. 254, 145, 449, 40, 62, 506.

8. Grossman, *James Fenimore Cooper,* p. 231.

9. S. F. Cooper, *The Cooper Gallery,* p. 390; *The Sea Lions,* p. 489.

10. For the history of Cooper's partnership with Dering in the *Union,* see Robert E. Spiller, *Fenimore Cooper: Critic of His Times* (New York, 1931), pp. 70–71; Henry W. Boynton, *James Fenimore Cooper* (New York, 1931), pp. 73–75; Clavel, *Fenimore Cooper: La jeunesse,* pp. 246–248. According to Boynton, Dering superintended the outfitting and manning of the vessel, but Spiller says that Cooper took over those duties when the *Union* was at Sag Harbor.

11. *The Monikins,* pp. 178, 98, 205; *The Sea Lions,* pp. 247, 158, 257–264.

12. *The Sea Lions,* pp. 82–83, 84, 220.

13. Quoted from the New York *Mercantile Register* in *Niles' Weekly Register,* September 30, 1820, p. 65. The writings of Poe's friend Jeremiah N. Reynolds offer many equally intriguing parallels to *The Sea Lions,* parallels that are too general to be conclusive evidence of Cooper's acquaintance with Reynolds' work. However, Cooper might have found the authority for his location of the secret sealing grounds in Reynolds' "Report . . . in Relation to Islands, Reefs, and Shoals in the Pacific Ocean, &c.," 23d Congr., 2d Sess., 1835, House Exec. Doc. No. 105, p. 26, for Reynolds observes that "Captain Pendleton of Stonington, Connecticut, one of the most practical and intelligent sealers I met with, and who has spent many years in the South Sea fur trade, is strongly of opinion that there are many valuable discoveries to be made in the seas southwest of the [South] Shetlands," the area in which the Deacon's sealing grounds lie. Certain passages in Reynolds' *Address on the Subject of a Surveying and Exploring Expedition to the Pacific Ocean and South Seas* (New York, 1836), too, seem to be echoed in *The Sea Lions:* see, for example, Reynolds' discussion of the priority of the sealers in southern discovery (*Address,* p. 95) and a similar discussion in *The Sea Lions,* p. 220. The most striking parallel between Reynolds and Cooper occurs in their descriptions of the wide-ranging activities of American maritime interests. According to the *Address,* pp. 24–25, Yankee mariners even venture "into the interior of benighted Africa . . . to drag the huge rhi-

noceros from his marshes, the ponderous elephant from his groves, and seize the Numidian lion in his lair." According to *The Sea Lions*, p. 111, they are always prepared "to carry a party out to hunt for camelopards, set nets for young lions, and beat up the quarters of the rhinoceros on the plains of Africa."

14. Benjamin Morrell, *A Narrative of Four Voyages to the South Sea, North and South Pacific Ocean, Chinese Sea, Ethiopic and Southern Atlantic Ocean, Indian and Antarctic Ocean* (New York, 1832), pp. 73, 67, 463; *The Sea Lions*, pp. 204, 309–311, 63.

15. Edmund Fanning, *Voyages round the World; with Selected Sketches of Voyages to the South Seas, North and South Pacific Oceans, etc.* (New York, 1833), pp. 428–429. Cooper could not have known that, as recent scholarship has shown, Fanning's memory was slightly at fault; the *Hersilia* did not make an independent discovery of the South Shetlands but had been diverted to them by news of William Smith's discovery of the islands in February, 1819. See Edouard A. Stackpole, *The Voyage of the Huron and the Huntress: The American Sealers and the Discovery of the Continent of Antarctica* (Mystic, Conn., 1955), pp. 10–13.

16. *The Sea Lions*, pp. 270–281; *Voyages round the World*, p. 300.

17. *The Sea Lions*, p. 8; *Early Critical Essays*, p. 43.

18. [Melville], rev. of *The Sea Lions* in *Literary World*, 4:370 (1849).

19. See "Cooper's *The Sea Lions* and Wilkes' *Narrative*," *PMLA*, 65:1069–1075 (1950.)

20. See *The Sea Lions*, pp. 207, 217, 290, 302–303, 307.

21. Gates, *PMLA*, 65:1075. It should be pointed out that some of the material that Gates assigns to Wilkes probably came from other sources. Thus he identifies the wedging of Daggett's schooner in the ice as a borrowing from Wilkes, but, as we have seen, Cooper uses substantially the same incident in *The Monikins*, published nine years before the *Narrative* appeared. Morrell's *Narrative of Four Voyages* offers closer parallels to some of the passages from *The Sea Lions* discussed by Gates than does Wilkes's *Narrative*, notably the recommendation of the Straits of Le Maire and the account of the capsizing iceberg.

22. William Edward Parry, *Journal of a Voyage for the Discovery of a North-West Passage from the Atlantic to the Pacific; Performed in the Years 1819–1820* (Philadelphia, 1821), pp. 87–89; *The Sea*

Lions, pp. 360, 363. Cooper's review of Parry originally appeared in the *Repository* for January 1822 and is reprinted in *Early Critical Essays,* pp. 65–96.

23. Parry, *Journal,* pp. 93–94, 128, 181–182; *The Sea Lions,* pp. 366–367, 413, 431, 447.

24. *The Sea Lions,* pp. 184–185, 187; W[illiam] Scoresby, *An Account of the Arctic Regions* (Edinburgh, 1820), II, 254–255, 519. Cooper's review of Scoresby's book originally appeared in the *Repository* for July 1821 and is reprinted in *Early Critical Essays,* pp. 42–64.

25. *The Monikins,* p. 197; *Excursions in Switzerland* (Paris, 1836), p. 21. The latter work was published in America in the same year under the title *Sketches of Switzerland.*

26. *The Sea Lions,* pp. 257–258, 306, 310–311, 367, 378, 374, 225, 303; cf. *Excursions in Switzerland,* pp. 164, 54–56, 173–175, and *A Residence in France,* pp. 253–268. For other comparisons of Antarctic scenery to the Alps in *The Sea Lions,* see pp. 221, 300, 302, 449.

27. *Excursions in Switzerland,* pp. 143, 41; *A Residence in France,* p. 209; *The Headsman,* p. 351.

28. Reynolds, *Address,* pp. 70, 99, 14–15.

29. Morrell, *A Narrative of Four Voyages,* pp. 29–30.

30. *Early Critical Essays,* p. 43.

31. *The Sea Lions,* pp. 6–8.

32. Charles Wilkes, *Narrative of the United States Exploring Expedition during the Years 1838, 1839, 1840, 1841, 1842* (Philadelphia, 1845), II, 295.

33. James Clark Ross, *A Voyage of Discovery and Research in the Southern and Antarctic Regions, during the Years 1839–43* (London, 1847), I, 282.

34. Cooper, *Correspondence,* II, 743.

35. *The Sea Lions,* p. 118.

36. Jude 12–13; cf. Melville's use of this passage in *Moby-Dick,* II, 180, where the infidel *Pequod,* her try-works blazing, plunges "into that blackness of darkness."

37. "Revaluations (XVI): James Fenimore Cooper," *Scrutiny,* 19:124 (Winter, 1952–1953). Cf. Howard Mumford Jones, "Prose and Pictures: James Fenimore Cooper," *Tulane Studies in English,* 3:146–147 (1952): "Not primitivism, not romanticism, not the influence of the frontier, not even the mere delight of employing his mythopoetic powers fundamentally shapes the fictional world of

Cooper, but a great religious vision, one comparable to that in the *Kosmos* of Alexander von Humboldt, a vision at once melancholy and sublime!"

38. *James Fenimore Cooper: A Re-Appraisal,* pp. 112–127.

39. *Tulane Studies in English,* 3:133–154.

40. "James Fenimore Cooper and Thomas Cole: An Analogous Technique," *American Literature,* 30:26–36 (1958).

41. *The Crater,* p. 491.

42. *The Sea Lions,* pp. 123–125, 465; 381, 397–398; 208, 457–458.

43. According to Susan Fenimore Cooper, "the book was written in the winter season" of 1848–1849 (*The Cooper Gallery,* p. 391). It was published in England on March 29, 1849, and in New York on April 10, 1849: see Robert E. Spiller and Philip C. Blackburn, *A Descriptive Bibliography of the Writings of James Fenimore Cooper* (New York, 1934), p. 155.

44. Quoted in Louis L. Noble, *The Course of Empire, Voyage of Life, and Other Pictures of Thomas Cole* (New York, 1853), pp. 224–225.

45. See S. F. Cooper, *The Cooper Gallery,* pp. 17, 72–73.

46. Quoted in Noble, *The Course of Empire,* pp. 287–289.

47. *The Sea Lions,* pp. 242, 223, 244, 262.

48. *Ibid.,* pp. 122, 403.

49. *Ibid.,* pp. 7, 395.

50. *Literary World,* 4:370.

51. See *Gleanings,* II, 246. The link between the character Stimson and Cooper's experience in the *Sterling* was first pointed out in Clagett, "Cooper and the Sea," I, 17.

52. See *Afloat and Ashore,* I, 210.

53. *The Sea Lions,* pp. 403, 405, 410.

54. *Ibid.,* p. 6.

55. *Ibid.,* pp. 361, 138.

56. *Ibid.,* pp. 407–412, 455–456. Cf. *Wing-and-Wing,* pp. 473–479, a tentative foreshadowing of the scene of Gardiner's conversion. As Raoul Yvard lies dying in the warm Mediterranean evening, "the Tramonta, as usual, had driven all perceptible vapor from the atmosphere, and the vault of heaven, in its cerulean blue, and spangled with thousands of stars, stretched itself above him, a glorious harbinger of the future, to one who died in hope." Raoul's eyes fix on one bright star, and his atheistic rationalism begins to ebb away. " 'That star haunts me,' " he tells Ghita; " 'if it really be a world, some all-powerful hand must have created it.' " He

dies, his eyes "still fastened on the star." The differences between this episode and the one in *The Sea Lions* are important. Cooper's concern in *Wing-and-Wing* is not so much for the expression of religious truth as for the evocation of a highly romantic and rather sentimental mood. The origin and nature of Raoul's "novel sensations" are left in vagueness, subordinated to the magic of the Mediterranean setting and the pathos of the young lover's death. Similarly, the religious differences that separate Raoul and Ghita exist primarily to produce a piquant situation; there is almost nothing of the deep commitment and stern urgency of *The Sea Lions* in the religious elements of the earlier novel.

57. Grossman, *James Fenimore Cooper*, p. 231; Cowie, *The Rise of the American Novel*, p. 154. Grossman is not the only critic whose response to *The Sea Lions* has been deadened and diminished by an annoyance with the surface manifestations of Cooper's theme. Melville, in an otherwise favorable review, observes with a slight sneer that "one of the subordinate parts of the book is the timely conversion of Roswell, the hero, from a too latitudinarian view of Christianity to a more orthodox, and hence a better belief" (*Literary World*, 4:370). Although he does not make Melville's mistake of underestimating the structural and thematic importance of Gardiner's conversion, Lounsbury condescendingly chides Cooper for his clumsy bigotry: Cooper "meant to inculcate a lesson, and the only lesson that can possibly be drawn is the sufficiently absurd one that dwellers in the chilly spiritual clime of Unitarianism can be cured of their faith in that icy creed by being subjected to the horrors of a polar winter"; see Thomas R. Lounsbury, *James Fenimore Cooper* (Boston, 1889), p. 260. No matter how the reader responds to Cooper's apparent insistence on a literal acceptance of the divinity of Christ, however, he should not be distracted by that response from an awareness that Cooper uses this particular doctrine as the specific occasion for the fictional examination of a far broader issue, the relationship of finite man to an infinite God.

58. *The Sea Lions*, pp. 15, 19–20, 25–26, 66.

59. *Ibid.*, pp. 71, 124.

60. *Ibid.*, pp. 202–307, *passim*.

61. *Ibid.*, pp. 430–448, *passim*.

62. *Ibid.*, pp. 55, 337, 362, 438.

63. Suggestions of the notion that guilt is attached to the slaughter of seals are common in the sealing narratives of Cooper's day. In an account of a sealing voyage to the South Shetlands in 1820–1821,

Nathaniel Ames tells of his horror at clubbing a seal which "uttered a piercing shriek, so exactly like a woman or child, that I leaped full two feet into the air" (*Mariner's Sketches,* p. 133). In *A Narrative of the Life, Travels and Sufferings of Thomas W. Smith* (Boston, 1844), p. 126, the narrator, who was sealing at South Georgia and the South Shetlands between 1817 and 1821, expresses a similar compassion for his victims: "Poor innocent animals! I could not but pity them, seeing the large tears rolling down from their eyes; they were slaughtered without mercy."

64. *The Sea Lions,* pp. 113–114, 73.

65. Lounsbury, *James Fenimore Cooper,* p. 258.

66. *The Sea Lions,* pp. 157–160.

67. *Ibid.,* pp. 173–186.

68. *Ibid.,* pp. 223, 247, 254, 258, 278, 333.

69. *Ibid.,* pp. 272–274.

70. *Ibid.,* pp. 413–443, *passim.* Daggett's lingering death gives Cooper the opportunity to develop other contrasts between the regenerate Gardiner and the unrepentant Daggett. Thus, when the dying Daggett hears of the return of the seals, which no longer awaken Gardiner's cupidity, his eyes brighten and his nature betrays "some of its ardent longings" (p. 439).

71. See Grossman, *James Fenimore Cooper,* p. 116.

72. Quoted from Cooper's correspondence with his publishers in William Charvat, "Cooper as Professional Author," *James Fenimore Cooper: A Re-Appraisal,* p. 142.

73. In "Cooper and the Sea," II, 629, Clagett complains of the awkwardness that results from the fact that, "for some unknown reason, Cooper chose to make the rival sealing vessels precisely alike in rig, size, and name."

74. *The Sea Lions,* pp. 132, 134. Historical authenticity did not require Cooper to rig his two sealers as schooners. Of the eight American vessels which took part in the second sealing season at the South Shetlands, 1820–1821, for example, two were ships, two were brigs, one was a sloop, and three were schooners; see Stackpole, *Voyage of the Huron and the Huntress,* pp. 78–80.

75. *The Sea Lions,* pp. 399, 437, 443.

76. *Ibid.,* pp. 439, 296, 463.

VII

A Literary Leviathan

1. Alexis de Tocqueville, *Democracy in America,* ed. Phillips Bradley (New York, 1945), I, 429.

2. See Henry Nash Smith, *Virgin Land: The American West as Symbol and Myth* (Cambridge, Mass., 1950), p. 12.

3. Cutler, *Greyhounds of the Sea,* p. 370.

4. It is worth noting that the relative unpopularity of Melville's later fiction, a phenomenon usually explained in terms of his ideological divergence from his audience and his refusal to repeat the formulas he had used in *Typee* and *Omoo* or in *Redburn* and *White-Jacket,* may also be a result of the fact that he was firmly established in the mind of the reading public as a *nautical* writer, a producer of the kind of fiction that was no longer in demand. Thus, if Melville had attempted to return to the methods and concerns of *Typee* or *White-Jacket* in the late 1850's, it seems unlikely that he could have regained his earlier popularity. Certainly no other American writer enjoyed popular acclaim for the serious treatment of similar nautical materials from the middle 1850's until the revival of interest in maritime affairs about the time of the Spanish–American War; see Charles Lee Lewis, *Books of the Sea: An Introduction to Nautical Literature* (Annapolis, 1943), p. 31.

5. Letter to Cooper dated July 29, 1830, *Correspondence,* I, 179.

6. Anon. rev. of *Wing-and-Wing* in *United States Magazine and Democratic Review,* 11:666 (1842); anon. rev. of *The Crater* in *United States Magazine and Democratic Review,* 21:440 (1847); anon. rev. of *Homeward Bound* in *Southern Literary Messenger,* 4:724 (1838); anon. rev. of *The Two Admirals* in *Southern Literary Messenger,* 8:361 (1842); [Grenville Mellen], rev. of *The Red Rover* in *North American Review,* 27:140, 145 (1828); [O. W. B. Peabody], rev. of *The Water-Witch* in *North American Review,* 32:516 (1831); [Francis Bowen], rev. of *Gleanings in Europe* in *North American Review,* 46:13 (1838); anon. rev. of *Homeward Bound* in *Knickerbocker,* 12:264 (1838).

7. G. Jean-Aubry, *Joseph Conrad: Life and Letters* (New York, 1927), II, 73; see also Conrad, *Notes on Life and Letters,* pp. 55–57.

8. Letter from Melville dated February 20, 1852, *Memorial of James Fenimore Cooper* (New York, 1852), p. 30.

9. Howard, *Herman Melville*, p. 152. Melville's review of *The Red Rover* first appeared as "A Thought on Book-Binding," *Literary World*, 6:276–277 (1850); it was reprinted by John Howard Birss in "A Book Review by Herman Melville," *New England Quarterly*, 5:346–348 (1932).

10. *Literary World*, 4:370.

Index